NAVIGATING LIFE TRANSITIONS FOR MEANING

NAVIGATING LIFE TRANSITIONS FOR MEANING

Edited by

ELIZABETH M. ALTMAIER

Department of Psychological and Quantitative Foundations, College of Education, University of Iowa, Iowa City, IA, United States

ELSEVIER

ACADEMIC PRESS

An imprint of Elsevier

Academic Press is an imprint of Elsevier
125 London Wall, London EC2Y 5AS, United Kingdom
525 B Street, Suite 1650, San Diego, CA 92101, United States
50 Hampshire Street, 5th Floor, Cambridge, MA 02139, United States
The Boulevard, Langford Lane, Kidlington, Oxford OX5 1GB, United Kingdom

British Library Cataloguing-in-Publication Data
A catalogue record for this book is available from the British Library

Library of Congress Cataloging-in-Publication Data
A catalog record for this book is available from the Library of Congress

ISBN: 978-0-12-818849-1

For Information on all Academic Press publications
visit our website at https://www.elsevier.com/books-and-journals

Publisher: Nikki Levy
Acquisitions Editor: Joslyn Chaiprasert-Paguio
Editorial Project Manager: Barbara Makinster
Production Project Manager: Omer Mukthar
Cover Designer: Mark Rogers
Cover image: Justin Salem Meyer

Typeset by MPS Limited, Chennai, India

Contents

4

Health transitions

5

Conclusions

List of contributors

Blake A. Allan Educational Studies, Purdue University, West Lafayette, IN, United States

Elizabeth M. Altmaier Department of Psychological and Quantitative Foundations, College of Education, University of Iowa, Iowa City, IA, United States

Keith M. Bellizzi Department of Human Development and Family Studies, University of Connecticut, CT, United States

Maja Bergman Division of Psychological and Educational Services, Graduate School of Education, Fordham University at Lincoln Center, New York, NY, United States

Cara E. Bigony Division of Psychological and Educational Services, Graduate School of Education, Fordham University at Lincoln Center, New York, NY, United States

Melissa Brenman Division of Psychological and Educational Services, Graduate School of Education, Fordham University at Lincoln Center, New York, NY, United States

Eric C. Chen Division of Psychological and Educational Services, Graduate School of Education, Fordham University at Lincoln Center, New York, NY, United States

Kate E. Dibble Department of Human Development and Family Studies, University of Connecticut, CT, United States

Areana Eivers School of Psychology and Counselling, Queensland University of Technology, Brisbane, QLD, Australia

Merle A. Keitel Division of Psychological and Educational Services, Graduate School of Education, Fordham University at Lincoln Center, New York, NY, United States

Adrian B. Kelly School of Psychology and Counselling, Queensland University of Technology, Brisbane, QLD, Australia

Tracie Liu Educational Studies, Purdue University, West Lafayette, IN, United States

Evgenia Milman School of Human Development & Education, St. Edward's University, Austin, TX, United States

Nicholas C. Neibergall Thompson Center, University of Missouri, Columbia, MO, United States

Robert A. Neimeyer Department of Psychology, The University of Memphis, Memphis, TN, United States; Portland Institute for Loss and Transition, Baltimore, MD, United States

Crystal L. Park Department of Psychological Sciences, University of Connecticut, CT, United States

Francisco J. Sánchez Educational, School & Counseling Psychology, University of Missouri, Columbia, MO, United States

Tara Sanft Medical Oncology, Yale University School of Medicine, New Haven, CT, United States

Sinead Sinnott Department of Psychological Sciences, University of Connecticut, CT, United States

Hannah Sugarman Division of Psychological and Educational Services, Graduate School of Education, Fordham University at Lincoln Center, New York, NY, United States

Preface

As psychology has increased the study of *meaning in life*, ways in which meaning is constructed, threatened, destroyed, and rebuilt are becoming clearer. Meaning at its foundation is *connection*—among events, thoughts, plans, goals, and the like. I may find meaning in my occupation because I am successful, because I have values that underlie my work, or because my occupational role confers status on me, all connections between one thing and another. Furthermore, at one end of that connection is stability, and at the other end is change. When new things occur, my meaning in life connects the change with the stable.

That connection happens when there is *purpose*, when events connect to hoped for goals and consequences. Meaning also is built when there is *mattering*, when I have value to others or when my decisions and actions have importance. When events have *continuity*, they connect across time. And when there is *coherence*, events connect across type of event. We are indebted to recent work by Park and colleagues who have argued for the multidimensionality of meaning (see George & Park, 2017).

One way to think about these types of connections is to consider an event demonstrated to threaten meaning in life. That type of event is *trauma*. In modern society, there are a wide variety of events traumatic to those who experience them: natural disasters such as tornado or hurricane, mass shootings, environmental disasters, and interpersonal violence are common examples. Statistics reveal that we are experiencing these events more frequently, and thus the likelihood of a concomitant erosion of meaning in life is increased.

Why do traumatic events erode meaning? One mechanism was described by Janoff-Bulman (1989), who posited that our assumptions about life may match our experience of life or may be in great conflict. For example, we have an assumption that the world is a benevolent place, that people are essentially good. We also assume that life is not random but rather is fair, that people "get what they deserve." When we experience being treated kindly, and having things generally "go our way," we feel confident in our predictions. But when the opposite happens, when a natural disaster sweeps away everything we own in life and the future is bleak, our assumptions simply do not line up with our experience. We are left with serious distress and arousal, with a distorted sense of reality, and with having lost our sense of identity and purpose. Thus traumatic events challenge and may destroy meaning in life.

This book considers another type of event, one that is universal among humans and yet may also hold challenges for meaning in life. That type of event is a *life transition*. Transitions occur as a discrete event, such as being laid off from work, or as a slow cumulative process, such as aging. Individuals may be aware of and actively processing the transition or may be less aware. It may be that the emotion of the transition interferes with its processing, as can occur in bereavement. Last, transitions are situated within contexts: examples are developmental transitions, the degree of challenge the transition poses to well-being, and the valence of the transition (positive or negative).

Do transitions affect meaning in life? And if so, how does that influence take place? These are the questions that chapter authors considered as they analyzed transitions in three general categories. The first is the category of development. Chapters focus on transitions in adolescence, a time of great change in development, and late life, another time of great change. Within development is identity, and a chapter analyzes how transgender individuals navigate transitions around identity. A second is the category of life role. Chapters analyze bereavement transitions and transitions that are forced on individuals in an uncertain labor market. The third is the category of health. Chapters consider three types of health transitions: that of chronic illness, that of surviving cancer, and that of acute cardiac events.

This book is needed for two distinct reasons. The first is that transitions are essentially what makes us human. And yet research documents the unsettling, even damaging, effects of transitions. If threats to meaning in life are the foundation of those difficulties, then individuals can be assisted to directly address meaning in life prior to and during the transitions. The second is that researchers, scholars, and clinicians all benefit from understanding meaning in life and how it is maintained or improved. Since meaning in life has been linked to physical and psychosocial well-being (see Heintzelman & King, 2014), its importance motivates our efforts to better understand it.

I thank the chapter authors for their insightful writing. Meaning can be a "squishy" construct, but their chapters are illuminating and provocative. The reader will look at transitions in life quite differently after following the authors' descriptions and insights, and that after all is the goal of this book.

References

George, L. S., & Park, C. L. (2017). The Multidimensional Existential Meaning Scale: A tripartite approach to measuring meaning in life. *The Journal of Positive Psychology, 6*, 613–627.

Heintzelman, S. J., & King, L. A. (2014). Life is pretty meaningful. *American Psychologist, 69*, 561–574.

Janoff-Bulman, R. (1989). Assumptive worlds and the stress of traumatic events: Applications of the schema construct. *Social Cognition, 7*, 113–136.

PART 1

Introduction

CHAPTER

1

Meaning in life amidst life transitions

Elizabeth M. Altmaier

[1]Department of Psychological and Quantitative Foundations, College of Education, University of Iowa, Iowa City, IA, United States

How do we discover, or create, meaning in life? When psychology and philosophy were closely related in the early 20th century, *meaning* was a concept considered to undergird thought itself. For example, Welby (1896) defined meaning as the combined influences of *sense* and *significance* [italics mine], thus locating meaning within the "great provinces of thought we call philosophy, poetry and religion" (p. 27). Meaning was a literal signal of the existence of perception and organization: "That a thing means something to us is equivalent to saying that it symbolizes something for us, that we are aware of some of the relations which it sustains to other things" (Angell, 1906, p. 204).

Some decades later during early years of experimental psychology, the study of meaning was virtually rejected, since meaning did not concord with "wholly observable phenomena and their causes" (Higginson, 1937, p. 503). For example, Tolman (1926) defined consciousness as "some moment or aspect in overt behavior" (p. 353), a distinction that would disallow the study of meaning without an overt expression. Further, meaning was thought to derive from the past experiences of the individual, and thus meaning as a product of life history was wholly subjective and its report, scientifically suspect.

Scholarly interest in meaning resumed during the middle 20th century, stimulated in large part by the writings of Viktor Frankl who reflected on his time imprisoned in concentration camps during World War II, where brutality and starvation eliminated mental and physical necessities. What remained was the choice of attitude in the face of

Navigating Life Transitions for Meaning
DOI: https://doi.org/10.1016/B978-0-12-818849-1.00001-1

those horrific circumstances, that choice of attitude being what he considered the only human freedom that cannot be taken away. His book (Frankl, 1963) was entitled *Man's Search for Meaning*, denoting an inner motivation to search for and create personal meaning. More recently, positive psychology (Seligman & Csikszentmihalyi, 2000), with its focus on strengths and virtues, generated further impetus to study meaning, particularly as it is present in human experiences of happiness and flourishing. For example, Seligman's model of PERMA (Seligman, 2017) defined happiness with meaning as an integral component—positive emotions, engagement, relationships, meaning, and accomplishment.

This chapter considers contemporary models of meaning, including their empirical support. Two challenges to meaning are then considered. First, the effect of trauma on meaning and the recreating of meaning after trauma are examined. Second, the potential of life transitions to affect meaning is discussed, including identification of potential mechanisms by which transitions might influence meaning. The chapter concludes with an overview of the remaining chapters.

Contemporary models of meaning

Contemporary scholars have attempted to define meaning, to understand its predictors, and to outline consequences of its presence or loss. One of the first psychologists to study meaning was Baumeister (1991) who approached the concept from the perspective of social psychology in understanding how people think and act. He defined meaning as "an imposition of a stable concept onto a changing biological process" (Baumeister & Vohs, 2002, p. 609). This stable concept is *connection*, the link between two entities. One entity is change, and the other entity is stability; meaning connects those processes for the individual.

According to Baumeister and Landau (2018), meaning, this stable link, incorporates four characteristics. The first is *purpose*, the orientation or motivation for actions, experiences, or activities. Meaning is present when events and circumstances connect to future goals or hoped for consequences. The second characteristic is *mattering*. Meaning denotes subjective value; meaning occurs when I matter, when my life brings value of some type, or when my decisions or actions have importance. The third is *continuity*; meaning is connection across time whereby disparate events become joined through shared meaning. The fourth characteristic is *coherence*. Meaning not only exists across time, but also across types of human experiences—events, thoughts and beliefs, history, activity.

Two of those characteristics, coherence and mattering, were considered further by Martela and Steger (2016). Their discussion presented coherence as comprehensibility, "making sense." In contrast, mattering signifies worth, positive or negative. Coherence is descriptive, mattering is evaluative. This distinction returns to Welby's (1896) view that meaning encompasses sense and significance. In support of this distinction are data from Davis, Nolen-Hoeksema, and Larson (1998) who interviewed 200 adults before and 6 and 12 months after a family member's death. Coders successfully categorized these adults' narratives regarding meaning into two types: making sense of the loss and finding something positive in the experience. Examples of responses in the type of making sense (coherence) were beliefs in God/fate, the death as predictable, and loss as part of a life cycle; examples of responses within the type of finding benefit (mattering) were growth in interpersonal bonds, gaining perspective, and giving to others in similar circumstances.

Are these two components of meaning the result of two different psychological processes? Davis and Novoa (2013) argued that making sense is part of our search for the confirmation of our basic assumption that life is fair, that events occur for a reason. Finding benefit may be an expression of dispositional traits (such as optimism) or other personal characteristics. However, these two processes may not delimit meaning making. For example, Meert et al. (2015) studied the meaning-making process that occurred as parents talked with their child's physician after the child's death. Finding benefit and sense making were aspects of meaning making but two additional components of meaning making were establishing continuing bonds with the deceased child and completing identity reconstruction (changes in the parents' sense of self).

An alternate way to define meaning making is through its operationalization in various measurement approaches. The most widely used measure of meaning is the Meaning in Life Questionnaire (Steger, Frazier, Oishi, & Kaler, 2006a, 2006b). This questionnaire assesses the degree to which an individual believes he or she has meaning in life, but items are not specific to any content in that meaning. For example, two items are "My life has a clear sense of purpose" and "I understand my life's meaning." Their validation research established two components of meaning—presence of meaning and search for meaning—represented by separate subscales.

A newer approach to measuring meaning in life was proposed by George and Park (2017) in their Multidimensional Existential Meaning Scale. Their operationalization of meaning in life encompasses three key dimensions—comprehension, purpose, mattering. Comprehension is the feeling that life "makes sense," that experiences are cohesive and fit within a personal story. Purpose is the degree to which individuals believe they have a clear view of their goals and of pathways toward achieving them. Mattering is the personal belief that existence has significance, that the individuals have value in their worlds. The development and validation research for their scale revealed that meaning in life judgments can be empirically differentiated among these three content dimensions.

Recent analytic scholarship supports meaning in life as multidimensional. Martela and Steger (2016) argued from their review of theoretical literature that meaning contains three facets: coherence, purpose, and significance. Coherence is the presence of "making sense," the comprehensibility of life within discernable patterns. The domain in which coherence operates is understanding. Purpose is derived from goals, aims, and directions; its domain is motivation. Significance is present when life is "worth living," and valued. Its domain is evaluation.

Meaning can be present or searched for, and therefore it can be prioritized as a value in itself. Russo-Netzer (2019) conducted two studies with 300 community-living adults to understand how prioritizing meaning in life is related to well-being. The assumption behind this research was that individuals vary in their approach to prioritizing meaning, from a general orientation to a specific intentionality, and in the degree to which meaning emphasis influences well-being. The findings documented individual differences in the degree of meaning prioritization, with the concurrent finding that prioritizing meaning leads to increased experience of meaning which in turn links to well-being including positive affect and life satisfaction.

In summary, meaning in life is connection among memory, events, and conceptions of the self. Meaning has a descriptive function, sense making, and an evaluative function, conferring gain or benefit. Models of well-being in life point to meaning as central to happiness. Meaning in life has also been empirically documented (see Hooker, Masters, & Park, 2018; Roepke, Jayawickreme, & Riffle, 2014) to be associated with physical and psychological benefits and its absence to be associated with physical and psychosocial problems.

Challenges to meaning

Traumatic events

One set of challenges to meaning is posed by individuals' experience of adverse and traumatic events. The term "trauma" was originally a medical term denoting physical injuries in and on the body, produced by suddenly occurring outside forces such as a motor vehicle accident or combat. Later use of the term expanded during World War I to cover psychological injuries, such as mutism and memory loss, presumed to be caused by those same external forces. In the case of combat, those forces were thought to be the soldiers' proximity to exploding shells. Most recently the term is used for psychological damage from external events. Trauma symptoms that cause significant life interference, including frequent and unwanted reliving of the experience, strong negative emotions such as anxiety and depression, and hyper vigilance, form the foundation for the diagnosis of Post-Traumatic Stress Disorder (American Psychiatric Association, 2013).

In modern society, a wide range of frequently experienced events can be disabling for individuals. Among those are mass shootings, sexual assault, bullying, mobbing (workplace bullying), natural disasters such as tornados and hurricanes, environmental disasters, accidents involving motor vehicles or trains or airplanes, and interpersonal violence. It is concerning that these events are occurring more frequently in people's lives. A national study conducted in 2010 (Kilpatrick et al., 2013) established that close to 90% of respondents had experienced a major traumatic event in their lifetime.

More broadly, events can also be traumatic because of the interaction of the event itself and the person experiencing it. If an event does not "fit," or cannot be accommodated within our core beliefs, it is experienced as traumatic. According to Janoff-Bulman (1989), all of us maintain core beliefs or assumptions about us, our world, and our interaction with the external world. Those beliefs are within three categories. The first category is that the world is a benevolent place; an example of a belief within this category is "people are essentially kind." The second category is that our interactions with the world are not random; a belief in this category is that "people get what they deserve." The last category is that we are decent people and have worth. Trauma violates these core beliefs. If the child of a caring parent is sexually abused by a "trustworthy" person such as a youth pastor, the world is no longer benevolent; rather, "decent" people are evil and bad things happen even to good people.

Trauma creates significant challenges to meaning in life. These challenges come from the disruption of previously held meanings, and from the damage to the whole person after the trauma. Experiencing severe arousal and disordered affect, having a distorted sense of reality, and losing one's sense of identity and purpose are frequent responses of traumatized individuals. Sometimes these responses are short-lived, but other times they are extended and pose ongoing impairment in life functions such as employment and interpersonal relationships. Psychology as a profession has devoted considerable effort to understanding meaning after trauma. For example, Park and Kennedy (2017) have outlined sequences by which trauma damages meaning, and by which the individual works to restore old meanings or create new ones (see Altmaier, 2017, for extended discussion.)

Triplett, Tedeschi, Cann, Calhoun, and Reeve (2012) examined pathways by which exposure to trauma could lead to growth and to life satisfaction, including a pathway of meaning. In their hypothesized model, rumination was postulated to lead to growth and then to meaning and then to satisfaction. Rumination is the process by which people repeatedly think about the event and its aftermath, including examining the core beliefs held prior to the trauma. Over 300 adults completed measures of trauma, core beliefs, growth, rumination, meaning, and life satisfaction. The results of path analyses supported the model, particularly the link between rumination and growth, although two types of rumination predicted two types of outcomes. Intrusive rumination—characterized by unintentional and unwanted thoughts and images—predicted distress and lower levels of meaning, while deliberate rumination—characterized by intentional analysis of an event—predicted higher levels of meaning and growth.

Life transitions

The purpose of this text is to consider whether and how life transitions affect meaning in life. The term "transition" originated from the Latin word *transire*, to go across. Thus, a transition is a change from one action to the next, or from one state of being to another, or from one place to another. Transitions occur as people make a change from employment to retirement; experience the intrusion of an illness into their everyday lives; as countries change from one political system to another; and as organizations alter their workplace expectations.

Bliese, Adler, and Flynn (2017) noted several characteristics of transitions that deserve consideration. The first is that a transition might be spurred by a discrete event or by a slow and cumulative process or by both. Aging, for example, is a cumulative process that creates transitions that are discrete in nature such as retirement, onset of illness, or bereavement. Second, individuals may be aware of and actively processing the transition event or they may be less aware. Some models of transitions (see Schlossberg, Waters, & Goodman, 1995) require active processing during transitions to stimulate a positive outcome from the transition. Last, interactions between the individual and the situation influence the outcome. Examples are the developmental stage of the individual (youth, adult, aging), the valence of the event (positive or negative), the centrality of the individual's beliefs affected by the event, and the degree to which meaning is impacted and, potentially, reestablished (Groleau, Calhoun, Cann, & Tedeschi, 2013).

The notion that transitions have an overall deleterious effect on humans was popularized by Holmes and Rahe in their work identifying life events that predict illness. The life events used in the Social Readjustment Rating Scale (Holmes & Rahe, 1967) include many transitions: divorce, retirement, pregnancy, illness, work role, child leaving home, death of close friend or family member. Rahe, McKean, and Arthur (1967) examined objective records of life change data and found severe illnesses correlated with preceding life changes, thus suggesting that transitions are experienced as stressful.

Why might transitions create challenges to meaning in life? One suggestion is that transitions create instability. By definition, meaning in life is a stable concept, so that measurement items such as "My life has meaning" are reliable over time. However, meaning in life can be subjectively and generally experienced ("I experience meaning in my life" "My life has purpose") or specifically experienced ("My success and achievements at work right now give my life meaning" "I have meaning in life due to my contributions to my community"). Transitions may impact one or both components of meaning. In two studies of adults sampled via the internet, Steger and Kashdan (2007) examined both daily meaning levels and global meaning and demonstrated that instability of both aspects of meaning negatively influenced well-being.

A second aspect of transitions is that they reduce or remove our ability to predict and control events. Transitions put us in situations with which we are unfamiliar, and that unfamiliarity can create a sense of threat. Coping theory (see Taylor & Stanton, 2007) suggests that coping responses related to approach and avoidance influence outcomes of stressful events. If stressors are not adequately managed, their negative influence on well-being may increase; conversely, adequate management of stressful events is associated with improved mental and physical health outcomes. When the transition imposes a loss of control, such as that occurring with a sudden health crisis or a significant bereavement, our well-being is at risk.

Many, if not most, transitions directly impact our personal identities. Our identities are achieved and maintained across many "selves." The term "self-concept differentiation" (Donahue, Robins, Roberts, & John, 1993) describes how an individual sees himself or herself as having different personality characteristics that vary by situation. In contrast, "self-concept clarity" (Campbell et al., 1996) refers to the extent to which one's self-concept is stable across time, consistent across situations, and clearly defined. Shin, Steger, and Henry (2016) examined self-concept clarity predicting meaning in life over an extended time among college students. In their study, self-concept clarity was associated with meaning in life, and students who reported an increase in clarity also reported increased meaning in life. In contrast, lowered clarity resulted in lessened meaning in life.

The social context of the transition is an additional influence on meaning. Many transitions are role transitions: role transitions can be entry transitions (getting married, becoming parents, starting college) or exit transitions (getting divorced, retiring). In a series of studies, Slotter and Walsh (2017) demonstrated several effects of role transitions. First, role exits and role entries both predicted confusion about self-identity. Second, persons who experienced negative emotions about the transition experienced greater confusion about their identity.

Transitions also create challenges as they occur in the context of developmental stage changes. As Erikson (1963) outlined, tasks we must navigate change as we develop, but each of those tasks involves the needs of the individual conflicting in some way with the needs of others. For example, the stage of identity versus role confusion occurs during adolescence. The child, becoming an adult, desires independence and autonomy, and must begin to establish his or her own ethics as opposed to the morality learned during childhood. Meaning in life, the sense of mattering, having purpose, and having coherence among selves, can be a central feature of the challenge of developmental transitions.

Even the "ending" of a transition has been implicated in the transition's effect on well-being and, potentially, meaning. Schworer, Krott, and Oettingen (2020) focused on whether people benefited from ending a transition in a well-rounded way. Well-rounded endings are marked by closure: by the belief that "everything was done that could be done," that loose ends were tied up, and that everything was completed to the fullest. These well-rounded endings are thought to contribute to ease of transition, positive affect, and selection of meaningful goals. In a series of studies, these hypotheses were supported. Well-rounded endings, including both presumably meaningful transitions (e.g., graduation from high school) and presumably less meaningful transitions (e.g., changing locations), resulted in more positive affect, less regret, and a self-reported easier transition.

In the chapters to follow, ten life transitions are presented. They are considered in the context of the type of transition and the impact of the transition on meaning in life. The transitions are of three essential types. First, there are developmental and identity transitions—those of adolescence and late life and of identity negotiation among transgender individuals. Second, there are role transitions—those of work and career choice, including meaningful work in an uncertain labor market, and those of relationship roles, specifically bereavement. Last, there are health transitions both sudden—cardiac arrest—and chronic. After consideration of these transitions, the last chapter revisits meaning in life through life's transitions and integrates the findings of specific transitions into a conceptual model.

References

Altmaier, E. M. (Ed.), (2017). *Reconstructing meaning after trauma: Theory, research, and practice.* San Diego, CA: Elsevier.

American Psychiatric Association. (2013). *Diagnostic and statistical manual of mental disorders* (5th ed.). Washington, DC: American Psychiatric Association.

Angell, J. R. (1906). *Psychology: An introductory study of the structure and function of human conscientiousness* (3rd ed.). New York: Henry Holt & Company.

Baumeister, R. F. (1991). *Meanings of life.* New York: Guilford Press.

Baumeister, R. F., & Landau, M. J. (2018). *Finding the meaning of meaning: Emerging insights on four grand questions. Review of General Psychology* (22, pp. 1–10).

Baumeister, R. F., & Vohs, K. D. (2002). The pursuit of meaningfulness in life. In C. R. Snyder & S. J. Lopez (Eds.), Handbook of positive psychology (pp. 608–618). Oxford, England: Oxford University Press.

Bliese, P. D., Adler, A. B., & Flynn, P. J. (2017). *Transition processes: A review and synthesis integrating methods and theory. Annual Review of Organizational Psychology and Organizational Behavior* (4, pp. 263–286).

Campbell, J. D., Trapnell, P. D., Heine, S. J., Katz, I. M., Lavallee, L. F., & Lehman, D. R. (1996). Self-concept clarity: Measurement, personality correlates, and cultural boundaries. *Journal of Personality and Social Psychology, 70,* 141–156.

Davis, C. G., Nolen-Hoeksema, S., & Larson, J. (1998). Making sense of loss and benefiting from the experience: Two construals of meaning. *Journal of Personality and Social Psychology, 75,* 561–574.

Davis, C. G., & Novoa, D. C. (2013). Meaning-making following spinal cord injury: Individual differences and within-person change. *Rehabilitation Psychology, 58,* 166–177.

Donahue, E. M., Robins, R. W., Roberts, B. W., & John, O. P. (1993). The divided self: Concurrent and longitudinal effects of psychological adjustment and social roles on self-concept differentiation. *Journal of Personality and Social Psychology, 64,* 834–846.

Erikson, E. H. (1963). *Youth: Change and challenge.* New York: Basic Books.

Frankl, V. E. (1963). *Man's search for meaning: An introduction to logotherapy.* Oxford, England: Washington Square Press.

George, L. S., & Park, C. L. (2017). The Multidimensional Existential Meaning Scale: A tripartite approach to measuring meaning in life. *The Journal of Positive Psychology, 12,* 613–627.

Groleau, J. M., Calhoun, L. G., Cann, A., & Tedeschi, R. G. (2013). The role of centrality of events in posttraumatic distress and posttraumatic growth. *Psychological Trauma: Theory, Research, Practice, and Policy, 5,* 477–483.

Higginson, G. D. (1937). The place of meaning in psychology. *Psychological Review, 44,* 491–504.

Holmes, T. H., & Rahe, R. H. (1967). The social readjustment rating scale. *Journal of Psychosomatic Research, 11,* 213–218.

Hooker, S. A., Masters, K. S., & Park, C. L. (2018). A meaningful life is a healthy life: A conceptual model linking meaning and meaning salience to health. *Review of General Psychology, 22,* 11–24.

Janoff-Bulman, R. (1989). Assumptive worlds and the stress of traumatic events: Applications of the schema concept. *Social Cognition, 7,* 113–136.

Kilpatrick, D. G., Resnick, H. S., Milanak, M. E., Miller, M. W., Keyes, K. M., & Friedman, J. J. (2013). National estimates of exposure to traumatic events and PTSD prevalence using DSM-IV and DSM-5 criteria. *Journal of Traumatic Stress, 26,* 537–547.

Martela, F., & Steger, M. F. (2016). The three meanings in life: Distinguishing coherence, purpose, and significance. *The Journal of Positive Psychology, 11,* 531–545.

Meert, K. L., Eggly, S., Kavanaugh, K., Berg, R. A., Wessel, D. L., Newth, C. J., et al. (2015). Meaning making during parent-physician bereavement meetings after a child's death. *Health Psychology, 34*, 453–461.

Park, C. L., & Kennedy, M. C. (2017). Meaning violation and restoration following trauma: Conceptual overview and clinical implications. In E. M. Altmaier (Ed.), *Reconstructing meaning after trauma* (pp. 17–27). New York: Elsevier.

Rahe, R. H., McKean, J. D., & Arthur, R. J. (1967). A longitudinal study of life-change and illness patterns. *Journal of Psychosomatic Research, 10*, 355–366.

Roepke, A. M., Jayawickreme, E., & Riffle, O. M. (2014). Meaning and health: A systematic review. *Applied Research in Quality of Life, 9*, 1055–1079.

Russo-Netzer, P. (2019). Prioritizing meaning as a pathway to meaning in life and well-being. *Journal of Happiness Studies, 20*, 1863–1891.

Schlossberg, N. K., Waters, E. B., & Goodman, J. (1995). *Counseling adults in transition: Linking practice with theory* (2nd ed.). New York: Springer.

Schworer, B., Krott, N. R., & Oettingen, G. (2020). Saying goodbye and saying it well: Consequences of a (not) well-rounded ending. *Motivation Science, 6*(1), 21–33.

Seligman, M. E. P. (February 24, 2017). *The PERMA model: Your scientific theory of happiness.* Available from https://positivepsychologyprogram.com/perma-model/.

Seligman, M. E. P., & Csikszentmihalyi, M. (2000). Positive psychology: An introduction. *American Psychologist, 55*, 5–14.

Shin, J. Y., Steger, M. F., & Henry, K. L. (2016). Self-concept clarity's role in meaning in life among American college students: A latent growth approach. *Self and Identity, 15*, 206–223.

Slotter, E. B., & Walsh, C. M. (2017). All role transitions are not experienced equally: Associations among self-change, emotional reactions, and self-concept clarity. *Self and Identity, 16*, 531–556.

Steger, M. F., Frazier, P., Oishi, S., & Kaler, M. (2006a). Meaning in Life Questionnaire. *Retrieved from PsycTESTS.*

Steger, M. F., Frazier, P., Oishi, S., & Kaler, M. (2006b). The Meaning in Life Questionnaire: Assessing the presence of and search for meaning in life. *Journal of Counseling Psychology, 53*, 80–93.

Steger, M. F., & Kashdan, T. B. (2007). Stability and specificity of meaning in life and life satisfaction over one year. *Journal of Happiness Studies, 8*, 161–179.

Taylor, S. E., & Stanton, A. L. (2007). Coping resources, coping processes, and mental health. *Annual Review of Clinical Psychology, 3*, 377–401.

Tolman, E. C. (1926). A behavioristic theory of ideas. *Psychological Review, 33*, 353–369.

Triplett, K. N., Tedeschi, R. G., Cann, A., Calhoun, L. G., & Reeve, C. L. (2012). Posttraumatic growth, meaning in life, and life satisfaction in response to trauma. *Psychological Trauma: Theory, Research, Practice, and Policy, 4*, 400–410.

Welby, V. (1896). Sense, meaning, and interpretation. *Mind, Vol. V, 24–37*, 186–202.

PART 2

Identity Transitions

CHAPTER

2

Navigating the teenage years: what do we know about how adolescents find meaning and purpose?

Areana Eivers and Adrian B. Kelly

School of Psychology and Counselling, Queensland University of Technology, Brisbane, QLD, Australia

Introduction

> I am 16 years old. I come from Sweden. And I speak on behalf of future generations. I know many of you don't want to listen to us – you say we are just children. But we're only repeating the message of the united climate science. ***Greta Thunberg, speech to the Houses of Parliament, United Kingdom, April 23, 2019***

Most conceptualizations of meaning and purpose are oriented toward adulthood. We know that meaning in life (MIL) is different across the lifespan (Steger & Dik, 2009). Older people generally report a greater sense of meaning, whereas young people describe higher levels of searching for meaning. Meaning commonly refers to making sense, coherence, or order of one's life, and having a purpose or goal toward which one can reach (Reker, Peacock, & Wong, 1987). Frankl (1963) conceptualized MIL as an innate desire to give as much meaning to one's life as possible, and to actualize as many values as possible. MIL can thus be thought of as having two main dimensions—the presence of meaning (perception that one's life is significant and has meaning) and the search for meaning (degree to which a person engages in efforts to understand or find meaning) (Steger, Frazier, Oishi, & Kaler,

Navigating Life Transitions for Meaning
DOI: https://doi.org/10.1016/B978-0-12-818849-1.00002-3

2006). MIL is typically associated with subjective well-being (high satisfaction with life, positive affect) and psychological well-being [autonomy, environmental mastery, personal growth, positive relationships, purpose in life (PIL), and self-acceptance]. However, whereas presence of meaning is often associated with life satisfaction, the search for meaning is often linked to depression (Steger et al., 2006). Moreover, Park, Park, and Peterson (2010) found that search for meaning can be associated with life satisfaction and more happiness when a person already has substantial meaning in their life. Similar to adults, adolescents who draw meaning from personal achievements, intimate relationships, religious values, self-acceptance, and a health community have higher life satisfaction. When adolescents haven't obtained a satisfactory level of meaning, a search for meaning can be problematic and frustrating. In this chapter on meaning-making in the context of adolescence, we will examine how these dimensions of MIL are observed specifically in the cognitive, behavioral, and social lives of adolescents, and whether underlying adult assumptions about MIL are appropriate or need revising.

Adolescence is well known to be a period of astonishing development and change. Typically beginning around age 10–12 years, adolescents undergo a host of puberty-related changes, including major physical growth, intellectual development, emerging capacity of the prefrontal cortex, menarche/gonadotrophy, increased sex drive, and the onset of reproductive capability (Li et al., 2014; Patton & Viner, 2007). Physical growth is often uneven in its proportions (e.g., height versus weight or muscle gain), and this is frequently a source of anxiety for adolescents as they search for social acceptance, approval, and potential sexual/romantic relationships. Early to middle adolescence is often characterized by preoccupations with body image and associated depression/anxiety (e.g., Hinchliff et al., 2016; Thomas et al., 2018). Intellectually, adolescents are close to reaching their pinnacle by the time they are 16, but ongoing development of the prefrontal cortex means that capacity to think conceptually, to inhibit impulses, to persist, and to plan are still in development (Kelly & Halford, 2007).

Accompanying physical changes, there are also social developmental changes, including curiosity about normative adult behaviors (e.g., Beiser, 1984), and more time spent with peers and less time spent with the family (e.g., Patton & Viner, 2007; Pinto, 2007). Adolescents are often curious about adult and forbidden behaviors. These are associated with a sense of "release" from childhood, freedom, and inclusion in peer groups with high social status (Borlagdan et al., 2010; Masterman & Kelly, 2003). Consistent with this, we have found that the ages of 14–16 years are when adolescents often first engage in sexual interactions, alcohol, tobacco, and other drug use (Chan, Kelly, Hides, Quinn, & Williams, 2016; Kelly et al., 2011; Thomas, Kelly, & Toumbourou, 2016). All of these factors make it difficult to even research the question of how adolescents develop a sense of meaning and purpose, because adolescents are grappling with multiple developmental tasks simultaneously, and may not have fully developed the conceptual language to provide a reliable measure or measures of life meaning: what it is, what it is for him/her, and where it can be found. Nevertheless, developmental markers point to adolescents being frequently engaged in a search for meaning and, beyond this, a search for PIL. The coming sections will outline what is currently understood about the developmental and ecological influences on meaning-making in adolescence.

Development of meaning-making in adolescence

Developmental theorists provide a framework for understanding the impact of enormous neurological, biological, cognitive, and social changes that occur during adolescence, and how these facilitate a growing capacity and drive for meaning-making during this phase of the human lifespan (Gilmore & Meersand, 2015; Jetha & Segalowitz, 2012; Moshman, 2011). Theorists such as Piaget, Kohlberg, and Erikson proposed an "age and stage" conceptualization of development—whereby incremental growth in cognitive capacity is associated with increasing chronological age, until by late adolescence a plateau is supposedly reached (Kunnen & Bosma, 2012). In rudimentary terms, this growth may be characterized as a movement from concrete to abstract, content to process, description to reasoning. As cognitive capacity expands, so too does adolescents' social experience, including engagement in more complex relationships and relationship networks, and both awareness of and interface with broader social-cultural contexts. This period of thick yet rapid change not only makes the process of meaning-making more accessible, it also makes it more relevant as young humans prepare themselves to be adult humans, with all the biological, social, and cultural implications of this transition.

Piaget's formal operational thought

According to Piaget's theory of cognitive development, by the age of approximately 10 years, most children will have consolidated their capacity for concrete operational thinking. By the end of this stage, children demonstrate an ability to think logically and systematically, and to consider multiple aspects of a situation or problem simultaneously (Moshman, 2011). This enables basic scientific method to be applied to problems, whereby different aspects of a task or situation are variously manipulated or held constant to test a hypothesis. Yet one key limitation of this stage of development is the continued reliance on concrete (i.e., that which is experienced through the senses) information to support the reasoning process. Piaget proposed that in many, but not all individuals, a further stage of cognitive development is achieved. This stage, proposed to extend from 12 years through to adulthood, is characterized by what Piaget called formal operational thinking. Movement from concrete operational to formal operational thought sees the young adolescent gaining an ability to think in abstract terms, with a capacity to manipulate ideas mentally rather than depending on concrete stimuli. With this capacity for abstract thought comes the ability to think about (e.g., imagine, plan, evaluate, compare) objects and experiences that have not been personally encountered. Moshman (2011) describes this ability as one that embraces "possibilities": "For the formal operational thinker, on the other hand, possibilities take on a life of their own. They are purposely and systematically formulated as a routine part of cognition. Reality is understood and evaluated as the realization of a particular possibility" (p. 9). One might argue that the adolescent processes of meaning-making are firmly grounded in this realization of possibilities.

What we know now that we did not fully know at the time that Piaget was forming his theory, is that the stages of adolescent cognitive development he proposed closely map on to underlying changes to neurological structure and activity occurring in the postpubertal brain (Blakemore & Choudhury, 2006; Jetha & Segalowitz, 2012). Not until the 1970s and 1980s did we begin to accumulate evidence that showed the frontal and prefrontal cortex regions of the brain, in particular, continue to develop past childhood and into early adulthood. Two main changes in the brain have been observed as occurring during adolescence: one is an increase in myelination, leading to greater insulation of neural cells and, hence, faster transmission of information between cells; the second is synaptic pruning, whereby redundant or relatively inactive neural connections are removed, making the brain more effective and efficient. Furthermore, changes in the brain during adolescence are associated with dramatic developments in executive functioning, capacity for logic and abstract reasoning, social information processing, and metacognition (Blakemore & Choudhury, 2006; Jetha & Segalowitz, 2012), all of which make possible both an expansion and deepening in meaning-making.

Personal narrative as meaning-making

One by-product of these cognitive developments is dramatic sophistication in the personal narratives of adolescents that incorporates more than just incremental changes to memory capacity. Personal narratives may be understood as the mental scripts we use to organize our meaning-making regarding self, other, and world, and then to communicate our meaning-making to others (Kunnen & Bosma, 2000; McLean, 2005; Nelson, 2018). Some authors have argued that personal narrative—also called the autobiographical self (Nelson, 2018) or autobiographical memory (Fivush, Habermas, Waters, & Zaman, 2011; McLean, 2005)—is the heart of meaning-making insofar as meaning-making is largely a construct of the self and the subjective. Yet even the most intrapersonal aspects of autobiography are derived from and reinforced by social experience, from the most proximal and dyadic forms of interaction (e.g., with caregivers and peers) to the influence of the collective (e.g., social norms and culture) (Fivush & Baker-Ward, 2005; Fivush et al., 2011). From birth, children are drawn into or witness stories about their own life, and about how this life is connected to the lives of others and to the world more generally (Habermas & Reese, 2015). These stories are built largely through language, but are also shaped by experience of routine and ritual, by unspoken expressions of mutual understanding between individuals or group members and by adaptations to one's environment (Nelson, 2018). Personal narratives begin as a means of mapping the self chronologically and relationally, but as the child becomes an adolescent, the narrative incorporates more and more elements of "how" and "why." Personal narrative assists in the development of identity and self-concept; during adolescence and via the capacity for abstract thought, personal narrative has the possibility of being at once more consolidated than during childhood, and more fluid and reflective, with an appreciation of moral relativity (Fivush et al., 2011; Genereux & McKeough, 2007; Habermas & Reese, 2015; Wood & Conway, 2006). Meaning-making is the glue that brings coherency to memories, impressions, and emotional responses that are not necessarily linked chronologically or even conceptually. It is the means by which we explain more than simply describe our history, to make sense of our present and future.

Constructive developmental theory

Kegan's constructive developmental theory is one attempt to explain how meaning-making develops, or is constructed, via social experience (Eriksen, 2006; Kegan, 1994; Kunnen & Bosma, 2012). Kegan's theory is based on the "age and stage" models of theorists such as Piaget, but is less concerned with the content of each stage and more with progressive changes in how individuals organize and construct their thinking, drawing on their personal experience (Eriksen, 2006; Kegan, 1994). In this process of organizing personal cognitions to suit the environment, meaning-making emerges. The theory (Kegan, 1994) proposes a series of six stages, or "orders of consciousness" that influence all aspects of an individual's social-emotional self. In the first two stages—the incorporative and impulsive—the infant and child develop from a basic consciousness that objects are outside of, or other than themselves, to a way of thinking and acting that is reflexive and driven by impulse. In the third stage—the imperial, thought to develop across the span from middle childhood to adolescence—the individual is aware that others have thoughts and feelings separate to their own, but their motivations and actions are driven by their own needs, wishes, and desires. Kegan proposed that in late adolescence it is possible, but not certain, that an individual will develop an "interpersonal" consciousness, whereby their sense of self is influenced by awareness of others' needs, interests, and desires, and a drive for mutuality in relationships.

Kegan also suggested two further stages of development in meaning-making associated with adulthood, although he argued that not all individuals will achieve these levels, or "balances" of consciousness. In the Industrial stage, individuals may define themselves according to the roles and duties they perform, or the industries and organizations to which they belong. Yet this is also the stage at which "self-authorship" becomes possible, and individuals can reflect on, modify, or discard their relationships; they can also choose to challenge social expectations and demands rather than being dependent on the expectations of others. In the final stage—the Interindividual—individuals no longer feel constrained by their personal history or by a single ideology; they are freed to reflect on multiple ideologies simultaneously and to live separately from the roles they inhabit.

While some might argue that Kegan's theory presents a developmentally pessimistic view of adolescents' meaning-making processes (Habermas & Reese, 2015; McLean, 2005), his model highlights how meaning-making is product of both intrapersonal and interpersonal experiences. In fact, most authors and researchers in the field agree that meaning-making, with its components of personal narrative and abstract reasoning, is both a social and a socialized construct. Adolescence is arguably the period, however, during which an individual not only becomes aware of the coalescence of personal and social experiences, but begins to sew these experiences together with a more coherent thread to make sense of themselves, their relationships, and the world they inhabit. To do this requires a systemic perspective. Bronfenbrenner's ecological systems theory (Bronfenbrenner, 1979) is a template for representing the systems within which adolescents (or any individuals) are embedded, and which exert dynamic influence on both the content and process of their meaning-making (Bronfenbrenner & Evans, 2000).

Systemic influences

According to ecological systems theory, individuals are constantly and concurrently engaged in transaction with multiple microsystems (e.g., family, peers, school), exosystems (e.g., legal and governing bodies), and macrosystems (e.g., mass media, cultural practice). They are also impacted by the mesosystemic interactions between subsystems, and by the chronosystemic influences of time, era, and developmental change. While the ecological systems theory heightens our appreciation of context, it also insists that we consider "the person in the center of the circles" and the way in which the individual coconstructs their social environment: "the central force in development is the active person: shaping environments, evoking responses from them, and reacting to them" (Darling, 2007, p. 204). This emphasis on the transactional processes between the developing person and the systems that they engage in and interact with is fundamental to an understanding of how meaning-making develops. While the following sections present theory and evidence of how meaning-making in adolescence is influenced by microsystemic and mesosystemic actors, it must be remembered that the adolescent, and the child before this, are not passive recipients of meaning, but rather, active contributors to it.

Influence of the caregiving environment

Arguably the earliest and hence the most powerful influence on adolescent meaning-making comes from parents or other key caregivers. From the moment of birth, children's developing narratives about their inner and outer worlds are built on the scaffolds of explanations and stories offered by the adults, and potentially older siblings, who are closest to them (Fivush et al., 2011; Fivush, Haden, & Reese, 2006; McLean & Mansfield, 2012; Reese, Yan, Jack, & Hayne, 2010). In this process, the child learns to derive meaning from their experiences based on the privileged discourses of their caregiving environment. For example, one child's parent explains a loss event, such as the death of a pet or elderly family member, as something that is "sad"; further, that this sadness is shared by others in the family or community and that it is appropriate to publicly demonstrate this sharing of sadness through acts of communal grieving (e.g., crying while reminiscing, attending a funeral and/or burial). Another child's parent explains a similar loss event as one that, while sad to some degree, is inevitable, unremarkable and possibly a relief, with efforts made to shield the child from any potential communal demonstrations of grieving. While the intent in both cases is to comfort and make things easier for the child, each of these children may develop a different meaning attached to death and experiences of loss as a consequence of exposure to different parental narratives.

Research has indicated that parental influences on processes of meaning-making persist into adolescence and beyond. In a study by McLean and Mansfield (2012), the way that mothers conversed with their adolescent children about sad, happy, and important events was significantly associated with the adolescents' meaning-making. More importantly, however, the effects varied according to the adolescents' age and gender: maternal scaffolding of meaning-making through the use of elaboration and questioning occurred more for young adolescents and for boys. Overall, more sophisticated meaning-making occurred for important events than for either sad or happy events, but the coconstruction of meaning-making was most complex with regards to sad events. For these types of events, more elaboration and questioning by mothers was associated with *less* meaning, especially for boys, which the authors suggest may indicate that conversations about sad events occur with the aim of eliciting emotional support rather than deriving meaning. Boys and girls did not differ in their level of meaning-making overall, but maternal scaffolding played a different role in supporting meaning-making according to gender. The authors conclude that girls may enter adolescence with a stronger foundation for meaning-making in the way of a more coherent personal narrative, such that they require less help from their mothers to develop their meaning-making style. This is consistent with a study (Fivush, Bohanek, Zaman, & Grapin, 2012) that showed adolescent girls tend to tell "longer, more elaborated, more coherent, and more reflective narratives that contain more internal-state language" (p. 315) than do adolescent boys. The authors of this study argue that this finding reflects gender differences in the ways that adolescents engage in the process of meaning-making; namely,

> Narratives are not just a product but are part of the process of creating meaning. Thus, a longer narrative suggests that females are working harder to create meaning than are males.... females' greater inclination to think about past events, to work through experiences to make sense of them, and to create more coherent evaluative understandings of one's past. Indeed, females report thinking about the past more frequently than do males and using past experiences in the service of understanding the self and current situations more so than do males (pp. 313–315).

2. Identity Transitions

An alternative interpretation may be, however, that these gender differences do not indicate significant differences in the capacity or desire for meaning-making, only that adolescent males and females go about the process of extracting meaning in different ways. There is scope for more exploration in this area.

In summary, despite the normal developmental drive toward differentiation and autonomy during adolescence, evidence suggests that adolescents still look to their parents to support the coconstruction of meaning through the sharing and scaffolding of narrative (McLean, 2005; McLean & Jennings, 2012; Pratt, Norris, Hebblethwaite, & Arnold, 2008). Of course, the favored narrative of a parent is itself shaped by the dominant *discourse of meaning* espoused by the community, society, and culture in which the parent and child are situated (Fivush et al., 2006, 2011). Parental reminiscing, explanation, and elaboration are, thus, the lenses through which sociocultural norms regarding meaning are focused in the individual (Fivush et al., 2006; Reese et al., 2010). Other members of the adolescent's extended family may also exert influence on meaning-making, such as grandparents and older siblings (Pratt et al., 2008; Pratt, Norris, Lawford, & Arnold, 2010), particularly in non-Western and more collectivist cultures where extended family and kin networks are often more actively engaged in caregiving (Bornstein & Güngör, 2009).

Influence of peers

One of the key aspects of development during adolescence is the growing importance and influence of peer relationships. In particular, adolescent friendships become a ground for the development and expression of intimacy and emotional support beyond the family boundary, which prepares individuals for ongoing life relationships including with romantic partners (Furman & Buhrmester, 1992; Smetana, Campione-Barr, & Metzger, 2006). Intimacy and support are often achieved through mutual self-disclosure (McLean & Jennings, 2012), making peers also, thus, significant actors in the processes of coconstructing meaning-making during this period. Importantly, however, adolescent peers are often engaged in their own, concurrent attempts at meaning-making. They may, therefore, coconstruct meaning but are limited in their capacity to provide the same degree of narrative, cognitive, and emotional scaffolding that parents and other key adult influences can provide (McLean & Mansfield, 2012). McLean and Jennings (2012) conducted a study in which they compared conversations about past events between 22 adolescents and their peers, and between the same adolescents and their mothers. The conversations were coded for degree of personal meaning communicated and amount of listener scaffolding behavior. The authors found that peers were less likely to provide scaffolding of narrative than mothers, although narrative scaffolding was found to be significantly associated overall with more evidence of meaning-making. There was also a difference in the quality of the shared meaning-making: friends were more likely than mothers to make suggestions about how their adolescent peers represented themselves to the world. Peers may also help adolescents to add shape to narratives and meanings away from the preconstructed narratives of influential adults, for example, constructing their own or at least alternative interpretations of key events, or assigning different priorities to the sources of information that have been used to construct meaning from these events by other family members. McLean and Jennings conclude,

> ...(adolescence) requires acquisition of an understanding of societal norms, as they will be the new standard for behavior outside of the family. Friends may play a critical role in this shift, providing a testing ground for how teenagers voice their identities. Friends can gently guide one another toward their age-specific norms in a way that mothers cannot (or perhaps choose not to) do (p. 1466).

Peers become, thus, both a buffer and a stepping stone for meaning that is socially constructed. They may provide a bridge between what meaning is offered by the family and other early microsystems (e.g., teachers) and the meaning available through engagement with the systems beyond these, such as social media, and sociocultural practices (Smetana et al., 2006).

It is also apparent that the influence of parents on adolescent meaning-making becomes weaker over time as adolescents engage in the developmentally normative process of separation from parents and differentiation of identity (Bokhorst, Sumter, & Westenberg, 2010). Increasingly, peers and not parents become both coach and audience in the meaning-making process (McLean, 2005). The psychological negotiation of these shifting relationship dynamics seems also to be reflected in the way memories are represented to make meaning. McLean and Thorne (2003) found that adolescents' recall of experiences of/with parents more often involved themes of separation and conflict than did peer memories, although both parent and peer memories included themes of closeness. By late adolescence, the proportions of closeness and separation themes in parent memories were more balanced, perhaps indicating that autonomy and relatedness sit more comfortably together in the parent–child relationship by this age, establishing a pattern to be continued into adulthood. Interestingly, themes of conflict in memories of either parents or peers were more strongly associated with meaning than were themes of closeness, emphasizing the importance of "struggle narratives" in meaning-making. Whether this association is a stronger feature of adolescent meaning-making versus meaning-making throughout the lifespan is unclear.

Purpose in life during adolescence

Some theorists have extended the concept of meaning to purpose: a PIL represents an intention to contribute to matters larger than the self. More particularly, PIL is a stable and generalized intention to accomplish something that is at once meaningful to the self and leads to productive engagement with some aspect of the world beyond the self (Bronk, 2012; Bronk & Finch, 2010; Damon, Menon, & Cotton Bronk, 2003). Bronk (2012) proposes that PIL, though based on MIL, varies from MIL in that purpose usually involves commitment at some level to a greater (often prosocial) cause with an other-oriented component, whereas MIL does not necessarily involve a cause beyond the individual (Bronk & Finch, 2010). As such, MIL is largely intrapersonal whereas PIL reaches across broader social systems. Bronk and Finch (2010) argue that it is purpose that makes an especially strong contribution to positive adolescent development. PIL also seems to serve a protective function, for example, higher purpose scores have been associated with lower levels of drug use during adolescence (Bronk, 2012; Noblejas de la Flor, 1997).

Bronk and Finch (2010) found evidence of consistent differences between youth reporting self-oriented MIL and those reporting other-oriented PIL. In a sample of 144 adolescents, four clusters were identified. The first group of youth was small (less than 5%) and consisted of those yet to identify a source of life meaning or purpose. The second group, or the self-focused cluster, consisted of youth who reported high scores for self-oriented sources of meaning (e.g., make money, be successful) and low scores for other-oriented sources of purpose. The third group of adolescents, or the other-focused cluster, exhibited essentially the opposite pattern of responses. These young people reported high scores for other-oriented sources of purpose (e.g., help others, make the world a better place) and low scores for self-oriented sources of meaning. Finally, the fourth group, or the both self- and other-oriented cluster, reported high scores for both self- and other-oriented long-term aims. Respondents in the latter two groups, who reported being drawn to at least some other-oriented long-term aims, are thought to represent youth with potentially purposeful interests. Youth with other-oriented long-term aims are more likely to be searching for a purpose, to have identified a purpose, to report higher levels of life satisfaction, and to score higher on openness (Bronk & Finch, 2010; Bronk, Hill, Lapsley, Finch, & Talib, 2010).

Adolescents who report strong MIL and PIL are innately impressive to most adults. Greta Thunberg (2019) noted this in her speech about the dangers of climate change to the United Kingdom's Houses of Parliament in 2019; she pointed out that she would prefer less attention be paid to her personal commitment to a cause or purpose, and more attention paid to the core problem of climate change: "People always tell me and the other millions of school strikers that we should be proud of ourselves for what we have accomplished. But the only thing that we need to look at is the emission curve. And I'm sorry, but it's still rising." Greta Thunberg is what one might call a "noble exemplar" (Bronk, 2012)—a young woman with a passionate PIL, and a clear sense of who she is and what she exists for. Purpose exemplars are perceived to have many character strengths or virtues, including hope and optimism, kindness, love and social intelligence, gratitude, perseverance, honesty and integrity, and openness to experience (Bronk, 2012; Bronk & Finch, 2010; Bronk et al., 2010; Malin, Liauw, & Damon, 2017).

Important to note, however, is that meaning and purpose are both often slow to develop and this process is unlikely to be smooth. In a study of early development of PIL (Bronk, 2012), three waves of in-depth, case study style interviews were conducted with nine adolescent "purpose exemplars" (young people with intense commitments to noble purposes). At Time 1, participants were between 12 and 23 years of age (M age = 19.11; SD = 3.37). Interviews were again conducted approximately 2.5 years later (Time 2), with a third round of interviews conducted 2 years later still (Time 3). The key findings were that purpose exemplars didn't have sudden or strong commitment to their causes during adolescence, and their initial level of interest was not especially intense. Young people in this study often reported inspirational narratives as triggering their interest or exploration of a cause. Capacity to maintain a positive attitude, to problem solve, to learn from mistakes, and to enact solutions are undoubtedly crucial to maintaining purpose (Toumbourou, 2016).

Summary and conclusions

For adolescents, biopsychosocial development occurs at a rapid rate, and the search for meaning and purpose in this context is often experienced as depressing and frustrating. Social experiences become more and more complex as adolescents become increasingly able to think abstractly, imagine, and realize possibilities. Meaning-making through social interactions are a key way in which adolescents build personal narratives—a key process in building a sense of self and purpose.

As adolescents grow, their narratives become more about the how and why of experience, more flexible, and more about self-authorship, contributing to a sense of agency as they seek to address social expectations, roles and demands. Parents and older siblings have key roles in scaffolding meaning through discourse, but the process of meaning-making seems to vary by child gender. Sons tend to have less rich, elaborate, and reflective personal narratives than daughters, and daughters tend to work harder to create meaning and are more reflective than boys. Peers, by virtue of being in a similar stage of development, are important sources of meaning-making, but the nature of meaning-making provided by peers is more about shaping behavior toward age-based social norms and become increasingly important as adolescents differentiate from their parents. Themes of closeness and struggle may pervade meaning-making, and this may be especially strong for adolescents compared to adults. A small proportion of adolescents move to other focused searches for meaning, and the journey toward passionate purpose is frequently incidental and incremental. Parents and older members of families have key roles in creating opportunities for exposure to inspirational sources and fostering values and character traits that align with other focused perspectives.

References

Beiser, H. R. (1984). An example of self-analysis. *Journal of the American Psychoanalytic Association, 32*, 3–12.

Blakemore, S. J., & Choudhury, S. (2006). Development of the adolescent brain: Implications for executive function and social cognition. *Journal of Child Psychology and Psychiatry and Allied Disciplines, 47*(3–4), 296–312.

Bokhorst, C. L., Sumter, S. R., & Westenberg, P. M. (2010). Social support from parents, friends, classmates, and teachers in children and adolescents aged 9 to 18 years: Who is perceived as most supportive? *Social Development, 19*(2), 417–426.

Borlagdan, J., Freeman, T., Duvnjak, A., Lunnay, B., Bywood, P. T., & Roche, A. M. (2010). *From ideal to reality: Cultural contradictions and young people's drinking*. Adelaide, Australia: National Centre for Education and Training on Addiction, Flinders University.

Bornstein, M. H., & Güngör, D. (2009). Organizing principles and processes from developmental science for culture and caregiving. In S. Bekman, & A. Aksu-Koç (Eds.), *Perspectives on human development, family, and culture* (pp. 69–85). New York: Cambridge University Press.

Bronfenbrenner, U. (1979). *The ecology of human development : experiments by nature and design*. Cambridge, MA: Harvard University Press.

Bronfenbrenner, U., & Evans, G. W. (2000). Developmental science in the 21st century: Emerging questions, theoretical models, research designs and empirical findings. *Social Development, 9*(1), 115–125.

Bronk, K. C. (2012). A grounded theory of the development of noble youth purpose. *Journal of Adolescent Research, 27*(1), 78–109.

Bronk, K. C., & Finch, W. H. (2010). Adolescent characteristics by type of long-term aim in life. *Applied Developmental Science, 14*(1), 35–44.

Bronk, K. C., Hill, P., Lapsley, K., Finch, H., & Talib, T. (2010). Purpose, hope, and life satisfaction in three age groups. *Journal of Positive Psychology*, *4*, 500–510.

Chan, G. C. K., Kelly, A. B., Quinn, C., Hides, L., & Williams, J. W. (2016). Does gender moderate the relationship between polydrug use and sexual risk taking among Australian secondary school students under 16? *Drug and Alcohol Review*, *35*, 750–754. Available from https://doi.org/10.1111/dar.12394.

Damon, W., Menon, J., & Bronk, K. C. (2003). The development of purpose during adolescence. *Applied Developmental Science*, *7*, 119–128.

Darling, N. (2007). Ecological Systems Theory: The Person in the Center of the Circles. *Research in Human Development*, *4*(3–4), 203–217. Available from https://doi.org/10.1080/15427600701663023.

Eriksen, K. (2006). The constructive developmental theory of Robert Kegan. *The Family Journal*, *14*(3), 290–298.

Fivush, R., & Baker-Ward, L. (2005). The search for meaning: Developmental prespectives on internal state language in autobiographical memory. *Journal of Cognition and Development*, *6*(4), 455–462.

Fivush, R., Bohanek, J. G., Zaman, W., & Grapin, S. (2012). Gender differences in adolescents' autobiographical narratives. *Journal of Cognition and Development*, *13*(3), 295–319.

Fivush, R., Habermas, T., Waters, T. E. A., & Zaman, W. (2011). The making of autobiographical memory: Intersections of culture, narratives and identity. *International Journal of Psychology*, *46*(5), 321–345.

Fivush, R., Haden, C. A., & Reese, E. (2006). Elaborating on elaborations: Role of maternal reminiscing style in cognitive and socioemotional development. *Child Development*, *77* (6), 1568–1588.

Furman, W., & Buhrmester, D. (1992). Age and sex differences in perceptions of networks of personal relationships. *Child Development*, *63*(1), 103.

Frankl, V. (1963). *Man's search for meaning: an introduction to logotherapy*. Boston, MA: Beacon Press.

Genereux, R., & McKeough, A. (2007). Developing narrative interpretation: Structural and content analyses. *British Journal of Educational Psychology*, *77*(4), 849–872.

Gilmore, K. J., & Meersand, P. (2015). *The little book of child and adolescent development*. New York: Oxford University Press.

Habermas, T., & Reese, E. (2015). Getting a life takes time: The development of the life story in adolescence, its precursors and consequences. *Human Development*, *58*(3), 172–201.

Hinchliff, G. L. M., Kelly, A. B., Chan, G. C. K., Toumbourou, J. W., Patton, G. C., & Williams, J. (2016). Risky dieting behaviors amongst adolescent girls: Associations with family relationship problems and depressed mood. *Eating Behaviors*, *22*, 222–224.

Jetha, M. K., & Segalowitz, S. J. (2012). Adolescent brain development: Implications for behavior. *Journal of Youth and Adolescence*, *43*(12), 2088–2090.

Kegan, R. (1994). *In over our heads: The mental demands of modern life*. Cambridge, MA: Harvard University Press.

Kelly, A. B., & Halford, W. K. (2007). Responses to ethical challenges in conducting research with Australian adolescents. *Australian Journal of Psychology*, *59*(1), 24–33.

Kelly, A. B., O'Flaherty, M., Connor, J. P., Homel, R., Toumbourou, J. W., Patton, G. C., & Williams, J. (2011). The influence of parents, siblings and peers on pre- and early-teen smoking: A multilevel model. *Drug and Alcohol Review*, *30*, 381–387.

Kunnen, E. S., & Bosma, H. A. (2000). Development of meaning making: A dynamic systems approach. *New Ideas in Psychology*, *18*(1), 57–82.

Kunnen, S. E., & Bosma, H. (2012). A logistic growth model: Stage-wise development of meaning making. In S. E. Kunnen (Ed.), *A dynamic systems approach to adolescent development* (pp. 117–130). London: Routledge.

Li, H. K., Kelly, A. B., Chan, G. C. K., Toumbourou, J. W., Patton, G. C., & Williams, J. W. (2014). Pubertal development and alcohol use: Does family relationship quality moderate this association? *Addictive Behaviors, 39*, 1389–1393.

Malin, H., Liauw, I., & Damon, W. (2017). Purpose and character development in early adolescence. *Journal of Youth and Adolescence, 46*, 1200–1215.

Masterman, P. W., & Kelly, A. B. (2003). Reaching adolescents who drink harmfully: Fitting intervention to developmental reality. *Journal of Substance Abuse Treatment, 24*(4), 347–355.

McLean, K. C. (2005). Late adolescent identity development: Narrative meaning making and memory telling. *Developmental Psychology, 41*(4), 683–691.

McLean, K. C., & Jennings, L. E. (2012). Teens telling tales: How maternal and peer audiences support narrative identity development. *Journal of Adolescence, 35*(6), 1455–1469.

McLean, K. C., & Mansfield, C. D. (2012). The co-construction of adolescent narrative identity: Narrative processing as a function of adolescent age, gender, and maternal scaffolding. *Developmental Psychology, 48*(2), 436–447.

McLean, K. C., & Thorne, A. (2003). Late adolescents' self-defining memories about relationships. *Developmental Psychology, 39*(4), 635–645.

Moshman, D. (2011). *Adolescent rationality and development: cognition, morality, and identity* (3rd ed.). New York: Psychology Press.

Nelson, K. (2018). Making memory: Meaning in development of the autobiographical self. In A. Rosa, & J. Valsiner (Eds.), *The Cambridge handbook of sociocultural psychology* (2nd ed., pp. 260–273). Cambridge: Cambridge University Press.

Noblejas de la Flor, M. (1997). Meaning levels and drug-abuse therapy: An empirical study. *International Forum for Logotherapy, 20*, 46–51.

Park, N., Park, M., & Peterson, C. (2010). When is the search for meaning related to life satisfation? *Applied Psychology: Health and Well-Being, 2*, 1–13.

Patton, G. C., & Viner, R. (2007). Pubertal transitions in health. *The Lancet, 369*(9567), 1130–1139.

Pinto, K. (2007). Growing up young: The relationship between childhood stress and coping with early puberty. *The Journal of Early Adolescence, 27*, 509–544.

Pratt, M. W., Norris, J. E., Hebblethwaite, S., & Arnold, M. L. (2008). Intergenerational transmission of values: Family generativity and adolescents' narratives of parent and grandparent value teaching. *Journal of Personality, 76*(2), 171–198.

Pratt, M. W., Norris, J. E., Lawford, H., & Arnold, M. L. (2010). What he said to me stuck: Adolescents' narratives of grandparents and their identity development in emerging adulthood. In K. C. McLean, & M. Pasupathi (Eds.), *Narrative development in adolescence: Creating the storied self* (pp. 93–112). New York: Springer.

Reese, E., Yan, C., Jack, F., & Hayne, H. (2010). Emerging identities: Narrative and self from early childhood to early adolescence. In K. C. McLean, & M. Pasupathi (Eds.), *Narrative development in adolescence: Creating the storied self* (pp. 23–43). New York: Springer.

Reker, G. T., Peacock, E. D., & Wong, P. T. P. (1987). Meaning and purpose in life and well-being: A life-span perspective. *Journal of Gerontology, 47*, 44–49.

Smetana, J. G., Campione-Barr, N., & Metzger, A. (2006). Adolescent development in interpersonal and societal contexts. *Annual Review of Psychology, 57*(1), 255–284.

Steger, M. F., & Dik, B. J. (2009). If one is looking for meaning in life, does it help to find meaning in work? *Applied Psychology: Health and Well-Being, 1*(3), 303–320.

Steger, M. F., Frazier, P., Oishi, S., & Kaler, M. (2006). The meaning in life questionnaire: Assessing the presence of and search for meaning in life. *Journal of Counseling Psychology, 53*(1), 80–93.

Thomas, H., Kelly, A. B., & Toumbourou, J. W. (2016). Prevention of alcohol-related harm for children and adolescents. In J. Fitzgerald, & G. Byrne (Eds.), *Psychosocial dimensions of medicine* (pp. 291–304). Melbourne, Australia: IP Communications.

Thomas, R., Kelly, A. B., Chan, G. C. K., Hides, L. M., Quinn, C. A., Kavanagh, D. J., & Williams, J. (2018). An examination of gender differences in the association of eating and weight loss attitudes and substance use. *Drug and Alcohol Review, 36*, 68–69.

Thunberg, G. (2019). 'You did not act in time': Greta Thunberg's full speech to MPs. The Guardian, 23rd April, 2019. Accessed 18th March, 2020.

Toumbourou, J. W. (2016). Prevention of adolescent risk behavior and promotion of positive youth development. In J. L. Romano, & M. Israelashvili (Eds.), *The Cambridge handbook of international prevention science* (pp. 432–455). Cambridge: Cambridge University Press.

Wood, W. J., & Conway, M. (2006). Subjective impact, meaning making, and current and recalled emotions for self-defining memories. *Journal of Personality, 74*(3), 811–845.

CHAPTER

3

Men's transitions in late life: exploring the influence of male norms

Nicholas C. Neibergall[1] *and Francisco J. Sánchez*[2]

[1]Thompson Center, University of Missouri, Columbia, MO, United States, [2]Educational, School & Counseling Psychology, University of Missouri, Columbia, MO, United States

Introduction

Aging for men has become an industry. Whereas before women drove the revenue for dermatologists, cosmetologists, and plastic surgery, today men are using these services at increasing levels, especially as they age. Yet unlike women who are in general trying to maintain their physical beauty, men are fighting to maintain their physical prowess. Consequently, age-related factors that affect men differ from those that affect women.

In this chapter we focus on issues related to men and aging. For most people, aging entails going through a variety of transitions such as retirement, death/loss, changes in mobility, health issues, changing family structures, and caring for aging loved ones. Several of these are covered in more detail in other chapters of this book. In this chapter we examine theories of men and masculinity to highlight ways that gender norms can serve to both help and hinder these and other types of transitions.

Of course, the individual process of transition is influenced by the person's appraisal of meaning (Thompson & Janigian, 1988) related to the transition process itself and the outcome following the process. For

Navigating Life Transitions for Meaning
DOI: https://doi.org/10.1016/B978-0-12-818849-1.00003-5

example, some people will relish in their ability to retire and shift their time and attention toward other interests while others identify a retirement transition with a loss of meaning in their life and a concrete signal of approaching elder years. Many people will likely fall somewhere in the middle of this spectrum or partially on each side of these two options simultaneously. Throughout this chapter, we examine ways in which traditional masculine norms influences these types of meaning appraisal processes. We begin with a review of foundational theories related to male norms. We then focus on relevant factors for transitions experienced by older men that have been identified in peer-reviewed literature.

Masculinity theories

Even into late adulthood, men continue to try to adhere to traditional masculine norms (Thompson & Langendoerfer, 2016). Yet, the realities of being an older man can interfere with fulfilling these traditional roles. In this section, we present a classic conceptualization of the construction of "traditional masculinity" among men in the United States. We then present three theories of masculine norms commonly used within the psychological study of men and masculinities that have psychometric scales to measure their constructs. Other theories can be found in Wong and Wester (2016).

One specific conceptualization was posited by Brannon (1976). It was primarily based on ideas of masculinity from the 1950s and 1960s, and it was comprised of four categories that outlined male roles (David & Brannon, 1976), which we describe below. Although that model is now over 40 years old, a content analysis of 98 qualitative studies published since 2000 including those focused on older men noted that participants' definitions continued to closely align with the four categories (Thompson & Langendoerfer, 2015). Furthermore, the subsequent theories that we will highlight exhibit similar categories as Brannon's model.

No "sissy stuff": the stigma of anything vaguely feminine

The first category focuses on avoiding stereotypical femininity. That is, any type of attitude, behavior, and outward characteristic that is considered stereotypically "feminine" should be avoided at all costs. Such prohibited traits can include appearing vulnerable, expressing sentimental emotions, being too emotionally intimate in relationships, and dressing in ways that are seen as feminine.

This category also includes the rejection of "homosexuality" and anything that is seen as "gay." Specifically, any kind of sexual or romantic relationship with another man is seen as antithetical to traditional notions of masculinity that dismisses one as feminine even though gender expression among gay and bisexual men varies along a continuum. To some degree, even befriending a man who is known or suspected of being gay can undermines one's standing as being masculine. Thus avoiding and confronting anything gay is often used as a strategy for preserving one's sense of masculinity.

Of course, popular notions regarding masculinity–femininity have evolved where today many view the binary gender system as a false dichotomy. Rather than being either/or and fixed, masculinity–femininity is increasingly seen as far more fluid. Nevertheless, it must be noted that many researchers, clinicians, and the general public continue to view these concepts as dichotomous and reject any challenges to that system.

The big wheel: success, status, and the need to be looked up to

The second category consists of indicators that a man has been successful. First, men must achieve status and power, which includes being admired and looked up to by others. Second, men should work to achieve and maintain high standing through competition and overpowering other people, especially other men. If a man does not have a sense of objective prestige in his community, this is seen as a threat to his identity as a man. The man should do whatever is necessary to push ahead and be seen as objectively successful in all that he does including school, work, community activities, family relationships, and hobbies. Third—and related to the prior two—a man should be able to provide for his family as the primary "breadwinner."

This category represents objectifying men in a utilitarian way, namely that they are only worth what they can produce. If men internalize the belief that they are only worth what they produce, then this process sets them up for psychological difficulties as they age and their ability to continue to be "successful" (in the way that they have been) begins to decrease. Although outsiders may see a man positively based on his lifetime achievements, a man's internal view is that perceived worth has been adversely affected by the limitations that come from aging.

The sturdy oak: a manly air of toughness, confidence, and self-reliance

The third category is the idea that men must be strong and tough, even in the face of great adversity. Men are expected to constantly project an image of self-confidence, self-reliance, great calmness, and the ability to handle difficult situations without being perturbed. Even if a man happens to feel unsure or incompetent, he should avoid exhibiting or admitting this. David and Brannon (1976) noted that this category is vague and harder to define; this may be due in part because this is an unrealistic and highly unachievable ideal. Nonetheless, boys socialized under these norms from an early age are expected to enact the idea of "being a man" despite the lack of clear instructions on what this means or how to do it. Thus boys are forced to rely on role models and imitate the behavior of those around them who are glorified as the ultimate personifications of "manliness."

One prototypical expression of "sturdiness" is through one's outward body appearance: Men who look strong and muscular personify what it means to be a "sturdy oak" (David & Brannon, 1976). This expression becomes challenging for older men who lose muscle mass and physical strength as a result of the aging process; this will be discussed in greater detail in later sections of this chapter. Older men may find themselves losing touch with their sense of perceived masculinity as it becomes more and more challenging to be the "sturdy oak" they once were.

Give 'em hell: the aura of aggression, violence, and daring

The final category of masculinity is defined through outward manifestations of strength and toughness. The intermingling of violence and what it means to "be a man" is learned from an early age as young boys and is reinforced over time. Although men are taught to be unemotional and to hide their emotions, anger is one of the few emotions that men are encouraged to express. In some Latinx communities, this is sometimes referred to as *machismo* (Arciniega, Anderson, Tovar-Blank, & Tracey, 2008); however, the specificity to how these terms are defined can vary greatly between regions, across disciplines, and among individual persons.

The overall theme of this category is dominance over other people and the expression of that dominance through overt and, in some cases, extreme ways. Over time, this aspect of masculinity has become particularly visible in television, movies, video games, and other forms of media. War is an ultimate expressions of this category both from an individual perspective as well as from a collective perspective (e.g., extreme pride in one's country at all costs necessary). Additionally, David and Brannon (1976) suggest that interpersonal violence through sports are key activities that exemplify this category. With few exceptions, these are activities that older men generally are not able to participate in directly. However, many older men still seek to participate in these activities indirectly through the consumption of media.

The work of David and Brannon (1976) and other scholars led to great interest in trying to measure norms associated with masculinity in the United States. Several key measures have been proposed and examined within the psychological study of men and masculinities. Although each theory has unique nuances, they generally include constructs similar to David and Brannon's four categories. Here we highlight a few key theories; the reader is referred to Walker, Tokar, and Fischer (2000) and Wong, Steinfeldt, Speight, and Hickman (2010) for additional information.

Gender role strain paradigm

Pleck proposed one of the major theoretical paradigms in the psychological study of men and masculinities (Cochran, 2010; Pleck, 1981, 1995). In this paradigm, gender roles are seen as socially constructed to protect patriarchal systems of power and oppression (Levant, 1996). Rather than arising naturally from a person, the performance of gender roles is instilled from a young age through a social system rewarding those who conform and sanctioning those who fail to conform. Pleck's theory furthered David and Brannon's theory, especially shifting the focus away from biological deterministic and essentialist views that had dominated psychoanalytic perspectives on sex differences for most of the 20th century (Levant & Richmond, 2016).

Research focused on this paradigm has identified three core sources of male gender role strain. The first strain is related to "gender role discrepancy" in which a man believes that he has failed to live up to a version of masculinity that is highly unattainable (Pleck, 1995). Consequently, most men experience feelings of being deficient for not meeting all these expectations, even if they are living successful lives (Liu, Rochlen, & Mohr, 2005; Rummell & Levant, 2014).

The second source of strain is referred to as "gender role dysfunction." This refers to the dysfunction experienced by men who strictly adhere to gender norms (Pleck, 1981, 1995). Research has found an association between conforming to masculine norms and a range of interpersonal problems (e.g., aggressive behavior, intimate partner violence, work problems; Amato, 2012; Seabrook, Ward, & Giaccardi, 2018) and mental health problems (Cournoyer & Mahalik, 1995; Wong, Ho, Wang, & Miller, 2017).

The third source of strain comes from "gender role trauma." This refers to the unique experience of certain groups of men for whom gender norms are particularly harsh. For instance, men who are part of a primarily fraternal group (e.g., elite sports, firefighters, military service members; Brooks, 1990; Steinfeldt, Gilchrist, Halterman, Gomory, & Steinfeldt, 2011) have additional expectations related to the norms of the groups that they identify with. Conversely, men from historically marginalized groups (e.g., men of color, men with disabilities, and gay/bisexual men; Good et al., 2006; Sánchez, Greenberg, Liu, & Vilain, 2009; Watkins, Walker, & Griffith, 2010) are often excluded from dominant conceptions of masculinity and they either struggle to meet societal expectations—which is seen as a futile goal—or they develop their own norms that further alienate them from the dominant group. These added expectations in the socialization process have been argued to be traumatic for men, even for the few who are able to complete the process with relative success (Pleck, 1995). Levant (1992) suggested that one negative outcome from this type of trauma is a stunted emotional development, labeled alexithymia, in which men have difficulty identifying and describing their feelings which in turn leads to significant difficulties in men's relationships.

Gender role conflict

O'Neil developed one of the first theories within the psychological study of men and masculinities that corresponded to Pleck's work (O'Neil, 1981a, 1981b). According to O'Neil, traditional gender role socialization coupled with society's "mystique" about what it means to be masculine instills a fear of femininity within males. This in turn fosters four primary patterns related to gender role conflict.

The first pattern of "success, power, and competition" refers to an individualist type of achievement in all areas regardless of the costs. Competition is also encouraged and is seen as essential for getting ahead. The second pattern is "restricted emotionality" where men learn not to be emotionally expressive, especially in front of other people. The third pattern is like the second pattern but is specific to "avoiding affectionate or intimate connection" with other men. That is, connecting with other men on an emotional level is seen as a threat to one's ability to maintain a strong sense of independence and invulnerability. The final pattern of this theory is the "competition" between devoting time to one's family versus devoting time to a job or education. Although men are socialized to be devoted to their family, they are also expected to be devoted to their careers to provide for their families. Consequently, men may have trouble balancing occupational and familial responsibilities.

Traditional masculinity in older men

The expression of masculine norms in older men is an understudied topic. In fact, much of how we understand masculinity ideology today is based on research with younger men. Complicating the issue is that many of the studies published in peer-reviewed journals have focused on the experience of "older men" using mixed gender samples (e.g., Baker & Gringart, 2009) and/or combined generational cohorts: That is, samples often include men who are markedly younger than 65 years old (e.g., Barken & Sims-Gould, in press). Nonetheless a few studies have identified how older men think about and practice their gender. In this section, we explore key aspects of masculine ideology that this research has identified as salient for older men. First, we present two qualitative studies focused on men 65 years of age or older that offer some general findings on the effects of aging. We then explore issues reported in these two studies in investigations with younger cohorts of men.

The effect of aging on men's masculine identity

Much of the research on older men's experience with gender norms have employed qualitative methodology. Although limited in generalizability, these studies have provided rich themes for future researchers to explore. For instance, in a study of 29 community dwelling men ages 65–89, Hurd Clarke and Lefkowich (2018) explored how these men defined masculinity and described the ways in which aging affected their sense as a man. Physical strength, leadership, and virility were three primary categories of masculinity identified in this sample of men. Yet, the men detailed how traditional notions of masculinity favor the young. In large part, this is because many attributes of traditional masculinity (e.g., strength, power, sexual prowess) become more difficult to attain given the natural progression of the male body. To counteract the effects of aging, many of the men used exercise and medications (e.g., Viagra and Cialis). Hurd Clarke and Lefkowich (2018) also noted that the older men were comfortable revealing intimate details from their lives that might make younger men feel vulnerable. Thus a potential positive from aging is an easing of restricting emotions and behaviors that previously prevented the men from expressing emotions and seeking help when they needed it.

In a subsequent study, Hurd and Mahal (in press) explored how older men experienced their aging bodies. In large part, their primarily heterosexual sample (only one participant identified as "homosexual") felt positive about their bodies, especially relative to what they had expected to look like at their age. However, many noted changes in their health, strength, cognitive abilities, and sexual functioning that naturally come with aging—all of which were seen as a threat to their masculine identities.

Holding on to the male body in late life

An important expression of gender for people of all ages is the physical appearance of one's body including body shape, hairstyle, and gait. This outward expression has been coined "doing gender" (West & Zimmerman, 1987). The unwritten societal "rules" about what is deemed masculine or feminine tends to be based on young to middle-aged adulthood although there are exceptions based on public personalities of older men (e.g., John Wayne, Marlon Brando, Clint Eastwood). These "rules" almost exclusively adhere to a strictly dichotomous binary gender system which ignores what younger generations are seeming to embrace, such as the concepts of gender fluidity and gender-nonbinary persons.

There are many biological transitions that occur as men age, over which they have no control, that challenge their identity in terms of what it means to be masculine (Calasanti & King, 2018). Some of the ways in which older men minimize the effects of aging are done via over-the-counter products marketed to both instill and address anxieties. For instance, an increasing number of older men are dying their hair, adopting dieting fads, purchasing antiaging creams, and using herbal supplements. Older men are increasingly accessing medical interventions historically used mostly by women, including plastic surgery and cosmetic injections like Botox (Ojala, Calasanti, King, & Pietilä, 2016). Perhaps the most common strategy to regain control over one's body is the use of erectile dysfunction drugs. Overall, more and more older men are using strategies to combat aging that were once seen as a female activity. Yet, rather than using the strategies to preserve their physical attractiveness, it seems that men engage in these behavior to preserve a healthy and strong outward appearance (Ojala et al., 2016).

Older men as caregivers

A dated estimate from 1990 approximates at least 1 million older adult male caregivers at that time (Kaye & Applegate, 1990). More recent estimates (2015–2016 data) are that there are 3.5 million men 65+ years providing unpaid care (Bureau of Labor Statistics, 2017). Although caregiving is not a universal experience of aging men, it is an important experience that will continue to increase in relevance as Americans are living longer and aging in place. It was noteworthy in reviewing the literature for writing this chapter that much of the peer-reviewed research on older adult men was related to their role as caregivers.

Transitioning to the role of caregiver can be challenging for men as they age because the emotional and practical duties of the role are usually relegated to women. Despite challenges, men tend to feel a sense of responsibility for the care of their spouse and this sense can deter men from hiring professional help or accessing resources that could help ease the burdens of the role (Black, Schwartz, Caruso, & Hannum, 2008). Although gender may not be the first thing a person may think of related to caregiving, it is relevant in a variety of different ways. Men who become caregivers are sometimes seen as particularly noble or selfless compared to women who take on the role (Milne & Hatzidimitriadou, 2003). This is yet another example of how societal "rules" or standards influence behavior, attitudes, and meaning of transition.

Given the challenges and "newness" of this role, older men may perform tasks in a way similar to how they would have performed tasks in their former career. This similarity can include having a managerial or task/mastery focused approach, avoiding feelings and focusing on tasks, working to maintain a sense of normalcy, self-medicating (e.g., alcohol), and distracting oneself from challenges with other hobbies/activities (Calasanti & King, 2007). Relying on gendered strategies that are familiar can help the coping process through the transition to the significant novel challenge of caregiving. Despite the many challenges of taking on a role that does not fit the traditional masculine man, men in one study (Ribeiro, Paúl, & Nogueira, 2007) noted that modern approaches to masculinity have allowed them to be more content in their role compared to how male caregivers would have been treated decades before in that role.

Caregiving is an inherently challenging role that entails tasks and responsibilities virtually round-the-clock. When men encounter significant difficulties, their sense of competence can be challenged, leading to depression, isolation, and loneliness (Milligan & Morbey, 2016). Rather than interpreting these challenges as normal or typical to the role of caregiving, some men internalize these challenges and struggle to express how they feel to others. An additional way gender can influence male caregivers is how they work to preserve the gender expression of their ailing partner (Calasanti & Bowen, 2006). Illness, frailty, and dementia can each be threats to gender expression.

A challenging aspect of being a caregiver for men is that it is an ongoing role without definable outcomes (Russell, 2007). Men often choose careers and hobbies which have a tangible product; examples include woodworking, athletics, manufacturing, and skilled trade jobs. It can be emotionally draining to complete the same tasks of caregiving-day in and day out without tangible end-products or recognition. Men may feel their work is unacknowledged and underappreciated since they may be used to positive praise for the more observable outcomes they had previously worked toward (Russell, 2007).

Despite transition challenges, men can also find a great deal of meaning through their role as caregivers. One key example is in understanding that their decision to provide care delayed or prevented the institutionalization of their partner (Russell, 2001). Relatedly, men may feel that no one knows their partner's needs and preferences in the same way they do, meaning they are best suited to provide direct care. Men may also see the role of caregiving as part of their duties as a man or husband. Men are certainly capable of providing adequate nurture and care despite being socialized that this is not an important part of being a man. In other words, societal expectations of men being unsuited to be good caregivers, including emotionally, is an artificially and socially constructed illusion that can be confronted.

Long-term care

One of the most challenging transitions for many older adults is the transition from their home to living in a long-term care (LTC) facility. Examples of these transitions are an older man entering LTC, an older man's spouse/partner entering LTC, and transitions from one LTC facility to another. Any of these situations can elicit shifts in identity that can be challenging; for example, when older men's wives are entering LTC, it can be difficult to adjust to strangers providing the majority of care that the husband once provided (Eriksson & Sandberg, 2008).

Some male LTC residents tend to isolate themselves rather than develop bonds with individuals as close/intimate friends (Moss & Moss, 2007). Men often rely on discussing previous work experiences/achievements and other tangible stereotypical representations of their identities as men in their interpersonal interactions. Although modern facilities attempt to support resident autonomy, entering LTC is one of the most tangible perceived losses of autonomy an older person can experience. Although challenging for men and women alike, this transition may be especially difficult for men given that independence is highly valued within traditional notions of masculinity (Smith, Braunack-Mayer, Wittert, & Warin, 2007).

Emotional expression and asking for help

The ability to be emotionally expressive and to seek support during difficult times is important for all people. For many men, it can be challenging because seeking emotional support goes against the expectations of men (Bennett, 2007). Men are taught from an early age that they either should not have certain emotions (e.g., "man up") or that the primary strategy for processing emotions should be to ignore or suppress them (e.g., "boys don't cry" but "get over it"). Being rational is an acceptable trait for men. Additionally, one strategy for processing and expressing emotions for older men is to assert their masculinity through actively engaging in a tangible activity rather than experience emotions (Bennett, 2007). This strategy, whether conscious or not, can help men to create meaning through suffering in ways that feel congruent with their identities as men.

One barrier to seeking help is the shift of identity from being a contributor to society to being primarily a receiver (Gregorčič, 2019). There are many communities (particularly rural communities) where there is not an abundance of resources for older people. For communities that do have resources for older people, some men may still refrain from engaging with these resources because of the identity shift to being a receiver. Many would argue that this shift is a natural and healthy one and that older people have earned their right to be in a receptive role. The meaning attributed by some older men to this identity change may skew negatively due in part to their sense of masculinity as independent men who earn their worth through providing.

Research has been relatively conclusive that men seek help at lower rates than women (e.g., Wendt & Shafer, 2014). Difficulty in asking for help is a problem of men of all ages, not just older adult men. However, stressors that can occur for older adult men can be significant. Furthermore, older adult men may be less able to work through problems independently due to health concerns, cognitive limitations, physical barriers/disabilities, and other impairing circumstances. Men may feel guilt or shame about needing to ask for help (Greenwood & Smith, 2015). When men delay asking for help, small problems can become transformed into large problems. For example, if an older man is unable to make mortgage payments, he may struggle to independently solve the problem over time. External sources of help that could have aided the identification of financial alternatives may only become involved too late as the man faces foreclosure. Men also have a greater tendency to avoid help seeking as a result of negative experiences asking for help in the past (Greenwood & Smith, 2015).

Widowed men

The loss of one's partner can be one of the most challenging transitions of late life. The death of one's partner also creates strong feelings of loss of control over one's life that can exacerbate the experience of suffering as a result of the loss (Canham, 2009). One common strategy for navigating this transition is by repartnering (Bennett, 2007). Repartnering can help men restore masculine roles related to sexuality, social roles, and practical domestic problems (e.g., such as not knowing how or preferring not to cook his own meals).

Religion can be one source of support during these trying times, but heterosexual men tend to be less religious than women and, in some studies, Gay men (García, Gray-Stanley, & Ramirez-Valles, 2008). Some men identify as religious because of available opportunities for leadership and/or social capital (Thompson & Remmes, 2003); this form of identification would suggest that older men rely on religious systems and communities to satisfy desires for social power and leadership rather than because of an internal sense of private devotion which is more common among women.

Older men and health

A consistent finding in research is that men access the health care system at a lower rate than women (Bertakis, Azari, Jay Helms, Callahan, & Robbins, 2000). Proportionally lower utilization of care throughout the lifetime may be an important variable influencing lower rates of life expectancy in among men (Pinkhasov et al., 2010). However, life expectancy is a complex issue with many variables and there are other factors that interact with low utilization rates. Within the United States some cultural groups, such as Black and Latinx men, have even lower utilization rates than White men (Dunlop, Manheim, Song, & Chang, 2002). Maintaining good health is important at any stage of life and medical problems can lead to difficult life transitions for older men, such as from relative independence to total dependence. A single health event for an older person can result in long-term reductions in the ability to care for oneself independently.

When it comes to men's health, evidence suggests that masculinity is less of a protective factor and is a strong risk factor for negative health outcomes (Levant & Wimer, 2014). One key difference in older men is the threat of loss of personal independence often outweighs the threat to masculinity of seeking help and going to the doctor (Smith et al., 2007; Tannenbaum & Frank, 2011). In other words, when having to "choose between two [perceived] evils" (i.e., seek help and potentially maintain independence or avoid help seeking and risk losing independence), loss of independence is a greater threat to masculinity than going to get professional help. Nonetheless, many men will continue to delay seeking health care and work to solve the medical problem they are having through self-help methods until they are certain beyond a doubt that they are unable to solve the problem on their own (Smith et al., 2007).

Masculinity can also influence how men navigate significant health transitions. Stansbury, Mathewson-Chapman, and Grant (2003) examined Veterans who had experienced prostate cancer. They found that patients who held strongly internalized societally defined values of masculinity experienced greater distress than patients who had flexible understandings of masculinity. This finding may not translate well to other health conditions given that the prostate is a significant part of the male biology. Good et al. (2006) found a variety of effects of masculinity on health outcomes after a serious injury. Within this study, increased masculinity resulted in lower life satisfaction, negative attitudes toward seeking help, and increased perceived functional barriers. An important finding in this study that did not appear to fit with these findings is that after 1 year, patients who identified as more masculine had better rehabilitation outcomes (Good et al., 2006). The researchers hypothesized this may have been a function of the perseverance and commitment to overcoming obstacles commonly associated with masculinity.

A note on late life suicide in older men

Suicide is an epidemic that disproportionately affects men. Older men are not immune from this trend and are in fact are one of the most vulnerable age groups to suicide (Canetto, 2017). The high rates of suicide among older adult men, and men in general, indicate masculinity likely plays at least some role in a significant disruption in meaning-making in one's life leaving a person to feel the only way out is to end their life. Many researchers have pondered the question "what makes men, and particularly older men, so vulnerable?" It is important we continue to work to better understand risk and protective factors for suicide and work to both prevent and intervene with older men to reduce suicide rates.

Positive expression of maleness

"Toxic masculinity" and "hegemonic masculinity" are terms and concepts often studied and discussed in both empirical research and the media. While it is important to better understand the darker side of masculinity, there are also researchers who are examining masculinity from a strengths-based/positive psychology approach. Given the relevance of positive psychology constructs to meaning in life, this approach may help understand and emphasize how strengths expressed through masculinity can counter the problematic elements of masculinity.

Kiselica and Englar-Carlson (2010) argued that identification of masculinity strengths may be more beneficial than focusing on the problematic elements of masculinity. They proposed that studying male "strengths" would increase understanding of masculinity. Among the strengths they identified, six related specifically to interpersonal patterns: male relational style focused on shared activities, male ways of caring including use of empathy, generative fatherhood, a group orientation toward common purpose, and the larger societal impact of fraternal organizations. Individual strengths are self-reliance, importance of work, courage and daring, and use of humor.

These strengths, with a positive psychology masculinity paradigm, were investigated by McDermott et al. (2019) in a large-scale survey (over 1000) of community living men and women. Using literature review and focus group methods, a large number of attributes were developed and presented for ratings on the degree to which the attribute was expected for women and expected for men. One notable finding was that almost all of the social-relational variables were expected more of women; a few exceptions were being a mentor and being a motivator, which were equally expected. Many attributes were rated as positive and as expected more for men; examples were being a leader, providing safety, being hardworking. However, of the male expectations, many were expressions of the traditional masculinity models; examples were being strong physically, driven to succeed, and finding ways to achieve goals despite obstacles.

Conclusion

Aging is an inevitable reality of life. Although our older years come with unique challenges, most people continue to experience lives of fulfillment. Nonetheless, cultural stereotypes and popular media present a slanted perspective on this time in life. Furthermore, marketing that promotes antiaging products by making us feel insecure about aging perpetuates negative perspectives.

For men, much of the focus in aging is on what has been "lost" in terms of capabilities and autonomy. For men who value stereotypical notions of masculinity, age-related impairments to fulfilling these notions result in distress. Some men respond to this distress by using interventions with potential health threats: hormone replacement therapy, androgenic–anabolic steroids, sexual enhancement medications, and other interventions.

In this chapter we have considered how gender norms contribute to younger and older men's sense of self. We examined theories of masculinity to offer a framework for understanding the nature of traditional norms and for the influence of those norms on older men. Qualitative and quantitative research highlights how older men are negatively affected by traditional norms.

As research in the psychology of men and masculinities continues, psychological scientists must intentionally sample older men to better understand their experience. There is also a need to examine male norms among aging men with subsets of underrepresented men: racial/ethnic minorities, men with disabilities, gay and bisexual men, and transgender men. Such research can help inform practitioners who are working with men in their later years.

References

Amato, F. J. (2012). The relationship of violence to gender role conflict and conformity to masculine norms in a forensic sample. *The Journal of Men's Studies, 20*, 187–208.

Arciniega, G. M., Anderson, T. C., Tovar-Blank, Z. G., & Tracey, T. J. G. (2008). Toward a fuller conception of machismo: Development of a traditional machismo and caballerismo scale. *Journal of Counseling Psychology, 55*(1), 19–33.

Baker, L., & Gringart, E. (2009). Body image and self-esteem in older adulthood. *Ageing & Society, 29*, 977–995.

Barken, R., & Sims-Gould, J. (in press). Home support workers and older men: The implications of masculinity for later life care. *Men and Masculinities*. https://doi.org/10.1177/1097184X18804308.

Bennett, K. M. (2007). "No Sissy Stuff": Towards a theory of masculinity and emotional expression in older widowed men. *Journal of Aging Studies, 21*(4), 347–356.

Bertakis, K. D., Azari, R., Jay Helms, L., Callahan, E. J., & Robbins, J. A. (2000). Gender differences in the utilization of health care services. *Journal of Family Practice, 49* (February), 147–152.

Black, H. K., Schwartz, A. J., Caruso, C. J., & Hannum, S. M. (2008). How personal control mediates suffering: Elderly husbands' narratives of caregiving. *The Journal of Men's Studies, 16*(2), 177–192.

Brannon, R. (1976). The male sex role: Our culture's blueprint of manhood, and what it's done for us lately. In D. David, & R. Brannon (Eds.), *The forty-nine percent majority: The male sex role* (pp. 1–45). New York: Random House.

Brooks, G. R. (1990). Post-Vietnam gender role strain: A needed concept? *Professional Psychology: Research and Practice, 21*, 18–25.

Bureau of Labor Statistics. (2017). *Unpaid eldercare in the United States 2015-16 summary*. Retrieved from <https://www.bls.gov/news.release/pdf/elcare.pdf>.

Calasanti, T., & Bowen, M. E. (2006). Spousal caregiving and crossing gender boundaries: Maintaining gendered identities. *Journal of Aging Studies, 20*(3), 253–263.

Calasanti, T., & King, N. (2007). Taking "women's work" "like a man": Husbands' experiences of care work. *Gerontologist, 47*(4), 516–527.

Calasanti, T., & King, N. (2018). The dynamic nature of gender and aging bodies. *Journal of Aging Studies, 45*(February), 11–17.

Canetto, S. S. (2017). Suicide: Why are older men so vulnerable? *Men and Masculinities, 20*(1).

Canham, S. L. (2009). The interaction of masculinity and control and its impact on the experience of suffering for an older man. *Journal of Aging Studies, 23*(2), 90–96.

Cochran, S. V. (2010). Emergence and development of the psychology of men and masculinity. In J. C. Chrisler, & D. R. McCreary (Eds.), *Handbook of gender research in psychology: Vol. 1. Gender research in general and experimental psychology* (pp. 43–58). New York: Springer.

Cournoyer, R. J., & Mahalik, J. R. (1995). A cross-sectional study of gender role conflict examining college-aged and middle-aged men. *Journal of Counseling Psychology, 42*, 11–19.

David, D. S., & Brannon, R. (Eds.), (1976). *The forty-nine percent majority: The male sex role.* New York: Random House.

Dunlop, D. D., Manheim, L. M., Song, J., & Chang, R. W. (2002). Gender and ethnic/racial disparities in health care utilization among older adults. *Journals of Gerontology – Series B Psychological Sciences and Social Sciences, 57*(4), 221–233.

Eriksson, H., & Sandberg, J. (2008). Transitions in men's caring identities: experiences from home-based care to nursing home placement. *International Journal of Older People Nursing, 3*(2), 131–137.

García, D. I., Gray-Stanley, J., & Ramirez-Valles, J. (2008). "The priest obviously doesn't know that I'm gay": The religious and spiritual journeys of Latino gay men. *Journal of Homosexuality, 55*(3), 411–436, h.

Good, G. E., Schopp, L. H., Thomson, D., Hathaway, S., Sanford-Martens, T., Mazurek, M. O., & Mintz, L. B. (2006). Masculine roles and rehabilitation outcomes among men recovering from serious injuries. *Psychology of Men & Masculinity, 7*(3), 165–176.

Greenwood, N., & Smith, R. (2015). Barriers and facilitators for male carers in accessing formal and informal support: A systematic review. *Maturitas, 82*(2), 162–169.

Gregorčič, M. (2019). Bottom-up strategies for community engagement and informal learning: Targeting men aged 60 years or more. *Andragoška Spoznanja, 25*(2), 19–35.

Hurd Clarke, L., & Lefkowich, M. (2018). 'I don't really have any issue with masculinity': Older Canadian men's perceptions and experiences of embodied masculinity. *Journal of Aging Studies, 45*(June), 18–24.

Hurd, L., & Maha, R. (in press). 'I'm pleased with my body': Older men's perceptions and experiences of their aging bodies. *Men and Masculinities.* https://doi.org/10.1177/1097184X19879188.

Kaye, L. W., & Applegate, J. S. (1990). *Men as caregivers to the elderly: Understanding and aiding unrecognized family support.* Lexington, MA: Lexington.

Kiselica, M. S., & Englar-Carlson, M. (2010). Identifying, affirming, and building upon male strengths: The positive psychology/positive masculinity model of psychotherapy with boys and men. *Psychotherapy, 47*(3), 276–287.

Levant, R. F. (1992). Toward the reconstruction of masculinity. *Journal of Family Psychology, 5*, 379–402.

Levant, R. F. (1996). The new psychology of men. *Professional Psychology: Research & Practice, 27*, 259–265.

Levant, R. F., & Richmond, K. (2016). The gender role strain paradigm and masculinity ideologies. In J. Y. Wong, & S. R. Wester (Eds.), *APA handbook of men and masculinities* (pp. 23–49). Washington, DC: American Psychological Association.

Levant, R. F., & Wimer, D. J. (2014). Masculinity constructs as protective buffers and risk factors for men's health. *American Journal of Men's Health, 8*(2), 110–120.

Liu, W. M., Rochlen, A. B., & Mohr, J. (2005). Real and ideal gender role conflict: Exploring psychological distress among men. *Psychology of Men & Masculinity, 6*, 137–148.

McDermott, R. C., Pietrantonio, K. R., Browning, B. R., McKelvey, D. K., Jones, Z. K., Booth, N. R., & Sevig, T. D. (2019). In search of positive masculine role norms: Testing the positive psychology positive masculinity paradigm. *Psychology of Men and Masculinities, 20*, 12–22.

Milligan, C., & Morbey, H. (2016). Care, coping and identity: Older men's experiences of spousal care-giving. *Journal of Aging Studies, 38*, 105–114.

Milne, A., & Hatzidimitriadou, E. (2003). "Isn't he wonderful?" Exploring the contribution and conceptualization of older husbands as carers. *Ageing International, 28*(4), 389–407.

Moss, S. Z., & Moss, M. S. (2007). Being a man in long term care. *Journal of Aging Studies, 21*(1), 43–54.

Ojala, H., Calasanti, T., King, N., & Pietilä, I. (2016). Natural(ly) men: Masculinity and gendered anti-ageing practices in Finland and the USA. *Ageing and Society, 36*(2), 356–375.

O'Neil, J. M. (1981a). Male sex-role conflicts, sexism and masculinity. *The Counseling Psychologist, 9*, 61–81.

O'Neil, J. M. (1981b). Patterns of gender role conflict and strain: Sexism and fear of femininity in men's lives. *Personnel and Guidance Journal, 60*, 203–210.

Pinkhasov, R. M., Wong, J., Kashanian, J., Lee, M., Samadi, D. B., Pinkhasov, M. M., & Shabsigh, R. (2010). Are men shortchanged on health? Perspective on health care utilization and health risk behavior in men and women in the United States. *International Journal of Clinical Practice, 64*(4), 475–487.

Pleck, J. H. (1981). *The myth of masculinity*. Cambridge, MA: MIT Press.

Pleck, J. H. (1995). The gender role strain paradigm: An update. In R. F. Levant, & W. S. Pollack (Eds.), *A new psychology of men* (pp. 11–32). New York: Basic Books.

Ribeiro, O., Paúl, C., & Nogueira, C. (2007). Real men, real husbands: Caregiving and masculinities in later life. *Journal of Aging Studies, 21*(4), 302–313.

Rummell, C. M., & Levant, R. F. (2014). Masculine gender role discrepancy strain and self-esteem. *Psychology of Men & Masculinity, 15*, 419–426.

Russell, R. (2001). In sickness and in health a qualitative study of elderly men who care for wives with dementia. *Journal of Aging Studies, 15*(4), 351–367.

Russell, R. (2007). The work of elderly men caregivers: From public careers to an unseen world. *Men and Masculinities, 9*(3), 298–314.

Sánchez, F. J., Greenberg, S., Liu, W. M., & Vilain, E. (2009). Reported effects of masculine ideals on gay men. *Psychology of Men & Masculinity, 10*, 73–87.

Seabrook, R. C., Ward, L. M., & Giaccardi, S. (2018). Why is fraternity membership associated with sexual assault? Exploring the roles of conformity to masculine norms, pressure to uphold masculinity, and objectification of women. *Psychology of Men & Masculinity, 19*(1), 3–13.

Smith, J. A., Braunack-Mayer, A., Wittert, G., & Warin, M. (2007). "I've been independent for so damn long!": Independence, masculinity and aging in a help seeking context. *Journal of Aging Studies, 21*(4), 325–335.

Stansbury, J. P., Mathewson-Chapman, M., & Grant, K. E. (2003). Gender schema and prostate cancer: Veterans' cultural model of masculinity. *Medical Anthropology: Cross Cultural Studies in Health and Illness, 22*(2), 175–204.

Steinfeldt, J. A., Gilchrist, G. A., Halterman, A. W., Gomory, A., & Steinfeldt, M. C. (2011). Drive for muscularity and conformity to masculine norms among college football players. *Psychology of Men & Masculinity, 12*(4), 324–338.

Tannenbaum, C., & Frank, B. (2011). Masculinity and health in late life men. *American Journal of Men's Health, 5*(3), 243–254.

Thompson, E. H., & Langendoerfer, K. B. (2015). Older men's blueprint for "being a man". *Men and Masculinities, 19*(2), 119–147.

Thompson, E. H. Jr., & Langendoerfer, K. B. (2016). Older men's blueprint for 'being a man.' *Men and Masculinities, 19*, 117–147. https://doi.org/10.1177/1097184X15606949.

Thompson, E. H., Jr., & Remmes, K. R. (2003). Does masculinity thwart being religious? An examination of older men's religiousness. *Journal for the Scientific Study of Religion, 41*(3), 521–532.

Thompson, S. C., & Janigian, A. S. (1988). Life schemes: A framework for understanding the search for meaning. *Journal of Social and Clinical Psychology, 7*(2–3), 260–280.

Walker, D. F., Tokar, D. M., & Fischer, A. R. (2000). What are eight popular masculinity-related instruments measuring? Underlying dimensions and their relations to sociosexuality. *Psychology of Men & Masculinity, 1*(2), 98–108.

Watkins, D. C., Walker, R. L., & Griffith, D. M. (2010). A meta-study of Black male mental health and well-being. *Journal of Black Psychology, 36*, 303–330.

Wendt, D., & Shafer, K. (2014). Gender and attitudes about mental health help seeking: Results from national data. *Health and Social Work, 41*(1), e20–e28.

West, C., & Zimmerman, D. H. (1987). Doing gender. *Gender and Society, 1*(2), 125–151.

Wong, Y. J., Ho, M.-H. R., Wang, S.-Y., & Miller, I. S. K. (2017). Meta-analyses of the relationship between conformity to masculine norms and mental health-related outcomes. *Journal of Counseling Psychology, 64*(1), 80–93.

Wong, Y. J., Steinfeldt, J. A., Speight, Q. L., & Hickman, S. J. (2010). Content analysis of *Psychology of Men & Masculinity* (2000–2008). *Psychology of Men & Masculinity, 11*(3), 170–181.

Wong, Y. J., & Wester, S. R. (Eds.), (2016). *APA handbook of men and masculinities*. Washington, DC: American Psychological Association.

CHAPTER

4

Transitions and transcendence: transgender individuals' identity negotiations and meaning construction in context

Eric C. Chen, Hannah Sugarman and Melissa Brenman

Division of Psychological and Educational Services, Graduate School of Education, Fordham University at Lincoln Center, New York, NY, United States

Societal norms, attitudes, and expectations regulating interpersonal behaviors are based on the assumption that sex is a dichotomous biological category; as such, transgender individuals often confront challenges in exploring their gender identity because of pressure to conform to a societal norm of gender expression (Bethea & McCollum, 2013). The term, "transgender," encompasses a broad spectrum of individuals whose gender identity or gender role or both do not match their assigned biological sex at birth (American Psychological Association (APA), 2015). Gender identity refers to an individual's deeply felt, inherent sense of being male, female, a blend of male and female, or another gender (ALGBTIC Transgender Committee, 2009). Gender identity is thus a personal, internal, and psychological experience of one's gender; a transgender individual may or may not concentrate on the outward expression of one's gender. Transgender individuals may also express "gender-variant" or "gender nonconforming" behaviors when their appearance or actions do not conform to the traditional norms for

Navigating Life Transitions for Meaning
DOI: https://doi.org/10.1016/B978-0-12-818849-1.00004-7

individuals of their biological sex (APA, 2009). It should be noted that the definitions of transgender-related constructs continue to evolve, as a result of shifting usage and contextual focus of terms.

Across the life span, all humans experience various types of life transitions, from developmental, personal, and career-related changes (e.g., college graduation, retirement), to those brought on by sudden or unexpected events (e.g., suffering from a severe illness, being laid off). For transgender individuals, "gender transitions" constitute significant life transitions that operate through both intra- and interpersonal channels and involve changes in sex category and gender identity. More specifically, gender transitions refer to "the process of changing from the gender roles and expectations associated with one's sex assigned at birth to align one's external appearance and behaviors more closely with gender identity" (Austin, 2016, p. 26). Gender transition is thus a potentially transformative and transcendent experience that may present changes and challenges spanning many aspects of one's life, including psychological, social, medical, and legal domains.

Gender transitions may, but do not always, involve changes to one's name and pronouns used, or surgical alterations to one's physical appearance or genitals (APA, 2015). At the interpersonal level, transgender individual's gender transitions, and the disclosure of their gender identity specifically, may be fraught with experiences of discrimination and victimization due to their status as a gender minority group in a transphobic societal culture (Hendricks & Testa, 2012). Misconceptions have proliferated regarding transgender individuals, and negotiations of their interpersonal relationships during gender transitions are often hampered by the fluidity and temporary nature of transgender identities. Contextual factors, such as laws and policies, reflect cultural and structural stigma against transgender individuals, further exacerbating the stresses involved in gender transitions and promoting internalization of stigmatic self-perceptions. Furthermore, experiences and anticipation of prejudice, discrimination, and harassment increase risks of mental and physical health complications (Bockting, Miner, Romine, Hamilton, & Coleman, 2013).

In the workplace, transgender individuals at various points in their gender transitions may be subjected to various forms of harassment and discrimination, which may be verbal, emotional, physical, or technological. According to the Human Rights Campaign (2019), 21 states in the United States prohibit employment discrimination based on sexual orientation and gender identity. It is illegal, for instance, under New York state law to harass an individual undergoing a gender transition regardless of the gender currently reflected on the individual's legal documentation. For transgender employees, their transitions may be intertwined with career decision-making processes, posing implications for their job-related stress and workplace satisfaction. Transgender employees' navigation of their gender identity expression and disclosure is thus affected by their relationships with colleagues, organizational policies, and barriers and support therein, in addition to the broader sociocultural context.

Regardless of the forms and levels of gender transitions, they can lead to difficulties in forming a coherent and positive personal identity, as well as in interpersonal relationships. Transgender individuals have to make sense of the meaning and implications of the changes involved in gender transitions as they navigate through them. As transgender individuals' self-definitions of their gender identity evolve, their appearances, behaviors, and communication patterns, both verbal and nonverbal, may change accordingly. Therefore they may need to confront others, from close family members to strangers in their daily encounters, with questions of how to respond appropriately. As a result of this process, their interpersonal connections may be forged, extended, or unraveled.

Within the family context, a transgender individual's gender transition is a period of uncertainty in which the intersection of what was previously assumed about the individual's identity and what is now known may provoke a search for new meaning for all members of the family. Family members may struggle with the ways in which they perceive and interact with the transgender individual, as well as with the meaning of their relationships before, during, and after the changes in sex category and gender identity. Thus transgender individuals and their families are confronted with a complex process of meaning-making surrounding transitions (Norwood, 2012), such as renegotiation of communication with one another about their changing roles and expectations (e.g., a daughter becomes a son, a brother becomes a sister, a husband becomes a wife).

Intrapersonally, gender transitions catalyze exploration of its implications on different elements of "meaning in life": *purpose* (having a goal of personal importance), *mattering* (being valued), *continuity* (holding true across time), and *coherence* (connecting disparate parts of life) (Altmaier, 2017). In the book, *The Evolving Self*, Kegan (1982) contends that all confrontations of human issues and concerns may be understood from the perspective of meaning-making. That is, being human involves the ongoing efforts of meaning-making in light of experience, which is a lifelong process that evolves over time. Kegan describes points of stability in meaning-making as "evolutionary truces," which establish a balance between self and other and present new solutions to the tension between an individual's desire for connection and distinctness. Furthermore, the heterogeneity of experiences among transgender individuals underscores the importance of considering developmental challenges and contextual factors in our understanding of their experiences of identity transitions and transcendence, and the evolution of meaning driven by those experiences. An individual's self-concept consists of multiple social identities and, as such, gender identity may move toward the center or periphery of the individual's self-concept in different contexts and stages in life.

The purpose of this chapter is to highlight transgender individuals' meaning-making as they confront issues related to their gender identity management, transition, and negotiations. In Kegan's (1982) terms, transgender individuals' psychological distress and resilience can be thought of as resulting from the emergence of a need to renegotiate the terms of their evolutionary truce. In the following sections, we first draw on the literature on stigma and minority stress to highlight how they affect transgender individuals' transitions in gender identity. Next, we examine the diversity of experiences among transgender individuals in identity management, expression, and disclosure through the lens of intersectionality and concealability of stigmatized identities. We conclude the chapter with suggestions for clinicians in school and mental health settings to support transgender individuals in their search for gender identity and to embrace its evolving nature over the life span.

Stigma, minority stress, and transgender identity

Transgender individuals' stress and health risks are often associated with gender-related stigma (Hatzenbuehler, Phelan, & Link, 2013). Stigma refers to an attribute or socially conferred mark that is perceived to discredit and reduce an individual "from a whole and usual person to a tainted, discounted one" (Goffman, 1963, p. 3); as such, stigma distinguishes individuals with this mark from others, portraying them as deviant and less valued (Link & Phelan, 2001). In the stigma literature, four distinct but related types of stigma processes produce and increase stress among members of stigmatized groups: *enacted, felt, internalized, and anticipated* (Major, Dovidio, Link, & Calabrese, 2018).

First, enacted stigma, according to Major et al. (2018), occurs at the interpersonal or structural level and communicates a bias against a person. At the interpersonal level, this refers to discrimination or the unfair treatment of stigmatized groups through prejudice. At the structural level, it refers to laws or cultural norms that limit opportunities, resources, and the overall well-being of stigmatized groups. Second, felt stigma refers to the perception that one's self is socially devalued based on membership in a stigmatized group. These perceptions stem from being treated unfairly, but can also occur in the absence of enacted stigma. Third, internalized stigma, also called "self-stigma," operates at the intrapersonal level. It occurs when an individual, consciously or unconsciously, adopts the negative societal beliefs and feelings connected with their stigmatized status. Finally, anticipated stigma is the expectation of encountering biases or discrimination on the basis of one's stigmatized mark before any bias actually occurs.

When individuals are at risk of being stigmatized, they may experience constant feelings of uncertainty and the need to be vigilant. As such, the stress in response to stigma influences one's affective, cognitive, behavioral, and physiological responses, often resulting in social isolation or community exclusion. Stigma and oppressive beliefs and attitudes toward transgender individuals' identity transitions also affect their family members. Transgender individuals' family members may have to confront enacted, felt, internalized, and anticipated stigma in their own negotiation of the transgender individual's transitions (Norwood, 2012).

Adding to the stigma literature, Hendricks and Testa (2012) expanded Meyer's (2003) minority stress model to deepen our understanding of the psychological mechanisms that underlie the negative consequences of societal biases against transgender individuals. In the adapted minority stress model for transgender individuals proposed by Hendricks and Testa, different types of minority stressors occur along a continuum, from the proximal, subjective, and direct to the distal, objective, and indirect. These stressors are (1) experiences of discrimination, in which transgender individuals are exposed to prejudice and harassment as they express, or are perceived to express, gender-variant or gender-nonconforming behavior; (2) expectation of stressful events, in which they expect to encounter harassment related to their gender identity or expression; (3) internalization of negative societal attitudes, otherwise known as internalized transphobia; and (4) concealment of their gender identity or expression.

Research has supported the role of minority stress in the development of maladaptive coping and mental health problems for transgender individuals (Breslow et al., 2015; Timmins, Rimes, & Rahman, 2017). There is also evidence, however, that transgender individuals may demonstrate resilience to negative health outcomes despite, or because of, minority stress (Bockting et al., 2013). Thus it is important to examine the complex dynamics between minority stressors and health outcomes as transgender individuals navigate their transition of gender expression and identity.

Intersectional nature of transgender individuals' identities

Because of the evolving view of gender identity and the diverse experiences of gender among transgender individuals, it is important to gain a more nuanced understanding of the intersection of transgender individuals' identities, and the combined effects of their specific social identities. The process of developing one's identity is based on a series of psychological events which occur both consciously and subconsciously over time (Chatman, Eccles, & Malanchuk, 2005), and help each individual reinforce a coherent sense of self. Buss (2001) further distinguished between personal identity and social identity, where personal identity refers to "the sense of being different from everyone else in appearance, behavior, character, or personal history," and social identity is "knowing oneself to be a member of a nation, religion, race, vocation, or any other group that offers a sense of belonging to something larger than oneself" (p. 358). In Chatman et al.'s (2005) view, an individual's personal self is a compilation of the meaning one makes from the individual's multiple identities and group memberships. Individuals are active and selective in accepting or rejecting beliefs, but also are influenced by the perceptions and assumptions of the groups they identify with (Swann, Johnson, & Bosson, 2009).

As humans encounter new physical and social contexts, they are challenged with the task of maintaining a balance between self-continuity and redefinition. When individuals are capable of negotiating their sense of self through new experiences, they are more likely to cultivate positive well-being (Chatman et al., 2005). Holding a marginalized identity increases the likelihood that individuals will encounter or anticipate stigmatization, contributing to more experiences that force them to negotiate their self-narrative with that being projected onto them from others. Transgender individuals who hold intersectional minority identities experience increased challenges to negotiating these identities, which, in turn, strains their ability to protect a healthy sense of self.

The intersection of group membership and exclusion not only influence the ways in which others will interact with an individual, it also affects the level of access to resources and social mobility they are able to achieve within a broader social context. According to a 2015 survey conducted by the National Center for Transgender Equality, 38% of black transgender individuals reported living in poverty, compared to just 12% of the US population. There were also disparities in housing instability, with 51% of black transgender women reporting that they have experienced homelessness at one point during their lives. The survey also found that 26% of black transgender participants were unemployed, twice the rate of the overall transgender sample and four times the rate of the general population. Thus the intersection of stigmatized identities resulting in experiences of racism and transphobia appears to contribute to lower levels of economic stability and social mobility. The prevalence of structural inequalities coupled with the numerous assaults that have occurred on transgender women of color in the United States and globally, highlights the lack of acceptance and safety for individuals holding these intersecting, marginalized identities. In 2018 alone, the Human Rights Campaign (2018) tracked at least 26 deaths of transgender people in the United States due to fatal violence, a majority of who held multiple intersectional minority identities. The continual aggression shown toward these women is likely to have a profound impact on their meaning-making process, perpetuating the message that society devalues their existence and is not willing to ensure their safety.

Personal and social identities shape individuals' experiences within and across groups, but also are experienced, at times independently, depending on the social contexts and interactions they encounter. As such, transgender individuals may identify more strongly with one social identity over another, and the meaning linked to one's identity may be activated by contexts or situations in which that identity is salient. Alvarado (2012) proposes that no one social identity can be understood in its entirety without examining the interactions it has with each of the other social identities an individual holds. Moreover, the intersectional nature of multiple social identities may compound systemic barriers for transgender individuals as a group at the fringes of society, such as transgender women of color being excluded from social groups due to sexism and racism. In a sample of transgender women of color in San Francisco, for instance, Latina and black transgender women were found to experience higher levels of exclusion and transphobia in comparison to other transgender women of differing racial backgrounds (Sugano, Nemoto, & Operario, 2006). In short, as a result of the intersectional nature of multiple identities, the experiences and consequences of transgender individuals' transitions and identity disclosures vary greatly both within and across groups.

Transgender individuals' stigmatized identities

When transgender individuals internalize society's negative messages about their gender identity, their transgender identity emerges as a largely concealable stigmatized identity (CSI). A CSI is defined as a critical aspect of one's identity that is socially devalued and hidden from others in social interactions (Quinn & Earnshaw, 2011). Individuals vary in the extent to which they conceal stigmatized aspects of their identity, as well as in the perceived severity of potential consequences if the identity is discovered (Pachankis, 2007). Transgender individuals' expressions of their gender identity may first involve disclosing or declaring their gender identity to others, followed by more visible or behavioral expressions of their authentic self. After transitioning, some transgender individuals may choose to "blend" in by concealing elements of their gender history, while others may choose to express their gender in ways outside of gender norms (Rood et al., 2017). Ultimately, concealment of their stigmatized identity is a complicated and individualized process for transgender individuals.

Concealment and disclosure

To understand and define the process of selectively concealing and revealing a stigmatized identity, Pachankis' (2007) comprehensive process model addresses the overall psychological impact of concealing a stigma, first elucidating which situations are likely to elicit stronger psychological impacts on individuals with CSIs, and then outlining the cognitive, affective, behavioral, and self-evaluative implications of these stressors. In Pachankis' (2007) view, individuals with a CSI experience most difficulty in situations where their stigmatized identity is particularly salient and likely to be discovered, and when that discovery would lead to significant challenges for that individual. Pachankis (2007) describes several cognitive challenges that arise from these situations, including a preoccupation with thoughts of the stigmatized identity, increased vigilance from anticipating the stigma being discovered, and suspiciousness. Individuals concealing stigmatized identities often expect more negative evaluations from others and may attempt to protect themselves by more closely monitoring their social interactions. This constant vigilance in social interactions can negatively impact interpersonal behavior of those with CSIs. Transgender individuals may engage in impression management behaviors, including lying or modifying their speech and mannerisms, which have been associated with barriers to connecting in communication, such as decreased eye-contact, speech errors, and extended pauses in conversation. Additionally, individuals who expend much cognitive energy in concealing their stigmatized identity may experience increased social avoidance and isolation. Gender identity concealment restricts the psychological support derived from group membership, such as attributing negative feedback to the stigmatized group rather than personal deficiencies (Pachankis, 2018).

Consequences of disclosure

Despite the risks of stress and stigma, disclosure has potential benefits including gaining access to appropriate medical care and transition-related resources, increased social support, and situational improvements such as the designation of gender-neutral bathrooms. Resilience is increasingly conceptualized as the development of an individual's capacity to use adversity as a catalyst for growth in the context of person–environment interactions (Roisman, 2005; Van Vliet, 2008). That is, an individual's resilience is enhanced as a result of successful adaptations to severe life stressors. Disclosure can thus bolster transgender individuals' sense of resilience—the ability to adapt effectively to risk exposure and to construct meaning out of threats to health (Austin, 2016).

For transgender individuals with experiences of discrimination, their marginalization may lead them to reach out to the online transgender community for a newfound "psychological sense of community," or "a feeling that members matter to one another and to the group, and a shared faith that members' needs will be met through their commitment to be together" (McMillan & Chavis, 1986, p. 9). Through this sense of connectedness to others, transgender individuals may recognize their shared identity, experience an increased level of social support, and form a commitment to combatting systemic injustices that lead to stigmatization and marginalization. Transgender individuals' membership in the transgender community is also likely to enhance their personal and in-group identity, encourage positive self-appraisal, and provide affirmation of their experiences as transgender individuals (Hendricks & Testa, 2012; Singh, Meng, & Hansen, 2014). Further, research has shown that transgender individuals' connection with the transgender community is negatively associated with anxiety and depression (Pflum, Testa, Balsam, Goldblum, & Bongar, 2015).

A developmental-contextual perspective of stigmatized identities

From a developmental-contextual perspective (Ford & Lerner, 1992), transgender individuals' negotiation of their CSIs varies depending on their developmental stage and contextual factors. A developmental-contextual perspective contends that human behavior changes over time and the meaning of behavior is embedded in, and inseparable from, contextual factors; an individual's needs, goals, and identities change across the life span often in response to contextual (e.g., family, school, work, community, society) change. The individual, however, is viewed "as an active agent of change and plays a major contributory role in shaping the surrounding environment across time" (Chen, Kakkad, & Balzano, 2008, p. 1272).

Likewise, for transgender individuals, the antecedents and consequences of gender identity disclosure are often affected by the social context within which it occurs (Brumbaugh-Johnson & Hull, 2018). During the disclosure process transgender individuals "teach others about trans-specific needs and experiences across a variety of contexts and situations" (Austin, 2016, p. 223). Opportunities and challenges exist at various points of transition for transgender individuals, during which others may respond positively or negatively to changes in their gender expression and identity.

Adolescence is a period where individuals experience a variety of normative development challenges, including maintaining a social network, negotiating autonomy within their family, and experiencing intimacy in personal relationships (Chen, Androsiglio, & Ng, 2010). Further, forming a coherent sense and understanding of self is an important developmental task for adolescents (Erikson, 1959), as they explore their identities (e.g., personal, career, and social), often through self-relevant questions (e.g., Who am I? Who I am going to be? Where will I be in the future?). As part of this exploration, disclosures constitute an important step in the reconciliation of different and evolving aspects of their social identities. Accordingly, a significant developmental challenge for transgender adolescents involves navigating the disclosure of their identity to others, whose responses may greatly affect their developing identities, and who may serve as gate-keepers to receiving appropriate medical and psychosocial treatment. Research indicates that adolescents have the tendency to focus on immediate desires, which results in frustration and disappointment when asked to tolerate delay in receiving gender-affirming treatment (APA, 2015).

In young adulthood, individuals begin to rapidly experience increased autonomy, maturity, and continued identity development (Erikson, 1959). This phase is a critical period for individuals to develop the necessary skills for self-sufficient living, stable long-term relationships, and life-long career paths. During this period, transgender individuals may still be struggling to reconcile their gender identity with societal expectations but may be simultaneously developing a more stable understanding of their own identity, perhaps gradually moving toward a more clear and certain identity (Austin, 2016).

Transgender young adults are not only continuing to navigate their understanding of their own gender identity, but also seeking a sense of purpose—whether that is found in starting a family or investing educational resources into a future career. Systemic barriers, however, may prevent finding meaning in work, as research indicates that transgender employees often face consequences for presenting themselves authentically in their workplaces, including discrimination, lack of support, and pressure to conform to social norms (Brewster, Velez, Mennicke, & Tebbe, 2014). When contending with romantic relationships and intimacy, transgender young adults have described the necessity and potential shame involved in educating potential romantic partners about their body, and some transgender individuals may choose to avoid romantic relationships due to fear of rejection or violence. Even once in committed romantic relationships, transgender young adults may have to navigate expectations around intimacy (Pulice-Farrow, Brown, & Galupo, 2017).

As adults enter the late stages of their lives, they often experience increased dependence on others, feelings of loneliness or isolation, and the challenge of "finding meaning" in their lives as they grapple with the inevitability of old age and death. Erikson (1959) characterizes the stage of late adulthood as a time of looking back and evaluating whether life has been meaningful. Significant challenges for older transgender adults may include receiving appropriate and affirmative health care, as well as balancing their desire to live out the end of their lives authentically, despite the struggle for societal and familial acceptance.

For transgender older adults, a main challenge may involve navigating disclosure in the health care system, as health-related complications increase with age. Some transgender elders who have transitioned may refuse medical care to avoid discrimination or judgment from health care providers, as their bodies may contain physical evidence of their transition. Similarly, they may face fear that they must reveal or "out" themselves to receive social security benefits (APA, 2015). Some transgender individuals who have concealed their identity throughout their lives may now choose to transition as older adults, as they begin to grapple with the fears and insecurities related to reaching the latter stages of their life, and worry that they will have never lived authentically (Cook-Daniels, 2015; Kimmel, Rose, & David, 2006). These individuals seek to develop a sense of coherence with their identity that they have been lacking throughout their lives; paradoxically, the longer an individual has experienced life under a set of traditional gender roles, the more difficult transitioning may be. Despite the variety of age-related challenges that transgender individuals may face, the majority of transgender individuals seem to share commonalities across the life span in attempting to live by their authentic self, navigate social pressures to conform to a particular gender role, and face discrimination and stigma as a result of their gender identity.

Practice implications

As this chapter has demonstrated, transgender individuals face a number of challenges across the life span associated with navigating the development of their gender identity, as well as the complex and ongoing decision-making process involved in concealment and disclosure of a stigmatized identity. Transgender individuals of all ages are at heightened risk for educational and economic consequences (James et al., 2016) as well as for developing health concerns (Bockting et al., 2013).

Some transgender individuals may turn to mental health professionals for support. However, all too often these individuals may receive clinical care that is inadequate or even harmful. Therefore it is vital that counselors and psychologists are well-educated in their roles as providers of trans-affirmative care and advocates for safer and more inclusive schools and workplaces. Providing affirmative care can help bolster resilience, increase a client's pride in their transgender identity, and help a client find meaning in the difficulties they have experienced.

Supporting transgender individuals in the context of schools

The literature has identified a number of protective factors that may help transgender youth to succeed in school, including school personnel intervention in harassment, the presence of lesbian, gay, bisexual, and transgender (LGBT) student groups, and systemic actions including comprehensive name change policies (McGuire, Anderson, & Toomey, 2010). Therefore, in addition to providing supportive, affirmative mental health care to transgender youth, mental health personnel in school settings must identify themselves as safe adults, combat bullying and harassment, provide psychoeducation for other school staff, and finally, advocate for more inclusive school policies.

One important factor for transgender youth has been identified as a connection to at least one trustworthy and supportive adult to help them to navigate safety issues and physical needs. Some youth may feel comfortable in their identity but are unsure of who is safe to share that identity with within the school setting (Johnson, Singh, & Gonzalez, 2014). Therefore school psychologists and counselors must feel empowered to serve as the advocate for youth and must make it clear to students that they are available as a confidante for gender-related concerns.

According to the position statement of the National Association of School Psychologists (NASP), additional responsibilities for a school psychologist in working with transgender youth include modeling school-wide acceptance and respect and intervening in bullying and harassment (NASP, 2014). Research has indicated that in the school setting, transgender youths are at risk for verbal and physical harassment and discrimination from peers (McGuire et al., 2010). This victimization has been linked to decreased school performance, school avoidance, and high dropout rates among the transgender community. School victimization has also been linked to negative long-term outcomes for LGBT adults; Greene, Britton, and Fitts (2014) found that adults who had been bullied due to their status as LGBT in school experienced increased fear of negative evaluation in their adult lives, indicating that school-based victimization can be highly damaging for transgender individuals. Therefore mental health professionals working in school settings must place special importance in combating bullying and harassment.

Another important facet of proactive care for school psychologists and counselors is to provide psychoeducation surrounding issues of gender identity for school staff and administrators with the goal of helping transgender youth to feel valued in the school setting. In a study of 68 transgender and gender nonconforming young adults, McGuire et al. (2010) concluded that the majority of these youth identified teachers as ineffective allies as teachers were not aware of how to best support them. According to the 2017 GLSEN National School Climate Survey,

42% of surveyed transgender students had been prevented from using their preferred name, and 46% of these students had been forced to use a bathroom that did not align with their gender identity. Psychologists in schools must encourage consistency among school staff in reinforcing a youth's chosen name and pronouns, as well as educate teachers on appropriate language and protocols for learning a student's preferred identity (Bowskill, 2017).

School psychologists and counselors must also advocate for and help design more inclusive curriculum and school-wide policies regarding gender-identity. School is commonly described by transgender individuals as a rigid, gendered space where the only option is male or female (Johnson et al., 2014). To create a safe school climate with these youth, special attention must be paid to deconstructing the gender binary. Ultimately, school psychologists and counselors play a vital role in supporting transgender individuals and helping to buffer them against negative outcomes.

Affirmative counseling for transgender clients

Affirmative counseling for LGBT clients in general is characterized by some common principles, including (1) gaining insight into the ways in which stigma-related stress affects one's mental health, (2) addressing shame and internalized stigma, and (3) promoting resilience and connection to the community as a buffer to stigma-related stress (APA, 2012; Pachankis, 2018). When transgender clients seek counseling for navigating challenges associated with their gender identity and expression, a central task of the clinician's affirmative practice is to point out the reciprocal interaction between the individual and their context. That is, clinicians need to validate transgender individuals' experiences of discrimination or pervasive victimization, helping them to understand their concerns within the broader context of sociocultural norms and policies that lead to stigmatization and marginalization. It is equally important for clinicians to reframe transgender clients' experiences from that of vulnerability to a sense of strength and resilience, in accordance with the view of the individual as an active agent of change, capable of shaping their relationships and life circumstances over time.

First, it is imperative for clinicians to gain insight into how stress related to stigma negatively impacts transgender individuals' mental health. Minority stress theory indicates that it is the continued exposure to the stigma around one's identity that contributes to increases in mental health disparities. Stigma includes the stress of being victimized, concealing one's identity, expecting rejection, and an overall compromise of mental health (Pachankis, 2018).

Second, for transgender individuals struggling with internalized stigma, their internalized stigma may be rooted in shame. Shame can be fostered through social rejection, a threat to self-esteem, or a threat to one's sense of identity and belonging (Van Vliet, 2008). Shame, in Van Vliet's (2008) view, can influence the core of an individual's being as it attacks one's positive self-image, posing risks to the individual's interpersonal connections.

Not living up to the expectations set by the self or others can result in a deep sense of shame and influence how transgender clients make meaning of their life. To address transgender clients' transphobia and shame, clinicians need to support them in demarginalizing their stigmatized identities by gaining insight and learning to attribute distress to stigma rather than self. Van Vliet (2008) views shame as "an assault on the self" (p. 237), and contends that the process of rebuilding of self involves shrinking shame from the core self, restoring and expanding one's positive self-concept, strengthening interpersonal connections, as well as an enhanced sense of personal power and control. Clinicians can help clients combat an internalized sense of shame through promoting self and other acceptance, connecting clients to community-building activities, and modeling supportive nonjudgmental environments.

Third, a central principle of transgender affirmative counseling involves promoting individuals' resilience. Factors that promote resilience among transgender individuals have been found to include an evolving definition of the self, finding self-worth, creating hope for the future, social activism, and being a positive role model for others (Singh, Hays, & Watson, 2011). The clinician can initiate the process of transforming transgender individuals' stigmatized identity by encouraging them to explore the edges or center of their experiences, and by helping them come to terms with the injustices at sociopolitical levels that contribute to their stigma. In particular, the counseling group, with its therapeutic value of, among others, instillation of hope, universality and interpersonal learning (Yalom & Leszcz, 2005), provides a catalyst for demarginalizing transgender individuals' stigmatized identities. Trans-affirmative care involves creating a safe environment for individuals to explore their own gender identity and extending this safe place in the group context serves as a buffer against internalized transphobia.

Disclosure of stigmatized identities to others who are similar to or different from transgender clients provides a high degree of personal validation and affirmation, particularly as they encounter challenges at different points of transition. With the support of others through the process of group therapy, transgender members also may receive psychoeducational and health resources, as well as transition-related legal information. As a social microcosm, the group fosters social advocacy and empowerment, where transgender members can practice their disclosure and experiment with expression and management of gender identity.

In the workplace, transgender individuals can experience transphobia depending on levels of perceived or explicit disclosure. Work provides opportunities for enhancing emotional well-being, meeting basic needs, and gaining social power (Blustein, 2008). Psychological, economic, and cultural factors, individually and collectively, influence one's ability to find sustaining work that is meaningful: however, marginalization and contextual forces often directly decrease a person's belief in the ability to make career choices (Duffy, Blustein, Diemer, & Autin, 2016). Due to the social stigma placed on transgender individuals, experiences of discrimination make it difficult for members of the community to thrive, acquire positions of power, or gain social capital and financial capital. Often lacking legal protection from employment discrimination, individuals who do not ascribe to the gender binary are left open to victimization. Given the interconnection between personal and career counseling (Hackett, 1994), clinicians need to be knowledgeable about the systemic barriers transgender individuals face in the workplace and outside, equipping clients with knowledge of their legal rights, and advocating for more inclusive protections.

Closing comments

Transgender individuals' gender and identity transitions spur a search for meaning. In the musical "My Fair Lady," once Eliza no longer perceives herself as an ignorant flower girl, the realization that "I am my own narrative" leads to questions and uncertainties about her view of self, her future, and her relationships with others: "Where am I to go? What am I to do? What's to become of me?" Conceptualized through Kegan's (1982) framework, the transgender individual's transitions and transcendence—as well as Eliza's—is a process of confirmation and contradiction, accepting one's authentic self while discovering its limits. Although transitions may lead to greater social isolation and questions about self-expression in social contexts, they may also prompt individuals to engage in thoughtful introspection, discover a sense of continuity of identity, and form close connections with others through shared experiences. Against the broader social-cultural contexts that often lead to stigmatization and marginalization, transgender individuals embarking on their journey of transition must wrestle with the uncertainties and challenges that lie ahead. With the support of affirming personal and counseling relationships, however, they will be poised and resilient in carving out their own paths, experiencing their gender transitions as coherent, purposeful, and significant.

References

Altmaier, E. M. (Ed.), (2017). *Reconstructing meaning after trauma: Theory, research, and practice.* Amsterdam, The Netherlands: Elsevier.

Alvarado, A. R. (2012). *Association for Studies in Higher Education. Salience at the intersection: Latina/o identities across different campus contexts* (pp. 1–31). Las Vegas, NV: UCLA.

American Psychological Association. (2009). *Report of the task force on gender identity and gender variance.* Washington, DC: Author.

American Psychological Association. (2012). Guidelines for psychological practice with lesbian, gay, and bisexual clients. *American Psychologist, 67,* 10–42.

American Psychological Association (APA). (2015). Guidelines for psychological practice with transgender and gender nonconforming people. *American Psychologist, 70,* 832–864.

Association of Lesbian, Gay, Bisexual, and Transgender Issues in Counseling. (2009). Competencies for counseling with transgender clients. Alexandria, VA: Author.

Austin, A. (2016). 'There I am': A grounded theory study of young adults navigating a transgender or gender nonconforming identity within a context of oppression and invisibility. *Sex Roles, 75,* 215–230.

Bethea, M. S., & McCollum, E. E. (2013). The disclosure experiences of male-to-female transgender individuals: A systems theory perspective. *Journal of Couple & Relationship Therapy, 12,* 89–112.

Blustein, D. L. (2008). The role of work in psychological health and well-being: a conceptual, historical, and public policy perspective. *American Psychologist, 63,* 228–240.

Bockting, W. O., Miner, M. H., Romine, R. E., Hamilton, A., & Coleman, E. (2013). Stigma, mental health, and resilience in an online sample of the US transgender population. *American Journal of Public Health, 103,* 943–951.

Bowskill, T. (2017). How educational professionals can improve the outcomes for transgender children and young people. *Educational & Child Psychology, 34,* 96–108.

Breslow, A. S., Brewster, M. E., Velez, B. L., Wong, S., Geiger, E., & Soderstrom, B. (2015). Resilience and collective action: Exploring buffers against minority stress for transgender individuals. *Psychology of Sexual Orientation and Gender Diversity, 2,* 253–265.

Brewster, M. E., Velez, B. L., Mennicke, A., & Tebbe, E. (2014). Voices from beyond: A thematic content analysis of transgender employees' workplace experiences. *Psychology of Sexual Orientation and Gender Diversity, 1,* 159–169.

Brumbaugh-Johnson, S. M., & Hull, K. E. (2018). Coming out as transgender: Navigating the social implications of a transgender identity. *Journal of Homosexuality, 66,* 1148–1177.

Buss, A. (2001). *Psychological dimensions of the self.* Thousand Oaks, CA: Sage.

Chatman, C. M., Eccles, J. S., & Malanchuk, O. (2005). Identity negotiation in everyday settings. In G. Downey, J. Eccles, & C. Chatman (Eds.), *Navigating the future: Social identity, coping and life tasks* (pp. 116–140). New York: Russell Sage Foundation.

Chen, E. C., Androsiglio, R. J., & Ng, V. (2010). Minority stress and health of lesbian, gay and bisexual individuals: A developmental-contextual perspective. In J. G. Ponterotto, J. M. Casas, L. A. Suzuki, & C. M. Alexander (Eds.), *Handbook of multicultural counseling* (3rd ed., pp. 531–544). Thousand Oaks, CA: Sage.

Chen, E. C., Kakkad, D., & Balzano, J. (2008). Multicultural competence and evidence-based practice in group therapy. *Journal of Clinical Psychology, 64,* 1261–1278.

Cook-Daniels, L. (2015). *Transgender aging: What practitioners should know. The lives of LGBT older adults: Understanding challenges and resilience* (pp. 193–215). Washington, DC: American Psychological Association.

Duffy, R. D., Blustein, D. L., Diemer, M. A., & Autin, K. L. (2016). The psychology of working theory. *Journal of Counseling Psychology, 63*(2), 127–148.

Erikson, E. H. (1959). *Identity and the life cycle: Selected papers*. Oxford: International Universities Press.

Ford, D. H., & Lerner, R. M. (1992). *Developmental systems theory: An integrative approach*. Thousand Oaks, CA: Sage.

Goffman, E. (1963). *Stigma: Notes on the management of spoiled identity*. Englewood Cliffs, NJ: Prentice-Hall.

Greene, D. C., Britton, P. J., & Fitts, B. (2014). Long-term outcomes of lesbian, gay, bisexual, and transgender recalled school victimization. *Journal of Counseling & Development, 92* (4), 406–417.

Hackett, G. (1994). Career counseling and psychotherapy: False dichotomies and recommended remedies. *Journal of Career Assessment, 1*, 105–117.

Hatzenbuehler, M. L., Phelan, J. C., & Link, B. G. (2013). Stigma as a fundamental cause of population health inequalities. *American Journal of Public Health, 103*, 813–821.

Hendricks, M. L., & Testa, R. J. (2012). A conceptual framework for clinical work with transgender and gender nonconforming clients: An adaptation of the Minority Stress Model. *Professional Psychology: Research and Practice, 43*, 460–467.

Human Rights Campaign. (2018). *Violence against the transgender community in 2018*. Retrieved September 15, 2019 from <https://www.hrc.org/resources/violence-against-the-transgender-community-in-2018>.

Human Rights Campaign. (2019). *State maps of laws and policies*. Retrieved September 13, 2019 from <https://www.hrc.org/state-maps/employment>.

James, S., Herman, J., Rankin, S., Keisling, M., Mottet, L., & Anaf, M. (2016). *The report of the 2015 US Transgender Survey*. Washington, DC: National Center for Transgender Equality.

Johnson, C. W., Singh, A. A., & Gonzalez, M. (2014). "It's complicated": Collective memories of transgender, queer, and questioning youth in high school. *Journal of Homosexuality, 61*, 419–434.

Kegan, R. (1982). *The evolving self*. Cambridge, MA: Harvard University Press.

Kimmel, D. C., Rose, T., & David, S. (2006). *Lesbian, gay, bisexual, and transgender aging: Research and clinical perspectives*. New York: Columbia University Press.

Link, B. G., & Phelan, J. C. (2001). Conceptualizing stigma. *Annual Review of Sociology, 27*, 363–385.

Major, B., Dovidio, J. F., Link, B. G., & Calabrese, S. K. (2018). Stigma and its implications for health: Introduction and overview. In B. Major, J. F. Dovidio, & B. G. Link (Eds.), *The Oxford handbook of stigma, discrimination, and health* (pp. 3–28). New York: Oxford University Press.

McGuire, J. K., Anderson, C. R., & Toomey, R. B. (2010). School climate for transgender youth: A mixed method investigation of student experiences and school responses. *Journal of Youth and Adolescence, 39*, 1175–1188.

McMillan, D. W., & Chavis, D. M. (1986). Psychological sense of community: A definition and theory. *Journal of Community Psychology, 14*, 6–23.

Meyer, I. H. (2003). Prejudice, social stress, and mental health in lesbian, gay, and bisexual populations: Conceptual issues and research evidence. *Psychological Bulletin, 129*, 674–697.

National Association of School Psychologists. (2014). Safe schools for transgender and gender diverse students. *[Position statement]*. Bethesda, MD: Author.

Norwood, K. (2012). Transitioning meanings? Family members' communicative struggles surrounding transgender identity. *Journal of Family Communication, 12*, 75–92.

Pachankis, J. E. (2007). The psychological implications of concealing a stigma: A cognitive-affective-behavioral model. *Psychological Bulletin, 133*, 328–345.

Pachankis, J. E. (2018). The scientific pursuit of sexual and gender minority mental health treatments: Toward evidence-based affirmative practice. *American Psychologist, 73*, 1207–1219.

Pflum, S. R., Testa, R. J., Balsam, K. F., Goldblum, P. B., & Bongar, B. (2015). Social support, trans community connectedness, and mental health symptoms among transgender and gender nonconforming adults. *Psychology of Sexual Orientation and Gender Diversity*, *2*, 281–286.

Pulice-Farrow, L., Brown, T. D., & Galupo, M. P. (2017). Transgender microaggressions in the context of romantic relationships. *Psychology of Sexual Orientation and Gender Diversity*, *4*, 362–373.

Quinn, D. M., & Earnshaw, V. A. (2011). Understanding concealable stigmatized identities: The role of identity in psychological, physical, and behavioral outcomes. *Social Issues and Policy Review*, *5*, 160–190.

Roisman, G. I. (2005). Conceptual clarifications in the study of resilience. *American Psychologist*, *60*, 264–265.

Rood, B. A., Reisner, S. L., Puckett, J. A., Surace, F. I., Berman, A. K., & Pantalone, D. W. (2017). Internalized transphobia: Exploring perceptions of social messages in transgender and gender-nonconforming adults. *International Journal of Transgenderism*, *18*, 411–426.

Singh, A. A., Hays, D. G., & Watson, L. S. (2011). Strength in the face of adversity: Resilience strategies of transgender individuals. *Journal of Counseling & Development*, *89*, 20–27.

Singh, A. A., Meng, S. E., & Hansen, A. W. (2014). "I Am My Own Gender": Resilience strategies of trans youth. *Journal of Counseling & Development*, *92*, 208–218.

Sugano, E., Nemoto, T., & Operario, D. (2006). The impact of exposure to transphobia on HIV risk behavior in a sample of transgendered women of color in San Francisco. *AIDS and Behavior*, *10*, 217–225.

Swann, W., Johnson, R., & Bosson, J. (2009). Identity negotiation at work. *Research in Organizational Behavior*, *29*, 81–109.

Timmins, L., Rimes, K. A., & Rahman, Q. (2017). Minority stressors and psychological distress in transgender individuals. *Psychology of Sexual Orientation and Gender Diversity*, *4*, 328–340.

Van Vliet, K. J. (2008). Shame and resilience in adulthood: A grounded theory study. *Journal of Counseling Psychology*, *55*, 233–245.

Yalom, I., & Leszcz, M. (2005). *The theory and practice of group psychotherapy* (5th ed.). New York: Basic Books.

PART 3

Role Transitions

CHAPTER

5

Meaning-making in bereavement transitions: review and clinical relevance

Evgenia Milman[1] *and Robert A. Neimeyer*[2,3]

[1]School of Human Development & Education, St. Edward's University, Austin, TX, United States, [2]Department of Psychology, The University of Memphis, Memphis, TN, United States, [3]Portland Institute for Loss and Transition, Baltimore, MD, United States

The case of Rosa

When Rosa received the impossible news that her middle son, Miguel, had experienced a "cataclysmic brain injury" in an automobile accident while returning to university in a distant city, her response was from the outset as intricately social as it was psychological. As she excused herself from the board meeting of her company to take the call from an unknown critical care physician, she found her world turned upside down by the news, and the need to mobilize both her internal and external resources to meet the crisis, regulating her own rising alarm as well as that of her family and social system. Hurriedly making a flurry of phone calls to arrange to fly to Miguel's side, she also received many more from panicked members of her network, trying all the while to take in and make sense of the welter of fragmentary and inconclusive communications from hospital staff to piece together an account of what had happened and was happening now. Beyond the immediate imperative to understand what had transpired and to participate in critical medical decisions when she arrived onsite at the hospital, Rosa struggled to bridge the world as it was with the world as it had been just 24 hours ago, before a tsunami of unprecedented grief and despair had washed away the vestiges of predictability and

Navigating Life Transitions for Meaning
DOI: https://doi.org/10.1016/B978-0-12-818849-1.00005-9

familiarity that once defined her worldview, and connected her securely to the people she loved. Now, in the rubble of what was once her life, she faced the nightmare decision of when to withdraw life support from her brain dead son, as she struggled to retain faith in a God and in a universe that seemed indifferent to suffering and loss, and as the web of compassionate connection to the beings and beliefs she cherished seemed to be torn irreparably by the trauma that was ending the life of her child.

Grief and growth: a research review

The transitions involved in the loss of a loved one are experienced by virtually all, and the experience of grief has been studied extensively in recent decades, providing insights into how adaptive and adverse responses to death-related loss progress and influence one another. Research confirms that the majority of bereaved individuals encounter transient and moderate distress, returning to baseline levels of functioning 18–24 months following the loss (Bonanno & Kaltman, 2001; Bonanno et al., 2002; Bonanno, Wortman, & Nesse, 2004; Davidson, 1979; Galatzer-Levy & Bonanno, 2012). Nevertheless, bereavement can also lead to disabling and chronic psychological suffering that results in a wide range of mental, physical, and functional impairments (Casey, 2011; Mezey, Evans, & Hobdell, 2002; Ott, 2003; Rheingold, Zinzow, Hawkins, Saunders, & Kilpatrick, 2012; Stroebe, Schut, & Stroebe, 2007). Chief among these is a prolonged and clinically significant form of grief that affects 10% of the bereft (Lundorff, Holmgren, Zachariae, Farver-Vestergaard, & O'Connor, 2017) and is characterized by a symptomatic profile commonly referred to as complicated grief (Shear et al., 2011) or prolonged grief disorder (PGD; Prigerson, Vanderwerker, & Maciejewski, 2008). PGD has been introduced as a mental health diagnosis in the most recent edition of the World Health Organization's International Classification of Disease (ICD-11; World Health Organization, 2018) and has been included as a condition for further study in the DSM 5 (American Psychiatric Association, 2013). The symptomatic profiles described by the DSM 5 and the ICD-11 represent the same diagnostic entity (Maciejewski, Maercker, Boelen, & Prigerson, 2016) defined by symptoms of profound separation distress, featuring marked and persistent yearning for and preoccupation with the deceased. PGD also presents with a variety of additional symptoms that reflect its severity and can be broadly categorized as bereavement-related distress (e.g., anger, numbness, etc.) or disrupted reengagement in life postloss (difficulty moving on, trusting others, etc.) (Lee, 2015; Lee & Milman, in press; Maciejewski et al., 2016).

Yet the prospect of enduring psychological devastation following the death of a loved one does not preclude the potential for resilient bereavement outcomes. Scholars have offered diverse perspectives on

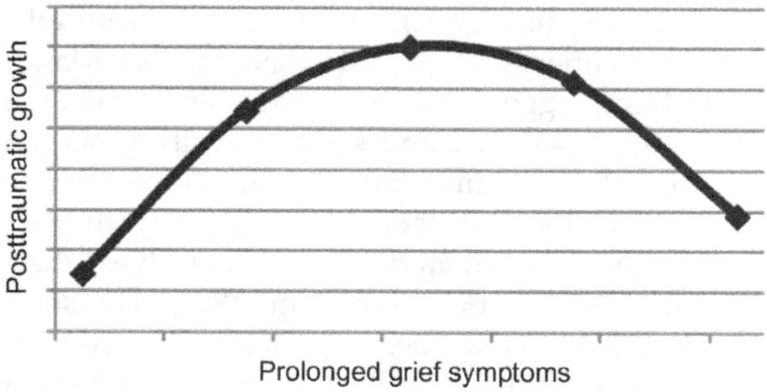

FIGURE 5.1 Graph depicting the curvilinear association between prolonged grief disorder symptoms and posttraumatic growth. Source: *Adapted from Currier, J.M., Holland, J. M., & Neimeyer, R.A. (2012). Prolonged grief symptoms and growth in the first 2 years of bereavement: Evidence for a nonlinear association.* Traumatology, *18(4), 65.*

how resilience manifests (Southwick, Bonanno, Masten, Panter-Brick, & Yehuda, 2014; Westphal & Bonanno, 2007). Some forms of resilience are defined by the recovery of health and well-being either in the immediate aftermath of an isolated stressful event or in the face of ongoing stressors (Bonanno & Diminich, 2013). However, the literature has also described resilience in terms of a positive personal change beyond mere recovery of previous functioning. In the literature, this phenomenon is widely referred to as *posttraumatic growth* (PTG), which is characterized as increased appreciation of life, sense of personal strength, improved interpersonal relationships, the realization of new possibilities, and spiritual development (Tedeschi & Calhoun, 1996, 2008).

Crucially, adverse and resilient bereavement outcomes do not represent opposite ends of a single outcome dimension (Calhoun, Tedeschi, Cann, & Hanks, 2010; Neimeyer, Bottomley, & Bellet, 2018). In other words, resilience is not simply the absence of psychopathology (Bonanno, 2004, 2012; Bonanno, Brewin, Kaniasty, & Greca, 2010; Bonanno, Westphal, & Mancini, 2011; Southwick et al., 2014). In fact, greater postloss growth has been shown to co-occur with more severe grief (Büchi et al., 2007). Building on this finding, research has demonstrated that the greatest growth occurs at intermediate levels of PGD symptomology, while the least growth occurs when PGD symptomology is at its lowest or at its highest (Currier, Holland, & Neimeyer, 2012). In other words, there seems to be a curvilinear association between PGD symptoms and PTG, such that PTG peaks when grief is significant, but not overwhelming (see Fig. 5.1).

Reconstructing meaning in the wake of loss

The meaning reconstruction paradigm provides a framework for understanding how growth emerges from the distress of grief during bereavement, but also how grief can become chronically impairing (Neimeyer, 2019; Neimeyer et al., 2018; Neimeyer, Klass, & Dennis, 2014). This paradigm suggests that individuals construct narrative systems that define their personal and social identities, orienting them to their ongoing life. After a significant loss, the bereft may find the loss experience is incompatible with their preexisting narrative systems, calling into question their understandings of themselves, their lives, and their worlds (Park, 2010; Park & Folkman, 1997). For such mourners, grief can be described as a meaning-making process wherein the mourner negotiates the impact of the loss by revising orienting narratives to develop a more nuanced and useful meaning system (Gillies, Neimeyer, & Milman, 2014).

When the bereft make progress in revising their orienting systems to accommodate the grief experience, they are understood to have made meaning of their loss. The manner in which meaning manifests varies depending on how the loss has challenged the bereaved and how they have addressed this challenge. Thus even though the transitions that characterize bereavement are universal, the grief experience is vastly diverse. For parents whose child committed suicide following an anguished struggle with mental illness, meaning may emerge as a narrative about their child's release from an existence of seemingly unebbing suffering. Alternatively, for a widower who has encountered the unpredictable and unjust nature of the world after an intoxicated driver took the life of his spouse, meaning might manifest in a sense of valuing life despite its uncertainty and a commitment to building a more just world through initiatives to end drunk driving.

Measuring meaning made in bereavement

In an effort to recognize diverse expressions of meaning, early research differentiated between meaning that manifests as *sense* made of the death event itself (e.g., suicide described as release from suffering) and meaning that manifests as an unsought *benefit* derived from the grief experience (e.g., increased valuation of life despite the uncertain world) (Neimeyer, 2019). Building on this pluralistic conceptualization of meaning, two self-report meaning measures were developed and validated with a bereaved population. The first of these is the *Integration of Stressful Life Experiences Scale* (ISLES; Holland, Currier, Coleman, & Neimeyer, 2010; Holland, Currier, & Neimeyer, 2014) which assess meaning using two subscales. The *Comprehensibility* subscale inquires as to whether the bereaved is struggling to integrate the death event into orienting narratives (e.g., "I have difficulty integrating this event into my understanding about the world") and the *Footing in the World* subscale probes whether the bereaved have restored challenged self-narratives (e.g., "I don't understand myself anymore since this loss"). As such, the ISLES provides a broad-gauge measure indicating how much meaning the bereaved has made of the loss, without necessarily specifying the manner in which this meaning is expressed (Holland et al., 2010; Holland et al., 2014).

Alternatively, in an attempt to capture diverse manifestations of meaning, Gillies, Neimeyer, and Milman (2015) developed the *Grief and Meaning Reconstruction Inventory* (GMRI) as a nuanced assessment of what meaning the bereaved has made. The GMRI probes the degree to which the bereft endorse a variety of specific meaning themes derived from a thematic analysis of participant grief accounts (Gillies et al., 2014). Four positively valanced subscales include: the *Continuing Bonds* subscale, which assesses the formation of a symbolic, life-affirming connection with the deceased, built in response to the threat presented by the physical absence of a central attachment figure (e.g., "Memories of my loved one bring me a sense of peace and solace"); the *Personal Growth* subscale, which refers to positive identity change derived from the adversity of grief (e.g., "Since this loss, I'm more self-reflective"); the *Valuing Life* subscale, which refers to increased appreciation of life gained through confrontation with its ephemeral nature (e.g., "I value and appreciate life more"); and the *Sense of Peace* subscale, which refers to the perception that, despite the devastating nature of the loss, the death event itself brought release from suffering for the deceased (e.g., following a debilitating illness) and/or for the bereaved (e.g., following a difficult caregiving experience) (e.g., "This death brought my loved one peace"). The final subscale of the GMRI, entitled *Emptiness and Meaninglessness*, captures themes of meaning that are negatively valanced in terms of the emotions that they engender. For example, the tragically premature death of a parent following a highly conflictual relationship might foster regret stemming from unresolved relational dynamics (e.g., "I feel pain from regrets I have in regard to this loss"). Together, the five subscales of the GMRI capture the content of meaning, allowing for a rich profile of how meaning manifests among the bereaved.

Meaning-making as the common explanatory pathway

A loss that poses a negligible challenge to the orienting system of the bereft is likely to result in low and transient grief-related distress, leaving little opportunity for the transformative experience of growth. Bonanno and Diminich (2013) have aptly referred to this mild grief reaction as *minimal-impact resilience*, defined not by a recovery of functioning following the disruption of loss but rather by the minimal perturbation of functioning despite loss. Minimal-impact resilience is experienced by a sizable percentage of grieving individuals (35–65%; Bonanno & Diminich, 2013; Bonanno, Wortman, et al., 2004). Unsurprisingly, research shows that these grievers are significantly less likely to engage in meaning-making for the simple reason that their losses were not associated with a crisis of meaning in the first place (Bonanno, Wortman, et al., 2004). A loss that leaves the mourner's orienting narrative system intact, producing only mild distress, allows little opportunity or need for PTG (Westphal & Bonanno, 2007), and so, low levels of PGD are associated with the lowest growth in Fig. 5.1.

By contrast, when the circumstances of the loss are tragic or violent or the mourner loses a relational figure who played a crucial role in his or her life story, such as a child or spouse, fundamental narratives regarding the nature of the world and the identity of the bereaved may be challenged. Such losses may require a sweeping reconstruction of the mourner's orienting narratives which can exacerbate the severity of grief causing PGD (Currier, Holland, & Neimeyer, 2006; Milman et al., 2018; Rozalski, Holland, & Neimeyer, 2017). Similarly, if the bereaved lacks a social network with which to coconstruct the meaning of loss or if the bereaved possess dispositional traits associated with self-defeating life narratives, such as neuroticism and insecure attachment, the process of rebuilding a life-affirming orienting system may be hindered, triggering the prolonged grief that characterizes PGD.

Indeed, research has suggested that violent loss, loss of a spouse or child, low social support, neuroticism, and insecure attachment—all risk factors with the strongest empirical support for their ability to predict PGD (Burke & Neimeyer, 2013)—increase PGD symptoms by undermining the mourner's ability to make meaning following the loss. For example, multiple studies have indicated that meaning-making represents the process by which violent death influences the severity of PGD (Currier et al., 2006; Milman et al., 2018; Rozalski et al., 2017). More recently, research has employed a prospective longitudinal design to identify meaning-making as the process mediating the detrimental impact of multiple risk factors on PGD symptomatology (Milman et al., 2019a). Specifically, violent death, spousal death, low social support, neuroticism, and insecure attachment were each found to co-occur with having made less meaning of the loss in the early stages of bereavement, and over time, those mourners who made less meaning of their loss reported higher PGD symptomatology. Such findings suggest that risk factors for PGD foster adverse bereavement outcomes by hindering the meaning-making process. Together, this research highlights the central role that disrupted meaning-making plays in the etiology of mental health disorders that can develop during bereavement transitions, particularly PGD.

While an intense and prolonged search for meaning predicts PGD (Coleman & Neimeyer, 2010), overcoming this process to successfully reconstruct the challenged orienting system can provide the basis for meaningful reengagement with life and an accompanying sense of growth. Indeed, recent "network analysis" of the system of PGD symptoms on the one hand and features of PTG on the other has demonstrated that a challenged and subsequently adapted worldview bridges the two domains, representing a potential "pivot point" from grief to growth (Bellet, Jones, Neimeyer, & McNally, 2018). It appears then, that an orienting system rendered sufficiently vulnerable by loss provides the necessary context for a distressing but ultimately transformative process of meaning reconstruction that may not so much assuage the severity of grief as engender a compensatory experience of growth.

Accordingly, in Fig. 5.1, the apex of growth co-occurs with intermediate levels of PGD symptomology—spanning just below to just above the cut-off for clinical diagnosis. Similarly, Westphal and Bonanno (2007) have suggested that PTG likely occurs among the 15–25% of mourners who experience a *recovery* trajectory (Bonanno & Diminich, 2013; Bonanno, Wortman, et al., 2004). Recovery is characterized by substantial and impairing distress postloss followed by a gradual improvement with a return of baseline functioning within 1–2 years. Presumably, this reduction in the severity of grief results in part from mourners' progress in negotiating the detrimental impact of the loss on their orientating systems.

In cases where the loss devastates the survivor's life narrative in a manner that is experienced as insurmountable, the quest for meaning can become anguishing, repetitive, intrusive, and unproductive. Prospective research has shown that when the struggle to make meaning takes on this ruminative quality, it moderates the impact of PGD risk factors on grief severity, producing the highest degree of PGD symptomology (Milman et al., 2019b). Specifically, mourners who were in the 90th percentile on rumination and made the lowest degree of meaning of their loss reported PGD symptoms that were a full standard deviation above the average for the sample. As demonstrated in Fig. 5.1, such elevated and disabling PGD symptomology is associated with a low degree of growth (Currier et al., 2012).

It appears that the meaning-making process represents a final, common explanatory pathway or mechanism accounting for how grief progresses over time, both in terms of its severity and its potential for fostering growth. If the orienting system remains relatively intact postloss, the mourner experiences little in the way of distress; by contrast, losses that deal a crippling blow to the orienting system of the bereft result in chronically impairing grief—crucially, at both of these extremes, there is a diminished capacity for growth. On the other hand, losses that are challenging but do not overwhelm the mourners' capacity to rebuild their orienting narratives are conducive to profound grief, but also equally profound growth.

The social construction of grief

Importantly, the meaning-making process does not occur in a vacuum, but rather is shaped by the mourner's social environment. In fact, the bereft are understood to coconstruct the meaning of a loss with individuals in their immediate social network and their larger community under the influence of cultural prescriptions regarding how grief should be expressed and enacted (Bellet, Holland, & Neimeyer, 2019; Neimeyer et al., 2014). In other words, meaning-making is defined as a situated, interpretive, communicative activity that occurs either in concert or in conflict with social influences (Neimeyer et al., 2014). In a judgmental or antagonistic interpersonal context, the mourner's attempt to make sense of the loss may be undermined and "disenfranchised," in the sense of being minimized, criticized or disqualified (Doka, 2002; Neimeyer & Jordan, 2002). Indeed, bereaved individuals frequently identify invalidating social interactions that minimize or misunderstand their grief experience as a primary barrier to meaning-making (Breen & O'Connor, 2009). Furthermore, spiritual crisis following bereavement has been characterized not only as a disrupted relation to the divine but also in terms of confrontations with an unsupportive spiritual community (Burke et al., 2014). In turn, alienation from the mourner's faith community consistently predicts greater bereavement complications (Burke, Crunk, Neimeyer, & Bai, 2019).

As noted previously, research has also identified meaning-making as a mediator of the relationship between low social support and PGD symptoms (Milman et al., 2019a). Specifically, lack of social support co-occurred with having made less meaning of the loss in the early stages of bereavement, and over time those mourners who made less meaning of their loss reported higher PGD symptomatology. Such findings suggest that low social support fosters PGD by hindering the meaning-making process. This notion is further reinforced by a study that differentiated the simple lack of social support from the *social invalidation* (SI) of meaning-making (Bellet et al., 2019). The researchers found that SI of meaning-making (as through misunderstanding mourners' experience or critiquing or judging their account of the loss) explained the degree of PGD symptomatology more strongly than general lack of social support for the mourner. In fact, when SI of meaning-making was taken into account, the effect of low social support on PGD symptoms was rendered insignificant. These results indicate that the passive absence of a social network may be less detrimental to bereavement outcomes than the active presence of social interactions that undermine the mourner's attempt to make meaning of a loss. Furthermore, social support has been found to moderate how strongly violent bereavement hinders meaning-making, and by extension, the degree to which it predicts PGD symptomatology over time (Milman et al., 2019a). It appears then, that diminished social resources can impact grief severity in-and-of-themselves and/or can exacerbate the detrimental effects of other risk factors.

While social impediments to meaning-making are relevant to negative bereavement outcomes, supportive social networks that provide the opportunity to coconstruct the meaning of loss in conversation with receptive individuals are likely to foster growth and resilience (Bellet et al., 2019; Neimeyer et al., 2018). In fact, *social validation* (SV) of meaning-making (e.g., helping the bereaved makes sense of the loss, offering useful perspectives) demonstrated a significant relationship with PTG, but was unrelated to PGD symptoms (Bellet et al., 2019). More generally, research suggests that satisfaction with social support is related to reduced emotional struggles throughout bereavement (Bottomley, Burke, & Neimeyer, 2015; Burke, Neimeyer, & McDevitt-Murphy, 2010; Dyregrov, 2006; Thuen, 1997; Vanderwerker & Prigerson, 2004) and that satisfactory social support is experienced within interactions that allow accurate and complete expression of one's grief to empathetic others (Davis, Lehman, Silver, Wortman, & Ellard, 1996; McMenamy, Jordan, & Mitchell, 2008; Nolen-Hoeksema & Davis, 1999; Toller, 2011). There is also growing evidence that the ability to adapt self-expression to elicit SV is predictive of resilient grief responses (Bonanno & Burton, 2013). Such research has shown that grieving individuals who can amplify or suppress their self-expression depending on the presence of perceived social threat demonstrate more resilient responses to acutely stressful events including bereavement (Bonanno & Burton, 2013; Bonanno, Papa, Lalande, Westphal, & Coifman, 2004; Westphal, Seivert, & Bonanno, 2010).

Taken together, this research suggests that although death-related loss is universal, grief is an experience that varies widely depending on how and with whom it is narrated. Transformative growth during bereavement is possible despite or, more accurately, because of a vulnerable struggle to reconstruct a meaningful reality in concert with social networks and in compliance with cultural scripts. However, if the bereft lack SV of their grief narrative, the meaning reconstruction process can be hindered resulting in enduring psychological distress and impairment that can render resilient growth impossible.

Meaning reconstruction in a clinical setting

The majority of those grieving a loss negotiate the meaning reconstruction process without the benefit of formal therapy, drawing on their own internal and social resources. However, if the loss represents a profound challenge to the narrative system of the bereft or if the grief experience is disabling, then the meaning-making process can become a target for therapeutic intervention. Accordingly, the meaning reconstruction paradigm has been proposed as a frame for grief therapy with individuals (Neimeyer & Sands, 2011), families (Hooghe & Neimeyer, 2013; Nadeau, 1998; Walsh & McGoldrick, 2004), and groups (MacKinnon et al., 2014; MacKinnon et al., 2015; Neimeyer, Milman, & Steffen, in press). In preliminary research, meaning-oriented techniques and protocols have shown promising outcomes with PGD (Neimeyer & Alves, 2016) and with risk factors for PGD including violent bereavement (Rheingold et al., 2015; Saindon et al., 2014), and suicide bereavement (Supiano, Haynes, & Pond, 2017). Meaning Centered Grief Therapy following the loss of a child, another risk factor for PGD, has also been proposed and the preliminary research indicates strong effect sizes on multiple outcome indices (Lichtenthal et al., 2019).

Meaning-oriented approaches to grief therapy are designed to facilitate meaning-making by examining how client's losses have challenged their orienting narratives and supporting clients in rebuilding these narratives to allow for a meaningful reengagement in life (Alves et al., 2014; Lichtenthal & Breitbart, 2015; e.g., MacKinnon et al., 2015; Neimeyer, 2012a; Rynearson & Salloum, 2011; Salloum & Overstreet, 2012; Steffen & Coyle, 2011; Supiano et al., 2017). This is accomplished by incorporating a dual focus on the *event story* of the death itself and the *back story* of the mourner's relationship with the deceased (Neimeyer, 2019).

A clinician working within the meaning-oriented framework commonly begins by inviting the client to provide a rich description of the deceased loved one. To assist in this, therapists can prompt the client with questions such as "What did having ___ in your life mean to you?" or "Are there particular stories that ___ would want us to know about her life?" (Hedtke, 2012). Questions of this sort presume the continuation of an attachment bond rather than detachment as the normative course of grieving (Hedtke, 2012), in effect reconstructing the meaning of the bond in a form that is sustainable in the physical absence of the deceased. Furthermore, because meaning-making arises out of experiential engagement with grief, the therapist might encourage the client to bring significant objects relevant to the deceased into the session. Such objects allow for a tangible and emotionally poignant exploration of the deceased's character and of significant moments in the relational narrative.

For example, in the context of a meaning-oriented group grief intervention, a participant brought her deceased mother's perfume bottle to the session (Neimeyer, 2016). The beautifully shaped bottle and its scent encapsulated the glamorous air the participant attributed to her mother, bestowing a visceral reality to her mother's qualities. In another instance, a participant who was heavily influenced to pursue anthropology by her deceased father brought a tattered book her father had gifted her as a child with depictions of ancient artifacts that inspired her childhood fascination with anthropology. The well-loved pages of this book ushered in an experientially vivid recognition of the prominent role this participant's father played in her career choices.

This "person-first" approach of inviting a "thick description" of the deceased and his or her relation to the client—as opposed to an immediate focus on grief-related suffering—serves several purposes. These include (1) honoring the personhood of the deceased and granting permission to speak of him or her freely in the interested presence of the therapist or group, (2) reaffirming a sense of attachment security that was challenged by the death, (3) clarifying for both client and therapist the meaning of the loss by understanding the unique meaning of the relationship, and (4) laying the groundwork both for deeper exploration of relational dynamics such as unfinished business with the deceased and for interventions aimed at helping the client integrate the circumstances that characterized the narrative of the death itself.

Depending on the client's implicit and explicit expression of *need* and *readiness* in the early sessions of therapy (Neimeyer, 2019), the therapist then can turn either toward assisting the client with further accessing the *back story* of the relationship with the deceased to reconstruct a meaningful bond or help resolve a problematic one, or to processing the *event story* of the dying to assist with its integration in the aftermath of a troubling or perhaps traumatic transition. In the former case tools like the *Life Imprint* (Neimeyer, 2012b) and various legacy projects (Lichtenthal et al., 2019) can help articulate and affirm the enduring impact of the loved one on the lives of the living. Alternatively, when an assessment of unfinished business in bereavement (Holland, Klingspon, Lichetnthal, & Neimeyer, 2018) brings to light unresolved relational issues such as unexpressed feelings and questions or unaddressed conflicts or disappointments, invoking the presence of the deceased to invite a symbolic dialogue about such matters may be in order. Here, tools such as *Correspondence with the Deceased* (Neimeyer, 2012c), in which the client is supported or prompted to write a heartfelt letter to the deceased, and then in a second step, respond to the letter as if from the vantage point of the deceased, can go some distance toward reopening a conversation foreclosed by the death. Likewise, *Chair Work* (Neimeyer, 2012d) can permit the powerful performance of healing dialogues that encourage forgiveness and understanding, or in the case of the most abusive of relationships, help the client assert necessary boundaries.

Often, however, the client's preoccupation with events surrounding the dying compels attention to the *event story* of the death itself, especially when the circumstances of the loss are sudden and/or violent in nature, shattering or violating the client's assumptions about how life is or should be. In this case, the clinician might introduce a meaning-oriented exposure exercise. One such technique, entitled the *Meaning Reconstruction Interview,* begins with visualization of critical death-related scenes, focusing on the associated embodied emotional reactions of the client (Neimeyer, 2006). As is the case in exposure-based work more generally, encouraging the client to attend to the evocative details of the death story builds tolerance of their distressing nature thereby enabling the bereft to engage with and adequately process these scenes. A meaning-oriented therapist would then examine and address how the death event has impacted and perhaps challenged the client's sense of self, the world, and the future using a series of *exploration* and *elaboration* questions.

Alternatively, the therapist could lead the client in a *Restorative Retelling* procedure (Rynearson & Salloum, 2011), carefully sifting through the previously unspeakable details of the dying story as witnessed or imagined, progressing at a "slow motion" pace that permits integration of critical scenes and associated meanings, helping the client self-regulate and articulate his or her own emotions while achieving greater mastery over a traumatic experience (Neimeyer, 2012g). Such work often benefits from between-session opportunities to further process the meaning and implications of the loss through *Directed Journaling* (Lichtenthal & Neimeyer, 2012), whose prompting questions promote greater emotion modulation and facilitate further sense-making and benefit-finding regarding the lessons of loss.

In addition, various arts-assisted modalities can be employed to support the review of the death event narrative. As one example, the therapist can direct clients to draw salient scenes of the dying as an aid to telling the event story, and then invite them to depict themselves at the scene of the dying in the way they wish they could have been, but unable to prevent the dying (e.g., caressing the deceased at the scene of the death or lifting their soul to heaven; Correa, 2016). Though such work does not erase the memory of the tragic dying, it does help balance it with imagery depicting the care and love that characterized the relationship with the deceased. Other techniques such as *Analogical Listening* (Neimeyer, 2012e) can be used to deepen accessing and articulation of the internal narrative of the loss, namely the embodied felt sense of the client's perturbing emotions at various junctures in the retelling.

As therapy progresses and the client achieves greater modulation of emotion, reconstruction of the continuing bond, and integration of the death story, the focus of meaning-oriented treatment might shift to an exploration of the overall life narrative within which the loss occurred. For example, the *Chapters of our Lives* exercise (Neimeyer, 2014) entails the construction of a "Table of Contents" for the client's life story, with distinct chapter titles revealing significant events or time periods, including that of the death. The therapist supports the client in the process of placing life experiences in chronological order and connecting them across time to relevant personal, family, cultural, or spiritual events and sources of resilience through the use of selected facilitative questions in session, or as prompts for reflective writing between sessions. This work provides a scaffold for integrating the client's loss into an overall life trajectory through recognition of how the grief experience might be shaped by and give shape to the recurring themes in the client's life story (e.g., survival, self-sacrifice, lessons learned).

Clinicians working with the meaning reconstruction paradigm might also focus on bolstering opportunities for meaning-making outside of the therapeutic context by strengthening existing positive relationships and/or building new supports. Interventions designed to build resilience in the acute stages of violent bereavement include encouraging the bereft to review their social network, identifying the types of support available from specific individuals so that the bereft can strengthen connections according to their evolving needs (Rheingold & Williams, 2018; Williams & Rheingold, 2018). For example, clients can be prompted to list several "Doers" in their social network who can provide practical assistance of various kinds, "Listeners" who can join them in compassionately sorting through their feelings and questions, and "Respite" figures who can provide a simple "time out" from grief through pleasurable social or physical activities, and then agree to contact relevant figures for needed support in the interval between sessions. Additionally, in the case of socially stigmatizing losses, such as death by violent means (homicide, suicide, overdose, or accident), it may be vital to work with bereft clients to facilitate disengagement from critical or dismissive individuals who might be contributing to a socially invalidating disenfranchised grief experience (Doka & Neimeyer, 2012).

The social network of the bereaved client can also be recruited to participate in therapy using a family or couple's format. Therapists can facilitate mutually supportive meaning reconstruction by creating a safe space for acknowledging divergent individual meanings and building communal family meanings of the loss (Hooghe & Neimeyer, 2013;

Nadeau, 1998). Much of the collective family (re)negotiation of meaning arises spontaneously, without prompting by the therapist, as the family discusses the dying process, the death, the deceased, the changed structure and roles of the family members as well as the postloss life of each. However, the therapist can also offer explicit invitations to in-session or between-session tasks and rituals that promote collective and positive engagement with the meaning of the loss (e.g., hosting an inclusive Christmas dinner to honor the loved one's affinity for this holiday, perhaps setting a symbolic place for the deceased at the table). For spiritually inclined mourners, this commonly includes accessing or inventing meaningful practices of both a private (e.g., reading religious devotionals, spiritual journaling) and public (e.g., participating in memorial services, joining a meditation or yoga group) nature.

Finally, the use of group therapy allows clinicians to introduce the bereft to a new social environment that validates attempts to make meaning of grief (Neimeyer, Milman, & Steffen, in press). Group formats are among the most common in grief therapy, particularly when death occurs in violent circumstances (Armour, 2007; Murphy et al., 1998; Neimeyer et al., 2020; Rheingold et al., 2015; Salloum, 2008; Salloum & Vincent, 1999; Supiano et al., 2017). The popularity of grief therapy groups is likely associated with the perception that proximity to other bereaved individuals decreases the likelihood of being misunderstood or exposed to societal stigma. Group therapists focus on managing interpersonal dynamics and guiding the process of therapy in a manner that elicits a lively constructive dialogue permitting validation of both shared perspectives on bereavement as well as unique expressions of grief. Beyond the illustrative techniques of grief therapy mentioned above, readers can consider the many dozens of tools and strategies concretely conveyed and illustrated in published handbooks devoted to such practices (Neimeyer, 2012a, 2016, in press).

We conclude by considering how several of these themes and practices found expression in Rosa's response to Miguel's grave injury and ultimate death.

A clinical coda

Rosa's anguishing quest to take in the reality of her son's cataclysmic injury was palpably evident, even at the most physical levels, as she struggled to recognize her child's broken body in the trauma center in the 3 days following the fateful accident. Under the press of great despair and equally fervent hope, she attempted to make sense of the extent of his injuries in a social field populated by the discourses of academic medicine, dire assessments, and the competing fears and hopes of friends and family. Thrust into the position of decision maker by her holding durable power of attorney for Miguel's health care, she bore the weight of the choice to remove life support from her brain dead son, hoping against hope for the unassisted functioning of his heart and lungs, which was not to be. The ensuing days brought a blur of necessary arrangements for his funeral and burial, culminating in moments of grace when the church swelled with supporters, and times of crushing grief, as when she placed the first shovelful of dirt on his casket in the freshly dug grave.

As the months passed without alleviation of her preoccupying grief, sleeplessness, and ruminative replaying of the accident as she imagined it and of the days in the hospital as she had experienced them, Rosa ultimately sought therapy with one of the authors (RAN). In keeping with the mandate to practice full presence to her pain with no attempt to rapidly assuage or reframe it (Neimeyer, 2012f), the therapist respectfully witnessed the depth of her suffering and assisted her in bearing it mindfully, as they engaged the hard existential questions for which she scarcely had words: *What sort of universe, what sort of God would visit such tragedy on the living? Where and in what form did Miguel now exist, and was a changed relationship with him still possible? Who was she as a mother, to Miguel and to her other children, in light of his death? How could she understand the inchoate, incomprehensible feelings that arose for her in her own body and world of emotion, and find words for conveying them to others who might offer useful empathy and understanding?* Gradually navigating the process of these incipient attempts at meaning-making, some helpful procedures began to emerge and complement the intensely relational base of the therapy, including Rosa's journaling and its processing with her therapist, written correspondence to Miguel and back to herself as if from his perspective, and restorative retelling of the scene of Miguel's dying in slow motion detail with considerable care to help with its integration. Additional sessions with her other young adult children complemented these individual efforts, addressing the unique struggles of each while also helping them respect and support the meaning of the loss to one another.

Importantly, much of Rosa's reconstruction of meaning occurred spontaneously in her social world, as she devoted the insurance money disbursed for the accident to a remarkable memorial to her son in the form of a bronze statue of his being lifted skyward by an angel at the cemetery, unveiled in a moving second memorial service. It included her organization of a gathering of Miguel's friends and her own to form what became a monthly meditation group in her home that held a sacred space for the multiple and ongoing losses of this small community, joined across time by many other bereaved parents. And most remarkably, it grew to involve the founding of *Fuerza Miguel*, whose "vigilante philanthropy" used social media to mobilize rapid and well-coordinated efforts to provide emergency assistance to victims of devastating natural disasters, to sick children, and to impoverished families during the holidays and other times of need. Therapy validated and celebrated these acts of meaning, ultimately embracing them as evidence of Rosa's resilient growth through grief, metabolizing her pain into a selfless form of service that affirmed the significance of her son's life, and its ongoing contribution to the lives of others.

References

Alves, D., Fernandez-Navarro, P., Baptista, J., Ribeiro, E., Sousa, I., & Goncalves, M. M. (2014). Innovative moments in grief therapy: The meaning reconstruction approach and the processes of self-narrative transformation. *Psychotherapy Research, 24*(1), 25–41.

American Psychiatric Association. (2013). *Conditions for further study. Diagnostic and Statistical Manual of Mental Disorders* (5th ed., pp. 806–831). Arlington, VA: American Psychiatric Pub.

Armour, M. (2007). Violent death: Understanding the context of traumatic and stigmatized grief. *Journal of Human Behavior in the Social Environment, 14*(4), 53–90.

Bellet, B. W., Holland, J. M., & Neimeyer, R. A. (2019). The Social Meaning in Life Events Scale (SMILES): A preliminary psychometric evaluation in a bereaved sample. *Death Studies, 43*(2), 103–112.

Bellet, B. W., Jones, P. J., Neimeyer, R. A., & McNally, R. J. (2018). Bereavement outcomes as causal systems: A network analysis of the co-occurrence of complicated grief and posttraumatic growth. *Clinical Psychological Science, 6*(6), 797–809.

Bonanno, G. A. (2004). Loss, trauma, and human resilience: Have we underestimated the human capacity to thrive after extremely aversive events? *American Psychologist, 59*(1), 20.

Bonanno, G. A. (2012). Uses and abuses of the resilience construct: Loss, trauma, and health-related adversities. *Social Science and Medicine, 74*(5), 753.

Bonanno, G. A., Brewin, C. R., Kaniasty, K., & Greca, A. M. L. (2010). Weighing the costs of disaster: Consequences, risks, and resilience in individuals, families, and communities. *Psychological Science in the Public Interest, 11*(1), 1–49.

Bonanno, G. A., & Burton, C. L. (2013). Regulatory flexibility: An individual differences perspective on coping and emotion regulation. *Perspectives on Psychological Science, 8*(6), 591–612.

Bonanno, G. A., & Diminich, E. D. (2013). Annual research review: Positive adjustment to adversity–trajectories of minimal–impact resilience and emergent resilience. *Journal of Child Psychology and Psychiatry, 54*(4), 378–401.

Bonanno, G. A., & Kaltman, S. (2001). The varieties of grief experience. *Clinical Psychology Review, 21*, 705–734.

Bonanno, G. A., Papa, A., Lalande, K., Westphal, M., & Coifman, K. (2004). The importance of being flexible: The ability to both enhance and suppress emotional expression predicts long-term adjustment. *Psychological Science, 15*(7), 482–487.

Bonanno, G. A., Westphal, M., & Mancini, A. D. (2011). Resilience to loss and potential trauma. *Annual Review of Clinical Psychology, 7*, 511–535.

Bonanno, G. A., Wortman, C. B., Lehman, D. R., Tweed, R. G., Haring, M., Sonnega, J., & Nesse, R. M. (2002). Resilience to loss and chronic grief: A prospective study from preloss to 18-months postloss. *Journal of Personality and Social Psychology, 83*(5), 1150–1164.

Bonanno, G. A., Wortman, C. B., & Nesse, R. M. (2004). Prospective patterns of resilience and maladjustment during widowhood. *Psychology and Aging, 19*(2), 260.

Bottomley, J. S., Burke, L. A., & Neimeyer, R. A. (2015). Domains of social support that predict bereavement distress following homicide loss: Assessing need and satisfaction. *OMEGA-Journal of Death and Dying, 75*(1), 3–25.

Breen, L. J., & O'Connor, M. (2009). Acts of resistance: Breaking the silence of grief following traffic crash fatalities. *Death Studies, 34*(1), 30–53.

Büchi, S., Mörgeli, H., Schnyder, U., Jenewein, J., Hepp, U., Jina, E., ... Sensky, T. (2007). Grief and post-traumatic growth in parents 2–6 years after the death of their extremely premature baby. *Psychotherapy and Psychosomatics, 76*(2), 106–114.

Burke, L. A., Crunk, A. E., Neimeyer, R. A., & Bai, H. (2019). Inventory of Complicated Spritual Grief 2.0 (ICSG 2.0): Validation of a revised measure of spiritual distress in bereavement. *Death Studies*. Available from https://doi.org/10.1080/07481187.2019.1627031.

Burke, L. A., & Neimeyer, R. A. (2013). Prospective risk factors for complicated grief. In M. Stroebe, H. Schut, & J. van den Bout (Eds.), *Complicated grief: Scientific foundations for health care professionals* (pp. 145–162). New York: Routledge.

Burke, L. A., Neimeyer, R. A., Holland, J. M., Dennard, S., Oliver, L., & Shear, M. K. (2014). Inventory of Complicated Spiritual Grief: Development and validation of a new measure. *Death Studies, 38*(4), 239–250.

Burke, L. A., Neimeyer, R. A., & McDevitt-Murphy, M. E. (2010). African American homicide bereavement: Aspects of social support that predict complicated grief, PTSD and depression. *Omega, 61*, 1–24.

Calhoun, L., Tedeschi, R., Cann, A., & Hanks, E. (2010). Positive outcomes following bereavement: Paths to posttraumatic growth. *Psychologica Belgica, 50*, 1–2.

Casey, L. (2011). *Review into the needs of families bereaved by homicide*. London: Ministry of Justice.

Coleman, R. A., & Neimeyer, R. A. (2010). Measuring meaning: Searching for and making sense of spousal loss in late life. *Death Studies, 34*, 804–834.

Correa, F. (2016). Drawing images of violent death. In R. A. Neimeyer (Ed.), *Techniques of grief therapy: Assessment and Intervention*, pp. 256–258. New York: Routledge.

Currier, J. M., Holland, J. M., & Neimeyer, R. A. (2006). Sense-making, grief, and the experience of violent loss: Toward a mediational model. *Death Studies, 30*(5), 403–428.

Currier, J. M., Holland, J. M., & Neimeyer, R. A. (2012). Prolonged grief symptoms and growth in the first 2 years of bereavement: Evidence for a nonlinear association. *Traumatology, 18*(4), 65.

Davidson, G. W. (1979). Hospice care for the dying. In H. Wass (Ed.), *Dying: Facing the facts* (pp. 158–181). Philadelphia, PA: Hemisphere Publishing Corporation.

Davis, C. G., Lehman, D. R., Silver, R. C., Wortman, C. B., & Ellard, J. H. (1996). Self-blame following a traumatic event: The role of perceived avoidability. *Personality and Social Psychology Bulletin, 22*(6), 557–567.

Doka, K. J. (2002). *Disenfranchised grief: New directions, challenges, and strategies for practice*. Champaign, IL: Research Press.

Doka, K. J., & Neimeyer, R. A. (2012). Orchestrating social support. In R. A. Neimeyer (Ed.), *Techniques of grief therapy: Creative practices for counseling the bereaved* (pp. 315–317). New York: Routledge.

Dyregrov, K. (2006). Experiences of social networks supporting traumatically bereaved. *OMEGA-Journal of Death and Dying, 52*(4), 339–358.

Galatzer-Levy, I. R., & Bonanno, G. A. (2012). Beyond normality in the study of bereavement: Heterogeneity in depression outcomes following loss in older adults. *Social Science & Medicine, 74*(12), 1987–1994.

Gillies, J., Neimeyer, R. A., & Milman, E. (2014). The Meaning of Loss Codebook: Construction of a system for analyzing meanings made in bereavement. *Death Studies, 38*(4), 207–216.

Gillies, J. M., Neimeyer, R. A., & Milman, E. (2015). The Grief and Meaning Reconstruction Inventory (GMRI): Initial validation of a new measure. *Death Studies, 39*(2), 61–74.

Hedtke, L. (2012). Introducing the deceased. In R. A. Neimeyer (Ed.), *Techniques of grief therapy: Creative practices for counseling the bereaved* (pp. 253–255). New York: Routledge.

Holland, J. M., Currier, J. M., Coleman, R. A., & Neimeyer, R. A. (2010). The Integration of Stressful Life Experiences Scale (ISLES): Development and initial validation of a new measure. *International Journal of Stress Management, 17*(4), 325.

Holland, J. M., Currier, J. M., & Neimeyer, R. A. (2014). Validation of the integration of stressful life experiences scale—Short form in a bereaved sample. *Death Studies, 38*(4), 234–238.

Holland, J. M., Klingspon, K. L., Lichetnthal, W. G., & Neimeyer, R. A. (2018). The Unfinished Business in Bereavement Scale: Development and psychometric evaluation. *Death Studies.*

Hooghe, A., & Neimeyer, R. A. (2013). Family resilience in the wake of loss: A meaning-oriented contribution. In D. S. Becvar (Ed.), *Handbook of family resilience* (pp. 269–284). New York: Springer.

Lee, S. A. (2015). The Persistent Complex Bereavement Inventory: A measure based on the DSM-5. *Death Studies, 39*(7), 399–410.

Lee, S.A., & Milman, E. (in press). The Persistent Complex Bereavement Inventory (PCBI). In R.A. Neimeyer (Ed.), Techniques of Grief Therapy: Bereavement and Beyond (3rd ed.). New York: Routledge.

Lichtenthal, W. G., & Breitbart, W. (2015). The central role of meaning in adjustment to the loss of a child to cancer: Implications for the development of meaning-centered grief therapy. *Current Opinion in Supportive and Palliative Care, 9*(1), 46–57.

Lichtenthal, W. G., Catarozoli, C., Masterson, M., Slivjak, E., Schofield, E., Roberts, K. E., ... Breitbart, W. (2019). An open trial of Meaning-Centered Grief Therapy: Rationale and preliminary evaluation. *Palliative and Supportive Care, 17*, 2–12.

Lichtenthal, W. G., & Neimeyer, R. A. (2012). Directed journaling to facilitate meaning-making. In R. A. Neimeyer (Ed.), *Techniques of grief therapy: Creative practices for counselling the bereaved* (pp. 165–168). New York: Routledge.

Lundorff, M., Holmgren, H., Zachariae, R., Farver-Vestergaard, I., & O'Connor, M. (2017). Prevalence of prolonged grief disorder in adult bereavement: A systematic review and meta-analysis. *Journal of Affective Disorders, 212*, 138–149.

Maciejewski, P. K., Maercker, A., Boelen, P. A., & Prigerson, H. G. (2016). "Prolonged grief disorder" and "persistent complex bereavement disorder", but not "complicated grief", are one and the same diagnostic entity: An analysis of data from the Yale Bereavement Study. *World Psychiatry, 15*(3), 266–275.

MacKinnon, C. J., Smith, N. G., Henry, M., Berish, M., Milman, E., Körner, A., & Cohen, S. R. (2014). Meaning-based group counseling for bereavement: Bridging theory with emerging trends in intervention research. *Death Studies, 38*(3), 137–144.

MacKinnon, C. J., Smith, N. G., Henry, M., Milman, E., Chochinov, H. M., Körner, A., ... Cohen, S. R. (2015). Reconstructing meaning with others in loss: A feasibility pilot randomized controlled trial of a bereavement group. *Death Studies, 39*(7), 411–421.

McMenamy, J. M., Jordan, J. R., & Mitchell, A. M. (2008). What do suicide survivors tell us they need? Results of a pilot study. *Suicide and Life-Threatening Behavior, 38*(4), 375–389.

Mezey, G., Evans, C., & Hobdell, K. (2002). Families of homicide victims: Psychiatric responses and help-seeking. *Psychology and Psychotherapy: Theory, Research and Practice, 75*(1), 65–75.

Milman, E., Neimeyer, R. A., Fitzpatrick, M., MacKinnon, C. J., Muis, K. R., & Cohen, S. R. (2018). Prolonged grief symptomatology following violent loss: The mediating role of meaning. *European Journal of Psychotraumatology, 8*(6).

Milman, E., Neimeyer, R. A., Fitzpatrick, M., MacKinnon, C. J., Muis, K. R., & Cohen, S. R. (2019a). Prolonged grief and the disruption of meaning: Establishing a mediation model. *Journal of Counseling Psychology, 66*(6), 714–725.

Milman, E., Neimeyer, R. A., Fitzpatrick, M., MacKinnon, C. J., Muis, K. R., & Cohen, S. R. (2019b). Rumination moderates the role of meaning in the development of prolonged grief symptomology. *Journal of Clinical Psychology, 75*(6), 1047–1065. Available from https://doi.org/10.1002/jclp.22751.

Murphy, S. A., Johnson, C., Cain, K. C., Gupta, A. D., Dimond, M., & Baugher, J. L. R. (1998). Broad-spectrum group treatment for parents bereaved by the violent deaths of their 12-to 28-year-old children: A randomized controlled trial. *Death Studies, 22*(3), 209–235.

Nadeau, J. W. (1998). *Families making sense of death* (Vol. 1). Newbury Park, CA: Sage.

Neimeyer, R. A. (2006). *Lessons of loss* (2nd ed.). New York: Routledge.

Neimeyer, R. A. (Ed.), (2012a). *Techniques of grief therapy: Creative practices for counseling the bereaved*. New York: Routledge.

Neimeyer, R. A. (2012b). The life imprint. In R. A. Neimeyer (Ed.), *Techniques of grief therapy* (pp. 274–276). New York: Routledge.

Neimeyer, R. A. (2012c). Correspondence with the deceased. In R. Neimeyer (Ed.), *Techniques of grief therapy: Creative practices for counseling the bereaved* (pp. 259–261). New York: Routledge.

Neimeyer, R. A. (2012d). Chair work. In R. A. Neimeyer (Ed.), *Techniques of grief therapy: Creative practices for counselling the bereaved* (pp. 266–273). New York: Routledge.

Neimeyer, R. A. (2012e). Analogical listening. In R. A. Neimeyer (Ed.), *Techniques of grief therapy: Creative practices for counselling the bereaved* (pp. 55–58). New York: Routledge.

Neimeyer, R. A. (2012f). Presence, process, and procedure: A relational frame for technical proficiency in grief therapy. In R. A. Neimeyer (Ed.), *Techniques of grief therapy: Creative practices for counselling the bereaved* (pp. 23–31). New York: Routledge.

Neimeyer, R. A. (2012g). Retelling the narrative of the death. In R. A. Neimeyer (Ed.), *Techniques of grief therapy: Creative practices for counselling the bereaved* (pp. 86–90). New York: Routlege.

Neimeyer, R. A. (2014). Chapters of our lives. In B. E. Thompson, & R. A. Neimeyer (Eds.), *Grief and the expressive arts: Practices for creating meaning* (pp. 80–84). New York: Routledge.

Neimeyer, R. A. (Ed.), (2016). *Techniques of grief therapy: Assessment and intervention*. New York: Routledge.

Neimeyer, R. A. (2019). Meaning reconstruction in bereavement: Development of a research program. *Death Studies, 43*, 79–91.

Neimeyer, R.A. (Ed.), (in press). *New techniques of grief therapy: Bereavement and beyond*. New York: Routledge.

Neimeyer, R. A., & Alves, D. (2016). Seeking meaning in loss: An online narrative constructivist intervention for complicated grief. *Grief Matters: The Australian Journal for Grief and Bereavement, 19*(3).

Neimeyer, R. A., Bottomley, J. S., & Bellet, B. W. (2018). Growing through grief: When loss is complicated. In K. J. Doka, & A. Tucci (Eds.), *When grief is complicated* (pp. 95–111). Washington, DC: Hospice Foundation of America.

Neimeyer, R. A., & Jordan, J. R. (2002). Disenfranchisement as empathic failure: Grief therapy and the co-construction of meaning. In K. J. Doka (Ed.), *Disenfranchised grief: New directions, challenges, and strategies for practice* (pp. 95–117). Champaign, IL: Research Press.

Neimeyer, R. A., Klass, D., & Dennis, M. R. (2014). A social constructionist account of grief: Loss and the narration of meaning. *Death Studies, 38*(8), 485–498.

Neimeyer, R., Milman, E., & Steffen, E.M. (in press), The meaning in loss group: Principles, processes and procedures. In R. Neimeyer (Ed.), *Techniques of grief therapy: Bereavement and beyond* (3rd ed.). New York: Routledge.

Neimeyer, R. A., & Sands, D. C. (2011). Meaning reconstruction in bereavement: From principles to practice. In R. A. Neimeyer, H. Winokuer, D. Harris, & G. Thornton (Eds.), *Grief and bereavement in contemporary society: Bridging research and practice* (pp. 9–22). New York: Routledge.

Nolen-Hoeksema, S., & Davis, C. G. (1999). "Thanks for sharing that": Ruminators and their social support networks. *Journal of Personality and Social Psychology, 77*(4), 801.

Ott, C. H. (2003). The impact of complicated grief on mental and physical health at various points in the bereavement process. *Death Studies, 27*, 249–272.

Park, C. L. (2010). Making sense of the meaning literature: An integrative review of meaning making and its effects on adjustment to stressful life events. *Psychological Bulletin, 136*(2), 257.

Park, C. L., & Folkman, S. (1997). Meaning in the context of stress and coping. *Review of General Psychology, 1*(2), 115.

Prigerson, H. G., Vanderwerker, L. C., & Maciejewski, P. K. (2008). A case for inclusion of prolonged grief disorder in DSM-V. In M. S. Stroebe, R. O. Hansson, H. Schut, & W. Stroebe (Eds.), *Handbook of bereavement research and practice: Advances in theory and intervention* (pp. 165–186). Washington, DC: American Psychological Association.

Rheingold, A. A., Baddeley, J. L., Williams, J. L., Brown, C., Wallace, M. M., Correa, F., & Rynearson, E. K. (2015). Restorative retelling for violent death: An investigation of treatment effectiveness, influencing factors, and durability. *Journal of Loss and Trauma, 20*(6), 541–555.

Rheingold, A. A., & Williams, J. L. (2018). A modular-based comprehensive approach for addressing heterogeneous mental health sequelae of violent loss survivors. *Death Studies, 42*(3).

Rheingold, A. A., Zinzow, H., Hawkins, A., Saunders, B. E., & Kilpatrick, D. G. (2012). Prevalence and mental health outcomes of homicide survivors in a representative US sample of adolescents: Data from the 2005 National Survey of Adolescents. *Journal of Child Psychology and Psychiatry, 53*(6), 687–694.

Rozalski, V., Holland, J. M., & Neimeyer, R. A. (2017). Circumstances of death and complicated grief: Indirect associations through meaning made of loss. *Journal of Loss and Trauma, 22*(1), 11–23.

Rynearson, E. K., & Salloum, A. (2011). Restorative retelling: Revising the narrative of violent death. In R. A. Neimeyer, H. R. Winokuer, D. L. Harris, & G. F. Thornton (Eds.), *Grief and bereavement in contemporary society: Bridging research and practice* (pp. 177–188). Abingdon: Taylor & Francis.

Saindon, C., Rheingold, A. A., Baddeley, J., Wallace, M. M., Brown, C., & Rynearson, E. K. (2014). Restorative retelling for violent loss: An open clinical trial. *Death Studies, 38*(4).

Salloum, A. (2008). Group therapy for children after homicide and violence: A pilot study. *Research on Social Work Practice, 18*(3), 198–211.

Salloum, A., & Overstreet, S. (2012). Grief and trauma intervention for children after disaster: Exploring coping skills versus trauma narration. *Behaviour Research and Therapy, 50*(3), 169–179.

Salloum, A., & Vincent, N. J. (1999). Community-based groups for inner city adolescent survivors of homicide victims. *Journal of Child and Adolescent Group Therapy, 9*(1), 27–45.

Shear, M. K., Simon, N., Wall, M., Zisook, S., Neimeyer, R., Duan, N., ... Ghesquiere, A. (2011). Complicated grief and related bereavement issues for DSM-5. *Depression and Anxiety*, *28*(2), 103–117.

Southwick, S. M., Bonanno, G. A., Masten, A. S., Panter-Brick, C., & Yehuda, R. (2014). Resilience definitions, theory, and challenges: Interdisciplinary perspectives. *European Journal of Psychotraumatology*, *5*(1), 25338.

Steffen, E., & Coyle, A. (2011). Sense of presence experiences and meaning-making in bereavement: A qualitative analysis. *Death Studies*, *35*(7), 579–609.

Stroebe, M., Schut, H., & Stroebe, W. (2007). Health outcomes of bereavement. *The Lancet*, *370*(9603), 1960–1973.

Supiano, K. P., Haynes, L. B., & Pond, V. (2017). The transformation of the meaning of death in complicated grief group therapy for survivors of suicide: A treatment process analysis using the meaning of loss codebook. *Death Studies*, *41*(9), 553–561.

Tedeschi, R. G., & Calhoun, L. G. (1996). The Posttraumatic Growth Inventory: Measuring the positive legacy of trauma. *Journal of Traumatic Stress*, *9*(3), 455–471.

Tedeschi, R. G., & Calhoun, L. G. (2008). Beyond the concept of recovery: Growth and the experience of loss. *Death Studies*, *32*(1), 27–39.

Thuen, F. (1997). Social support after the loss of an infant child: A long-term perspective. *Scandinavian Journal of Psychology*, *38*(2), 103–110.

Toller, P. (2011). Bereaved parents' experiences of supportive and unsupportive communication. *Southern Communication Journal*, *76*(1), 17–34.

Vanderwerker, L. C., & Prigerson, H. G. (2004). Social support and technological connectedness as protective factors in bereavement. *Journal of Loss and Trauma*, *9*, 45–57.

Walsh, F., & McGoldrick, M. (2004). *Living beyond loss: Death in the family*. New York: WW Norton & Company.

Westphal, M., & Bonanno, G. A. (2007). Posttraumatic growth and resilience to trauma: Different sides of the same coin or different coins? *Applied Psychology*, *56*(3), 417–427.

Westphal, M., Seivert, N. H., & Bonanno, G. A. (2010). Expressive flexibility. *Emotion*, *10* (1), 92.

Williams, J. L., & Rheingold, A. A. (2018). Novel application of skills for psychological recovery as an early intervention for violent loss: Rationale and case examples. *Omega: Journal of Death and Dying*. Available from https://doi.org/10.1177/0030222818766138.

World Health Organization. *International classification of diseases 11th revision ICD-11 beta draft 2017*. (2018). Retrieved from <https://icd.who.int/dev11/lm/en>.

CHAPTER

6

Transitions in an uncertain labor market: implications for meaningful work

Blake A. Allan and Tracie Liu
Educational Studies, Purdue University, West Lafayette, IN, United States

Introduction

Scholars are increasingly recognizing meaningful work as a central variable in facilitating positive workplace outcomes, including work engagement, commitment, job satisfaction, and performance (Allan, Batz-Barbarich, Sterling, & Tay, 2019). As a result, finding ways to establish and maintain meaningful work is an important target for scholarship. However, current transitions in the labor market have significant implications for meaningful work in the 21st century. The current chapter outlines historic and cultural roots of meaningful work, the contemporary demand for meaningful work, and the unique challenges for maintaining meaningful work in the current environment. We also review theoretical perspectives relevant to meaningful work in the transitioning labor market and discuss how technology and other factors will continue to present unique challenges and opportunities to workers seeking meaningful work.

Meaningful work

Scholars have defined meaningful work in different ways, and distinguishing various terms is important. Often scholars differentiate between the terms "meaning" and "meaningful" (Pratt & Ashforth, 2003).

Navigating Life Transitions for Meaning
DOI: https://doi.org/10.1016/B978-0-12-818849-1.00006-0

While "meanings" refer to the cognitive representations of stimuli in the environment or of internal experiences (Pratt & Ashforth, 2003), "meaningfulness" refers to the personal experience that certain activities are valuable, significant, or important (Lips-Wiersma, Wright, & Dik, 2016; Steger, Dik, & Duffy, 2012). Meaningful work, therefore, broadly refers to work that people perceive as significant and worthwhile (Pratt & Ashforth, 2003).

While this conceptualization of meaningful work is unidimensional, other conceptualizations of meaningful work are multidimensional and outline specific meaningful experiences (Allan et al., 2019). Often these multidimensional models integrate self-oriented experiences, such as personal growth, with other-oriented experiences, such as contributing to the greater good (e.g., Lips-Wiersma & Wright, 2012; Steger et al., 2012). Building off this previous work, Allan and colleagues (2019) argued that experiences are meaningful when people perform behaviors or have experiences that are congruent with their deeply held values. For example, people who help others at work are likely to judge this as meaningful if they highly value improving the welfare of others and if helping others is an important part of their identity and meaning in life. Moreover, when conducting value-congruent actions, people may experience positive emotions, such as self-transcendence and inspiration. When people consider whether their work is meaningful, they consider a variety of meaningful and meaningless experiences at work and integrate these into overall beliefs about the meaningfulness and value of their work (Bailey & Madden, 2017; Kahneman & Krueger, 2006). Meaningful work, therefore, is also an individual retrospective evaluation that one's work fulfills one's deeply held values and is therefore significant and worthwhile (Allan et al., 2019).

Meaningful work as a modern cultural phenomenon

Broadly speaking, the cultural ideology that work can, and perhaps should, be meaningful is a modern, culturally bound phenomenon. Specifically, the modern and Western idea that work is special and can be meaningful is embedded within the culture of the protestant work ethic, beginning with the protestant reformation in the 14th and 15th centuries, which placed work as central to people's lives (Donkin, 2010). Martin Luther introduced the idea that work was not just about survival and earthy penance but about fulfilling sacred, godly purposes on earth, elevating work to a calling whereby people could find salvation through their labor (Donkin, 2010). Other protestant philosophers, like Thomas Carlyle, echoed this sentiment by proclaiming that all work, particularly hard labor, was sacred and meaningful (Donkin, 2010). Puritans and other protestant groups fleeing persecution in Europe brought these ideals of work to the United States, where they became a fundamental part of American culture.

These cultural underpinnings coincided with a transition through different economic paradigms (i.e., hunter-gatherer to agrarian to industrial to postindustrial), which brought different conceptions of the value and meaning of working (DeBell, 2006). Specifically, as societies progress, the values of industrial society, such as economic security and loyalty, often transition to postindustrial values, such as quality of life, secularism, self-actualization, well-being, and meaningfulness (Inglehart & Baker, 2000; Inglehart, 2008). Accordingly, while the idea of meaningful work has religious roots, society is becoming increasingly secular (Hackett et al., 2015). Given the decline of religion as source of meaningfulness, people are increasingly turning toward their work or organizations to provide a sense of meaningfulness in their lives (Ashforth & Vaidyanath, 2002). For example, people are willing to accept significantly less pay to have meaningful work (Hu & Hirsh, 2017), and the majority of college students prioritize meaningful work over other work values (Allan, Owens, & Duffy, 2017). Having meaningful work is also significantly associated with being less likely to leave an organization, even if staying requires significant sacrifice (Bunderson & Thompson, 2009; Hu & Hirsh, 2017; Steger et al., 2012). Taken together, this evidence suggests that meaningful work is culturally bound and in high demand.

Challenges in obtaining meaningful work

Despite cultural ideologies that prioritize meaningful work, the current work environment may paradoxically make meaningful work more difficult to obtain. Industrial and postindustrial societies led to the increasing specialization of work (DeBell, 2006). Rather than in preindustrial societies where people often created a product from beginning to end, the industrial revolution led to the specialization of labor where people became good at a narrow collection of tasks. For example, in the early 20th century, movements such as scientific management broke down work into separate tasks performed by different workers, with the goal of improving economic efficiency and labor productivity (Donkin, 2010). This specialization degraded the extent to which a job involves the holistic creation of a product, a key predictor of meaningful work (Hackman & Oldham, 1976; May, Gilson, & Harter, 2004). Specialization also separated workers from the consequences and beneficiaries of their work, further degrading the likelihood of experiencing meaningfulness (Allan, Duffy, & Collisson, 2018; Skinner, 1986).

Beyond specialization of labor, today's postindustrial society is rapidly transitioning with uncertain futures, presenting even more challenges to meaningful work. Unstable work conditions, such as unemployment, underemployment, and working poverty, remain problems in most parts of the world, including the United States (ILO, 2017). Moreover, trends related to the degradation of work quality, such as the exponential growth of technology and automation, the rise of platform economies, globalization, population growth, and income equality, will continue to catalyze accelerated transitions of labor markets throughout the world (ILO, 2017). These conditions make the future of work increasingly precarious for workers, especially for vulnerable and marginalized populations, such as people of color, immigrants, people with low-incomes, and people with disabling conditions (e.g., Das-Munshi, Leavey, Stansfeld, & Prince, 2012). Additionally, an increasingly individualistic and neoliberal context in the United States has led to the erosion of collective bargaining rights and the social security net in the United States (Lott, 2014), putting even more pressure on individuals to maintain employment and meet their basic needs.

People experiencing this instability may be unable to prioritize or experience meaningful work due to constant fear that they may not be able to meet their basic needs (Duffy, Blustein, Diemer, & Autin, 2016). For example, unemployment by definition robs people of the ability to engage in collective purpose and experience the benefits of meaningful work (Jahoda, 1981). Underemployment and working poverty are also associated with having less meaningful work (Allan, Tay, & Sterling, 2017) as is job insecurity, lack of decent work, and deprivation of basic needs (Allan, Tebbe, Bouchard, & Duffy, 2018; Duffy et al., 2016; Stander & Rothmann, 2010). This association suggests that the volatility of the economic environment may add another factor that makes obtaining meaningful work difficult in the modern age.

In addition to instability in labor markets, the fundamental structure of organizations has changed. Beginning in the 1980s and accelerating through the 1990s, organizations transitioned from traditional, hierarchical structures to decentralized ones with fewer permanent employees and more contract workers (Katz & Krueger, 2019). As a result, the number of part-time and contract positions increased sharply, with some industries having a near complete transformation into a contract-based workforce (Katz & Krueger, 2019). This change marks a stark contrast to the 20th century where the working norm was to choose an occupation and stay loyal to one company, slowly rising up the ranks until retirement (Herr, 2001). In this context, work fit into well-defined roles within autonomous organizations (Oldham & Hackman, 2010). Manufacturing jobs in the United States provided good benefits, steady incomes, and a predictable middle-class life, and due to this loyalty and consistent employment, workers tended to identify strongly with their organization (Hall, 2004). This identification facilitated meaningful work as deriving from loyalty to a company and from a personal connection to its aspirations (Carton, 2018). For example, with effective organizational leadership, people could connect their daily work tasks to concrete goals, which in turn connected to the broader mission of the company (Carton, 2018).

Today the responsibility has shifted to individual workers to maintain meaningfulness in their work lives (Hall & Moss, 1998; Hall, Feldman, & Kim, 2013). People are changing jobs and careers at a faster rate than ever and often move rapidly between contract or gig jobs. Without stable organizations to house people's work, people's sense of meaningfulness may be the thread that runs between these temporary positions. Given its deep connection to the self, meaningfulness is motivating (Chalofsky, 2003), and enacting one's deepest values through a diversity of tasks leads workers to be engaged (Kahn, 1990) and empowered (Spreitzer, 1995). As workers market their "selves," their skills, knowledge, and abilities, understanding the significance of their work becomes more central to productivity and positive affective states at work. These positive states during work might lead, in turn, to general well-being and functioning (Rodríguez-Muñoz, Sanz-Vergel, Demerouti, & Bakker, 2014).

Maintaining meaningful work in the modern era

Given this background, perspectives that update traditional theories and enhance understanding about how people maintain meaningfulness in this context are particularly important. One traditional theory that integrated meaningful work was job characteristics theory (JCT; Hackman & Oldham, 1976; Oldham & Hackman, 2010). JCT identified characteristics of jobs, established by organizations, that cause people to become intrinsically motivated and productive at work. JCT specifically proposed that five job characteristics (skill variety, task identity, task significance, autonomy, and feedback) lead to three psychological states (meaningful work, responsibility, and knowledge of results), which then lead to positive outcomes (internal work motivation, quality work performance, job satisfaction, and low absenteeism). Stated broadly, workers feel positive emotions when they perform well on a meaningful task for which they are responsible and receive feedback. This positive affect is intrinsically motivating and creates a feedback loop of productivity, job satisfaction, and other positive work outcomes.

Despite strong support for its propositions and the identification of meaningful work as a central variable in promoting positive outcomes

(Allan et al., 2019; Humphrey, Nahrgang, & Morgeson, 2007), JCT is fundamentally embedded within a 20th century perspective on work (Oldham & Hackman, 2010). Job characteristics are no longer static, and people are not passive recipients of work conditions. Addressing these concerns, Kahn (1990) extended the JCT to identify how people personally engage in their work and experience meaningfulness. He viewed work engagement as the expression of workers' preferred selves in their job and meaningfulness as the sense that this expression of their selves is worthwhile. Kahn (1990) affirmed that job characteristics facilitate meaningful work, but also suggested that job roles that offer attractive identities, lead to positive interpersonal interactions, and promote positive self-perceptions also increase meaningfulness. Therefore, for Kahn (1990), experiencing meaningful work is not the passive result of job characteristics but includes people's core identities, including their values and goals. Specifically, when workers' job characteristics and tasks match their values and personal identities, they experience meaningful work (Lips-Wiersma, 2002; Steger & Dik, 2010). In essence, this "self-in-role" perspective furthered JCT by arguing that the experience of meaningful work is the outcome of a person interacting with their environment.

Building on this work, the protean career orientation (PCO) highlights the role of the individual in finding meaningful work. The PCO is an attitude toward work whereby people are self-directed and value-driven (Hall, 1996), a contrast to the more traditional, 20th century career orientations where organizations controlled people's careers and success (Hall et al., 2013). Specifically, with a PCO, people guide their own careers and work toward goals that accomplish deep, personal values (Hall, 1996). Rather than relying on organizations to determine and provide external markers of success (e.g., promotions and raises), people with a PCO aim to achieve psychological success, a sense of fulfillment and meaningfulness from accomplishing important life goals (Hall, 1996). The two defining metacompetencies of the PCO are self-awareness (i.e., knowing one's identity and values) and adaptability (i.e., being able to change), which allow people to pursue and accomplish their goals (Akkermans & Tims, 2017; Hall et al., 2013).

People with PCOs may be particularly able to maintain meaningful work in today's environment. First, aligning with the contention that people experience meaningful work when accomplishing value-consistent goals (Allan et al., 2019), people with PCOs are by definition driven to experience meaningful work. Moreover, this meaningful work is not located within a specific organization or tied to specific work tasks. Rather, people with a PCO are pursuing broader aspirations connected to their meaning in life, which they can accomplish with different organizations and tasks across time. As a result, if they are not experiencing meaningful work and have both self-awareness and adaptability, they may be particularly motivated to change jobs, redesign their work, or transform their organizations to meet their personal goals (Hall et al., 2013).

This willingness to modify and develop their own work, also known as job crafting (Wrzesniewski & Dutton, 2001), has particular relevance for fostering meaningful work (Berg, Dutton, & Wrzesniewski, 2013). In today's labor market, jobs are transitioning rapidly—not just disappearing and appearing but changing their structures. In this environment, jobs and their features are in a constant state of flux, and people are not passive recipients of these job characteristics (Oldham & Hackman, 2010). Rather, people who job craft actively change their jobs to be more meaningful (Berg et al., 2013). For example, workers may change the degree to which they focus on meaningful work tasks, add new tasks that are personally meaningful, or reframe their job roles as connected to broader meaningful purposes (Berg, Grant, & Johnson, 2010). This may affect the meaningfulness of work directly, but people who job craft may also experience greater person-environment fit over time, which may further lead to increased meaningful work (Tims, Derks, & Bakker, 2016).

In summary, the transition of labor markets from the 20th to 21st century has put increasing pressure on individuals to maintain and guide their own careers. Not surprisingly, those who adopt a PCO and are able to job craft may be particularly able to thrive in this environment. However, a PCO is not "good" in and of itself but might only function as adaptive in an increasingly individualistic labor context in the United States (Hamamura, 2012). This view is consistent with studies showing that people valuing freedom and self-expression within more individualistic nations experience greater life satisfaction than people holding the same values in more collectivistic nations (e.g., Oishi, Diener, Lucas, & Suh, 1999). Therefore, people who are able to adapt to the current economic context in the United States may be more successful in maintaining meaningful work.

The future of meaningful work

As discussed previously, technological growth and the rise of platform economies are central drivers of transitions in the labor market. Understanding the future of meaningful work involves examining these forces, which will have uncertain implications for workers' ability to maintain meaningful work. These forces will likely create both challenges and opportunities.

Technological growth is perhaps the most salient factor in the future of meaningful work. Advances in machine learning and artificial intelligence (AI) technology are leading to an increasing automation of the workforce (Lent, 2018). Automation, using machines to carry out the critical functions of a job (Parasuraman, Sheridan, & Wickens, 2000), is a priority for many companies that seek to reduce labor costs and increase productivity. Projections of the impact of automation vary, but all of them guarantee a significant shift in the structure of work—research shows that 45% of work activities have the potential to be automated with current technology, with about 23% of work activity hours likely to be automated by 2030 (Chui, Manyika, & Miremadi, 2015). Although fewer than 5% of occupations can be entirely automated, around 60% of occupations could have 30% or more of total activities automated (Chui et al., 2015). Although there may be a stereotype that only low-skilled jobs are at risk for automation, Chui et al. (2015) noted that certain low-income, low-skilled jobs cannot be automated, such as home health aides, landscapers, and maintenance workers, while 20% of executives' working time could be automated with current technology.

These findings suggest that AI will not claim the majority of jobs. Instead, most people will likely work collaboratively with AI in the workplace, with the processing capabilities of AI harnessed to streamline tasks. Automation is already present in many jobs—for example, companies use AI systems to collect and process large amounts of data, which human workers then use to make decisions (Gray & Suri, 2017). Social media websites also use AI bots to survey social media content and detect inappropriate or controversial content, even though humans make the final decision to delete these posts (Gray & Suri, 2017). Overall, automation may primarily complete paperwork and logistical tasks, leaving creative and emotion-based tasks to human works. For example, automated triage systems in emergency rooms may allow doctors to focus more on patient care (Chui et al., 2015).

Freed from routine and repetition, workers may be able to shift their attention to working with the holistic concept of their jobs, specifically in relational and creative domains, and use free time to job craft or connect with others. This shift may allow workers to connect with the broader mission of their work and thereby increase the salience and relevance of their job tasks. Essentially, as the early 20th century moved to increase productivity by breaking tasks down into components (Donkin, 2010), automation may eventually complete these repetitive (and perhaps more meaningless) tasks and subsequently allow workers to focus on meaningful work.

However, automation will not necessarily lead to uniform benefits. For example, a growing problem pertains to the need for specialization, education, and training. Although automation will reach all fields, it will have the greatest impact on jobs accessible to those with high-school degrees and under. Researchers project that by 2020 the United States may have one and a half million too few workers with the college or graduate degrees necessary for jobs and nearly six million lacking high-school diplomas (Manyika, Lund, Auguste, & Ramaswamy, 2012). As machines become more capable of filling these jobs without the need of humans, workers may enter fields that cannot be easily automated, such as health care. However, many of these "safer" fields require significant amounts of education and specialization. Moving forward, more people may pursue higher education only because of an association of a college degree to employment after graduation. Given barriers to education that already exist, for example financial barriers, those marginalized in higher education are in danger of being left behind as automation demands a more educated labor force.

Taken together, automation might present some opportunities for meaningful work while continuing to displace workers from jobs and putting pressure on individuals to obtain an increasingly more expensive secondary education (Archibald & Feldman, 2008). Without understanding what steps are necessary to secure a job in the changing marketplace, workers may find themselves struggling to adjust. Moreover, this insecurity in finding and maintaining stable employment is a fundamental threat to meaningful work, perhaps preventing workers from focusing on their desire for meaningfulness (e.g. Allan et al., 2017).

This difficulty relates to the rise of another significant factor in the future job market—the platform economy, also known as the sharing economy, the gig economy, or the on-demand economy. The word "platform" here refers to technological frameworks and digital matchmakers that recruit human workers, such as Uber, Lyft, Etsy, Twitch, YouTube, Airbnb, and Patreon. Platform economies operate with platforms employing workers to monetize labor, services, and assets owned by the individual. Workers join platform economies because they desire flexible hours, financial opportunities without formal hiring processes, and career self-management. These platforms are also cheap or free to join and many, such as Amazon's Mechanical Turk, include people of all ages and different geographic areas (Manyika et al., 2017).

Platform jobs are becoming increasingly popular, especially with the younger generation. People want positions that allow them to monetize their creative passions, whether it be selling jewelry online or streaming their video gaming to thousands of viewers. Through these platforms, influencers and content creators are also capable of reaching wide audiences, receiving social, psychological, and monetary reinforcement. People may benefit from work through platforms because of the opportunity to create meaningful work by engaging in self-employment based on their own values, goals, and interests (Oliver, 2015). As a result, people with a PCO may be able to capitalize on these opportunities by choosing jobs that meet deeper needs and values. For example, people with a desire to serve and connect with others might drive for Uber or Lyft or rent through Airbnb and subsequently find meaningfulness in the connections they make with consumers. Indeed, Airbnb workers are often motivated to meet and interact with their guests, regardless of monetary benefits (Frenken & Schor, 2019). Other studies indicate that social motivations to share and connect with others may make platform work particularly appealing (Böcker & Meelen, 2017; Fitzmaurice et al., 2016).

However, similar to automation, platform jobs create difficulties as well as opportunities. For example, people may be forced into the platform economy to earn extra money to meet basic needs. As a result, people may work on several different platforms at once or work through a platform in addition to a traditional part-time or full-time job (Törhönen, Hassan, Sjöblom, & Hamari, 2019). People who hold these types of alternative work arrangements by choice are protected against their potential negative effects on well-being, whereas people forced into these positions often experience negative outcomes (Barling, Inness, & Gallagher, 2002). Multiple jobholding has always been present in the workforce, but with the rise of platform work, future research needs to focus on this area. The impact of holding multiple jobs, working significantly beyond traditional hours, and being forced to work in the platform economy may be a significant source of job stress and lead to poorer well-being, which may erode meaningful work and meaning in life (Allan, Douglass, Duffy, & McCarty, 2016; Barling et al., 2002). In addition, some of these platform economies capitalize on social image. For example, YouTube live streamers experience a significant amount of emotional and physical labor to maintain their image and maintain high levels of productivity with no clear structure or set hours (Guarriello, 2019). This characteristic may blur the boundaries of work and life, further eroding the meaningfulness of work (Munn, 2013).

Above all, the biggest concern in platform economies lies in the platform companies themselves. Platform companies can change their terms of service or terminate user accounts with minimal warning (Van Doorn, 2017). Moreover, these companies do not provide employee benefits to platform workers. Worker classification, specifically the distinction between employees and contractors, has been a challenge for years, but scholars note how critical this issue is for platform companies in particular (Pinsof, 2015; Van Doorn, 2017). Considering that worker benefits such as disability, health insurance, job security, and maternity leave are all contingent on employment status, the fact that platform companies do not acknowledge their users as employees places these workers in a constant state of precarity. Whereas traditional companies sign contracts with their employees to protect both parties, platform economies are inherently imbalanced. For example, full-time YouTubers may find that their compensation primarily comes from the support of their viewers, with no guarantees or financial support from the platform itself. Indeed, there are no agreements between YouTube and their users to protect content creators from having their channels taken down overnight, losing them their entire audience. As noted previously, this uncertainty may hinder people's ability to experience meaningful work as they experience significant associated stress and anxiety (Allan et al., 2016).

Conclusion

In the modern era, many people want meaningful work, but rapid transitions in the labor market make obtaining and maintaining it difficult. Theoretical perspectives, such as the PCO and job crafting, may help individuals, scholars, and practitioners understand how to promote meaningful work in the current context. Regardless, as technology and new economic systems develop, the future of meaningful work is increasingly uncertain. Automation and platform economies offer challenges and opportunities for meaningful work, whether they be through increased precarity, delegating clerical work to machines, or pursuing dreams of being self-employed in one's passion. Either way, research and scholarship must continue to examine these issues to help people find meaningful work in an ever-transitioning world.

References

Akkermans, J., & Tims, M. (2017). Crafting your career: How career competencies relate to career success via job crafting. *Applied Psychology*, *66*(1), 168–195.

Allan, B. A., Batz-Barbarich, C., Sterling, H. M., & Tay, L. (2019). Outcomes of meaningful work: A meta-analysis. *Journal of Management Studies*, *56*(3), 500–528.

Allan, B. A., Douglass, R. P., Duffy, R. D., & McCarty, R. J. (2016). Meaningful work as a moderator of the relation between work stress and meaning in life. *Journal of Career Assessment*, *24*(3), 429–440.

Allan, B. A., Duffy, R. D., & Collisson, B. (2018). Helping others increases meaningful work: Evidence from three experiments. *Journal of Counseling Psychology*, *65*(2), 155–165.

Allan, B. A., Owens, R. L., & Duffy, R. D. (2017). Generation me or meaning? Exploring meaningful work in college students and career counselors. *Journal of Career Development*, *44*(6), 502–515.

Allan, B. A., Tay, L., & Sterling, H. M. (2017). Construction and validation of the Subjective Underemployment Scales (SUS). *Journal of Vocational Behavior*, *99*, 93–106.

Allan, B. A., Tebbe, E. A., Bouchard, L. M., & Duffy, R. D. (2018). Access to decent and meaningful work in a sexual minority population. *Journal of Career Assessment, 27*(3), 408–421.

Archibald, R. B., & Feldman, D. H. (2008). Explaining increases in higher education costs. *The Journal of Higher Education, 79*(3), 268–295.

Ashforth, B. E., & Vaidyanath, D. (2002). Work organizations as secular religions. *Journal of Management Inquiry, 11*(4), 359–370.

Bailey, C., & Madden, A. (2017). Time reclaimed: temporality and the experience of meaningful work. *Work, Employment and Society, 31*, 3–18.

Barling, J., Inness, M., & Gallagher, D. G. (2002). *Alternative work arrangements and employee well-being. Historical and current perspectives on stress and health* (pp. 183–216). Bingley, UK: Emerald Group Publishing Limited.

Berg, J. M., Dutton, J. E., & Wrzesniewski, A. (2013). Job crafting and meaningful work. In B. J. Dik, Z. S. Byrne, & M. F. Steger (Eds.), *Purpose and meaning in the workplace* (pp. 81–104). Washington, DC: American Psychological Association.

Berg, J. M., Grant, A. M., & Johnson, V. (2010). When callings are calling: Crafting work and leisure in pursuit of unanswered occupational callings. *Organization Science, 21*(5), 973–994.

Böcker, L., & Meelen, T. (2017). Sharing for people, planet or profit? Analysing motivations for intended sharing economy participation. *Environmental Innovation and Societal Transitions, 23*, 28–39.

Bunderson, J. S., & Thompson, J. A. (2009). The call of the wild: Zookeepers, callings, and the double-edged sword of deeply meaningful work. *Administrative Science Quarterly, 54*(1), 32–57.

Carton, A. M. (2018). "I'm not mopping the floors, I'm putting a man on the moon": How NASA leaders enhanced the meaningfulness of work by changing the meaning of work. *Administrative Science Quarterly, 63*(2), 323–369.

Chalofsky, N. (2003). An emerging construct for meaningful work. *Human Resource Development International, 6*(1), 69–83.

Chui, M., Manyika, J., & Miremadi, M. (2015). Four fundamentals of workplace automation. *McKinsey Quarterly, 29*(3), 1–9.

Das-Munshi, J., Leavey, G., Stansfeld, S. A., & Prince, M. J. (2012). Migration, social mobility and common mental disorders: Critical review of the literature and meta-analysis. *Ethnicity & Health, 17*(1-2), 17–53.

DeBell, C. (2006). What all applied psychologists should know about work. *Professional Psychology: Research and Practice, 37*(4), 325–333.

Donkin, R. (2010). *The history of work*. New York: Springer.

Duffy, R. D., Blustein, D. L., Diemer, M. A., & Autin, K. L. (2016). The psychology of working theory. *Journal of Counseling Psychology, 63*(2), 127–148.

Frenken K., & Schor J. (2019) Putting the sharing economy into perspective. In: O. Mont (Ed.), *A research agenda for sustainable consumption governance* (pp. 121–135). Edward Elgar Publishing.

Gray, M. L., & Suri, S. (2017). The humans working behind the AI curtain. *Harvard Business Review, 9*, 2–5.

Guarriello, N. B. (2019). Never give up, never surrender: Game live streaming, neoliberal work, and personalized media economies. *New Media & Society, 21*(8), 1750–1769.

Hackett, C., Connor, P., Stonawski, M., Skirbekk, V., Potancoková, M., & Abel, G. (2015). *The future of world religions: Population growth projections, 2010-2050*. Washington, DC: Pew Research Center.

Hackman, J. R., & Oldham, G. R. (1976). Motivation through the design of work: Test of a theory. *Organizational Behavior and Human Performance, 16*(2), 250–279.

Hall, D. T. (1996). Protean careers of the 21st century. *Academy of Management Perspectives, 10*(4), 8–16.

Hall, D. T. (2004). The protean career: A quarter-century journey. *Journal of Vocational Behavior, 65*(1), 1–13.

Hall, D. T., Feldman, E., & Kim, N. (2013). Meaningful work and the protean career. In B. J. Dik, Z. S. Byrne, & M. F. Steger (Eds.), *Purpose and meaning in the workplace* (pp. 57–78). Washington, DC: American Psychological Association.

Hall, D. T., & Moss, J. E. (1998). The new protean career contract: Helping organizations and employees adapt. *Organizational Dynamics, 26*(3), 22–37.

Hamamura, T. (2012). Are cultures becoming individualistic? A cross-temporal comparison of individualism–collectivism in the United States and Japan. *Personality and Social Psychology Review, 16*(1), 3–24.

Herr, E. L. (2001). Career development and its practice: A historical perspective. *The Career Development Quarterly, 49*(3), 196–211.

Hu, J., & Hirsh, J. B. (2017). Accepting lower salaries for meaningful work. *Frontiers in Psychology, 8*(1649).

Humphrey, S. E., Nahrgang, J. D., & Morgeson, F. P. (2007). Integrating motivational, social, and contextual work design features: A meta-analytic summary and theoretical extension of the work design literature. *Journal of Applied Psychology, 92*, 1332–1356.

Inglehart, R. F. (2008). Changing values among western publics from 1970 to 2006. *West European Politics, 31*(1-2), 130–146.

Inglehart, R., & Baker, W. E. (2000). Modernization, cultural change, and the persistence of traditional values. *American Sociological Review, 65*, 19–51.

International Labour Organization. (2017). *World employment and social outlook: Trends 2017.* Geneva, Switzerland: ILO.

Jahoda, M. (1981). Work, employment, and unemployment: Values, theories, and approaches in social research. *American Psychologist, 36*(2), 184–191.

Kahn, W. A. (1990). Psychological conditions of personal engagement and disengagement at work. *Academy of Management Journal, 33*(4), 692–724.

Kahneman, D., & Krueger, A. B. (2006). Developments in the measurement of subjective well being. *Journal of Economic Perspectives, 20*(1), 3–24.

Katz, L. F., & Krueger, A. B. (2019). The rise and nature of alternative work arrangements in the United States, 1995–2015. *ILR Review, 72*(2), 382–416.

Fitzmaurice, C. J., Ladegaard, I., Attwood-Charles, W., Cansoy, M., Carfagna, L. B., Schor, J. B., & Wengronowitz, R. (2016). Domesticating the market: moral exchange and the sharing economy. *Socio-Economic Review*, 1–22.

Lent, R. W. (2018). Future of work in the digital world: Preparing for instability and opportunity. *The Career Development Quarterly, 66*(3), 205–219.

Lips-Wiersma, M. (2002). The influence of spiritual "meaning-making" on career behavior. *Journal of Management Development, 21*(7), 497–520.

Lips-Wiersma, M., & Wright, S. (2012). Measuring the meaning of meaningful work: Development and validation of the Comprehensive Meaningful Work Scale (CMWS). *Group & Organization Management, 37*(5), 655–685.

Lips-Wiersma, M., Wright, S., & Dik, B. (2016). Meaningful work: differences among blue-, pink-, and white-collar occupations. *Career Development International, 21*(5), 534–551.

Lott, B. (2014). Social class myopia: The case of psychology and labor unions. *Analyses of Social Issues and Public Policy, 14*(1), 261–280.

Manyika, J., Lund, S., Auguste, B., & Ramaswamy, S. (2012). Help wanted: The future of work in advanced economies, McKinsey Global Institute.

Manyika, J., Lund, S., Chui, M., Bughin, J., Woetzel, J., Batra, P., ... Sanghvi, S. (2017). *Jobs lost, jobs gained: Workforce transitions in a time of automation*. McKinsey Global Institute.

May, D. R., Gilson, R. L., & Harter, L. M. (2004). The psychological conditions of meaningfulness, safety and availability and the engagement of the human spirit at work. *Journal of Occupational and Organizational Psychology, 77*(1), 11–37.

Munn, S. L. (2013). Unveiling the work–life system: the influence of work–life balance on meaningful work. *Advances in Developing Human Resources, 15*(4), 401–417.

Oishi, S., Diener, E. F., Lucas, R. E., & Suh, E. M. (1999). Cross-cultural variations in predictors of life satisfaction: Perspectives from needs and values. *Personality and Social Psychology Bulletin, 25*(8), 980–990.

Oldham, G. R., & Hackman, J. R. (2010). Not what it was and not what it will be: The future of job design research. *Journal of Organizational Behavior, 31*(2-3), 463–479.

Oliver, B. (2015). Redefining graduate employability and work-integrated learning: Proposals for effective higher education in disrupted economies. *Journal of Teaching and Learning for Graduate Employability, 6*(1), 56.

Parasuraman, R., Sheridan, T. B., & Wickens, C. D. (2000). A model for types and levels of human interaction with automation. *IEEE Transactions on Systems, Man, and Cybernetics – Part A: Systems and Humans, 30*(3), 286–297.

Pinsof, J. (2015). A new take on an old problem: employee misclassification in the modern gig economy. *Michigan Telecommunications and Technology Law Review, 22*, 341–373.

Pratt, M. G., & Ashforth, B. E. (2003). Fostering meaningfulness in working and at work. In K. S. Cameron, J. E. Dutton, & R. E. Quinn (Eds.), *Positive organizational scholarship: Foundations of a new discipline* (pp. 309–327). San Francisco, CA: Berrett Koehler Publishers.

Rodríguez-Muñoz, A., Sanz-Vergel, A. I., Demerouti, E., & Bakker, A. B. (2014). Engaged at work and happy at home: A spillover–crossover model. *Journal of Happiness Studies, 15*(2), 271–283.

Skinner, B. F. (1986). What is wrong with daily life in the western world? *American Psychologist, 41*(5), 568.

Spreitzer, G. M. (1995). Psychological empowerment in the workplace: Dimensions, measurement, and validation. *Academy of Management Journal, 38*(5), 1442–1465.

Stander, M. W., & Rothmann, S. (2010). Psychological empowerment, job insecurity and employee engagement. *SA Journal of Industrial Psychology, 36*(1), 1–8.

Steger, M. F., & Dik, B. J. (2010). Work as meaning: Individual and organizational benefits of engaging in meaningful work. In N. Garcea, S. Harrington, & P. Alex Linley (Eds.), *Oxford handbook of positive psychology and work* (pp. 131–142). New York: Oxford University Press.

Steger, M. F., Dik, B. J., & Duffy, R. D. (2012). Measuring meaningful work: The work and meaning inventory (WAMI). *Journal of Career Assessment, 20*(3), 322–337.

Tims, M., Derks, D., & Bakker, A. B. (2016). Job crafting and its relationships with person–job fit and meaningfulness: A three-wave study. *Journal of Vocational Behavior, 92*, 44–53.

Törhönen, M., Hassan, L., Sjöblom, M., & Hamari, J. (2019, January). Play, playbour or labour? The relationships between perception of occupational activity and outcomes among streamers and YouTubers. In *Proceedings of the 52nd Hawaii International Conference on System Sciences.*

Van Doorn, N. (2017). Platform labor: On the gendered and racialized exploitation of low income service work in the 'on-demand' economy. *Information, Communication & Society, 20*(6), 898–914.

Wrzesniewski, A., & Dutton, J. E. (2001). Crafting a job: Revisioning employees as active crafters of their work. *Academy of Management Review, 26*(2), 179–201.

PART 4

Health Transitions

CHAPTER

7

Meaning-making and chronic illness: understanding through narratives

Cara E. Bigony and Merle A. Keitel

Division of Psychological and Educational Services, Graduate School of Education, Fordham University at Lincoln Center, New York, NY, United States

> I choose to spend my time differently. I spend more time with the people I cherish. Before [my illness], I was on the highway but didn't see the landscape...I had been going too fast trying to be productive and not enjoying my time. I wasn't going slowly enough to see anything. Then, suddenly, I was [diagnosed] and standing on the side of the road. Now, I try to enjoy my life more, while driving the same path, but driving slower. I try to enjoy it in another way, and have more aspects of my life.

Meaning-making in relation to chronic illness has been shown to be a key process for patients. The above quote is from a young man with Crohn's disease, recounting how illness had a significant impact on him and prompted him to reprioritize his life. Chronic illness disrupts a sense of self, sense of time, and anticipated life trajectories. It can challenge highly valued personal goals and triggers feelings of vulnerability (Bury, 1982). It forces individuals to write an unexpected theme into their life story, often at an unexpected time. Even more, it offers the possibility of reevaluating one's life and goals, and making meaning from the illness experience. As Charmaz (1991) expressed, chronic illness "often crystallizes vital lessons of living" (p. vii).

In recent years, various fields have shown renewed interest in illness narratives, how individuals with chronic illness tell their stories. Illness narratives are being studied in health psychology, medical sociology,

Navigating Life Transitions for Meaning
DOI: https://doi.org/10.1016/B978-0-12-818849-1.00007-2

medical anthropology, and narrative medicine as a way to understand patients' experience of illness (Charon, 2008). They give voice to the lived experience of chronic illness and its many effects on health and vitality, daily life, and sense of self. Specifically, illness narratives have become an important lens through which to study how individuals make meaning, or make sense, of chronic illness. Meaning-making also has been shown to play an important role in coping with chronic illness (Frank, 1995; Roussi & Avdi, 2008). Constructed meanings through illness narratives have been studied at length in cancer, diabetes, and HIV/AIDS (e.g., Haidet, Kroll, & Sharf, 2006), as well as transdiagnostically. This chapter will address meaning-making processes through illness narratives of individuals with inflammatory bowel diseases (IBDs) and will include quotes from participants in a Consensual Qualitative Research (CQR) study conducted by the first author under the supervision of the second author. There have been many studies about the physical and psychological well-being of individuals with IBD (e.g., Jordan, Sin, Fear, & Chalder, 2016); however, few have focused on patient narratives and meaning-making.

Meaning-making and IBD

IBD is a group of inflammatory autoimmune conditions of the colon and small intestine; the two major types of IBD are Crohn's disease and ulcerative colitis (UC). According to the Crohn's and Colitis Foundation (2019), these conditions affect 1.6 million Americans and 5 million individuals worldwide. Both conditions are characterized by disabling symptoms including diarrhea with blood or pus, increased frequency of bowel movements to upward of 20 times per day, rectal bleeding, and weight loss. IBD follows a relapse-remission structure, waxing and waning at unknown times, with most individuals diagnosed before age 35. While it is of unknown cause, recent studies show that some combination of genetic and environmental factors may cause IBD.

Individuals with IBD are at greater risk for anxiety and depression (Byrne et al., 2017). Empirical evidence has found that lifetime prevalence rates of anxiety and depression for individuals with IBD are as high as 35.8% (Neuendorf, Harding, Stello, Hanes, & Wahbeh, 2016). IBD has also been widely shown to decrease health-related quality of life (due to factors such as psychological distress) and to have negative effects on self-esteem, relationships, daily activities, and social participation (Lönnfors et al., 2014).

Characterization of the illness is important to consider when studying meaning-making processes and IBD. The unpredictability and appraisals of IBD as highly stressful influence the individuals' experience of the illness. Specifically, uncertainty about the future and high stress appraisals have both been identified as key elements of meaning-making in chronic illness (Wiener, 1982). Given the uncertain disease trajectory, the idiosyncratic and unpredictable presentation of symptoms, and the lack of known causes, IBD does not fit Leventhal's common-sense model of illness, a frequently cited theoretical framework for understanding individuals' concepts of health and illness (Leventhal, Meyer, & Nerenz, 1980). This model consists of health-specific domains of knowledge and posits that individuals develop narratives composed of beliefs related to the causes and treatments of illness concepts (Leventhal et al., 1980; Leventhal, Phillips, & Burns, 2016). However, without an understanding of the causes of IBD and without known effective treatments, IBD is challenging for patients to conceptualize.

It follows that patients often identify IBD as a major life stressor (Singh et al., 2011). It is worth noting that more severe appraisals of the stressfulness of an illness can lead to higher reports of meaning-making and positive meaning found, even when controlling for the objective threat of the illness (Sears, Stanton, & Danoff-Burg, 2003). IBD presents individuals with not only a new normal, but also a new and uncertain normal that threatens the coherence of their life narrative. As a result, illness narratives become an especially important vehicle through which to study individuals' lived experience of the disease.

This chapter reviews the research on meaning-making processes in the context of IBD by both reviewing the literature on illness narratives and meaning-making, and by featuring voices of individuals with IBD from a qualitative study examining meaning-making processes in this population. Interviews were conducted with 10 individuals diagnosed with moderate to severe IBD (UC or Crohn's disease), ranging from 20–38 years old. Participants had been diagnosed 1–5 years prior, did not have comorbid chronic illnesses, and were in remission at the time of the interview. The interview protocol, which included open-ended questions regarding illness experience and meaning, was informed by clinical experience and knowledge of the literature. Data were analyzed using the CQR method (Hill, Thompson, & Williams, 1997). Throughout the chapter, participants' illnesses are referred to as IBD, given the similar meaning-making processes established across diagnoses. Pseudonyms are used to protect participants' anonymity.

The first author's interest in this illness experience developed partly as a result of her own experience of IBD. Many shared dimensions of the illness experience were carefully bracketed. As a patient, she too experienced biographical disruption and loss of self. Like many of the voices featured in this chapter, she too felt the shame of incontinence in her twenties, the fear of the trial-and-error approach to treatment, and betrayed by her body. The first author also bracketed her own experiences of meaning-making, including her experiences navigating relationships as someone who is chronically ill and as someone who provides psychological services for patients.

Cognitive and narrative introduction to meaning-making

Meaning-making in reaction to chronic illness has been addressed through both narrative and cognitive lenses. As it is beyond the scope of this chapter to address both lenses, we will focus primarily on the narrative study of meaning-making in chronic illness. The chapter will then discuss how chronic illness threatens personal and social meaning, and the ways that meaning can be reconstructed in the wake of chronic illness.

Numerous studies have attempted to understand the cognitive processes of meaning-making in the face of chronic illness. Given the interactive nature of narrative and cognitive processes, it is important to review a seminal theory. One influential theory is the General Meaning-Making Model posited by Park (2010), which is among the most commonly cited in cognitive meaning-making literature. This model asserts that before the onset of a trauma or illness, an individual has a *global meaning,* which is one's general orienting system in life, including beliefs, goals, and subjective feelings. The onset of an illness, acting as a major life stressor, creates a painful discrepancy between one's global beliefs, and one's *appraised meaning* of the illness (Park, 2010). This discrepancy creates strong discomfort and emotional pain, leading to coping and a drive toward meaning-making.

The model predicates that individuals are driven to have a unified global meaning. To recreate unified meaning after trauma, individuals must either adjust their global meaning to accommodate their appraised meaning of the illness, or alter their appraised meaning of the illness assimilate it into one's global meaning. These revisions occur through a constellation of purposeful coping efforts, which are used to restore meaning. Through a narrative lens, these coping strategies are understood as an attempt to integrate the illness into the narrative of one's life story.

Cognitive and narrative processes are at times parallel and arguably intertwined processes. As asserted by Neimeyer (2004), narrative processes provide a fundamental organizing structure for cognition. Cognitive and narrative approaches have also been described as distinct but compatible and complementary ways of approaching meaning-making (Roussi & Avdi, 2008). In the field of posttraumatic growth, Tedeschi and Calhoun (2004) have a similarly integrationist understanding that growth after trauma is a process of cognitive rebuilding to incorporate the traumatic event into one's life story. They specify that this narrative reconstruction is an aim of cognitive rebuilding after trauma. Additionally, coping and illness narratives are linked through the experience of talking about how they cope with a chronic illness, and asserting that the mundane daily challenges of living with the disease influence how they construct a sense of self and a public narrative of their experience (Bury, 2001).

Loss of meaning

Narrative inquiry into chronic illness rests on the assumption that storytelling is a universal and fundamental part of what makes us human. It assumes a desire to tell a coherent story of one's life. Storytelling has been identified as a reaction to illness and way of finding meaning in an illness (Early, 1982; Good et al., 1994). In stories of illness, we can learn how the illness has changed the individual's daily life and sense of self, and can begin to recognize the "infinite reservoir of meanings" conveyed in their stories (Gellner, 1992, p. 124). Two influential theories in narrative studies of meaning-making are Bury's (1982) concept of biographical disruption and Charmaz's (1983) concept of loss of self in chronic illness.

Biographical disruption

Bury's seminal concept of "biographical disruption" posits that chronic illness is a disruptive experience in one's life story, creating a disjuncture between *past/healthy* and *present/ill* self. According to Bury (1982), chronic illness disrupts by (1) forcing people to face pain, suffering and possibly death; (2) changing relationships by pushing them beyond the normal bounds of reciprocity and mutual support; and, (3) forcing plans and expectations for the future to be reexamined and adjusted. Bury (1988) later nominally distinguished that the disruption in everyday life from one's sense of self. Meaning *as concept* refers to the effects of treatment, symptoms, and lived challenges of the disease on everyday life, whereas meaning *as significance* refers to how the illness has impacted sense of self and relationships. For individuals with IBD, one form that meaning *as concept* takes is through the effects of physical symptoms such as daily bowel symptoms, stomach pain, and restricted diet that precipitate restructuring of daily life. Meaning *as significance* for these same individuals can be seen in their shifting understanding of self as chronically ill.

Bury (1982) asserted, with a nod toward the temporal dimension of the onset of chronic illness, that the early stages of illness show signs of biographical disruption. This is especially salient given the uniquely insidious onset of chronic illnesses. As noted above, IBD, much like Bury's study of rheumatoid arthritis, does not follow common-sense guidelines for illness. During early stages, there are three unfolding elements of the illness that cause significant disruptions. First, the chronic illness disrupts taken-for-granted assumptions and behaviors, which are thrown into question by the challenges posed by the symptoms. Second, there is a fundamental rethinking of one's self-concept and expected biography. Third, there is a response to this disruption of daily life and sense of self that requires the individual to face a new reality. In the face of this new reality, future goals and ambitions are challenged or called into question. Bury calls this a *biographical shift* from a perceived normal trajectory through chronological steps to one that is abnormal and damaging (p. 171).

A changed relationship with one's body is an important dimension of biographical disruption, a topic on which Charmaz has written at length. To externalize the disease, medical knowledge can play an important role in allowing individuals to perceive the disease as something separate (Bury, 1982). This is complicated, however, by the presence of daily symptoms that disrupt many aspects of daily life. This new and uncertain normal can only be calmed so much by medical treatments, given that there is no cure. Ivy, a participant in the CQR study, reflected how medical information has not sufficiently explained why and how the disease has disrupted her life:

> My doctor tries his best, but there's so many unanswered questions surrounding this disease...there hasn't been a person that could give me a definitive answer on why certain things happen [to my body]...[it] is a very unpredictable disease.

Ivy, like many others, navigates a changing relationship with her body that is idiosyncratic and hard for doctors to explain. Tasked with learning how to live with the illness and integrate it into her biography, there is a desire to use medical information to help explain the new normal. Incomplete medical knowledge and lack of guarantees for disease management force individuals to rely on their knowledge and biographical experience to navigate and make sense of their illness experience.

Disruption extends beyond daily life and sense of self, affecting friendships and community involvement. Social isolation has been identified as a main feature of chronic illness, due to functional limitations and to feelings about being disabled (Bury, 1982). For IBD patients, functional impairment often include fatigue, frequent bowel movements, and fear of leaving one's home in case of incontinence.

According to Bury, everyday life becomes a burden, something tiring that requires deliberate action. This theme was heard repeatedly in the narratives of individuals with IBD. One participant, Amina, addressed the toll of IBD on her social life:

> I either see friends that are doing what we've always done. . .or I sit at home and distance myself from the people I love. I try to figure out: How do I live life in this, in this new normal? It puts a strain on me internally to try to reconcile those feelings, since other people just want me to be who I used to be. I want to be who I was before diagnosis too, but I can't. I still have that feeling of unfairness every time I go to a social situation that I can't fully participate in.

The dietary restrictions of IBD forced Amina to reprioritize her social life, leading her at times to resent her illness for the limitations it puts on her social life, and at other times, wishing she could unshackle herself from its limitations to preserve social dynamics that existed prior to diagnosis. The changes in one's social life due to chronic illness is closely tied to Bury's (1982) process of *mobilization of resources*, in which the individual is "inevitably drawn into rearranging his or her wider personal and community involvement" (p. 175).

Disruption in one's professional life is prominent in illness narratives of individuals with IBD, and can appear in different forms based on whether or not there is perceived support in these environments (Bury, 1982). Participants in the CQR study expressed ambivalence about disclosure of illness to supervisors, fear of not being able to achieve premorbid career goals, and worry about performance. There is often an attempt to normalize the illness and its disruption in the spheres of work and school. However, even if coworkers and peers are supportive, their willingness to redistribute work to lighten the patient's workload can reinforce fears of not achieving or having to face that the illness disrupted the anticipated career trajectory (Bury, 1982). Jean-Paul struggled greatly with how his illness would influence his career and work relationships:

> I have a lot of questions. Like, should I tell my boss? I can probably get a card for being handicapped. . .but that has a long-term impact. Once I choose that, I cannot go back. I don't know if it's going to affect promotions or raises. . .What I fear most is people not understanding the difficulty of it. If I thought that my employer knew that everyone experiences [IBD] differently, then I wouldn't mind sharing. I also wouldn't want people to think that I abuse the advantages that he might give me. But the thing is, I don't know if I'll always be able to do the work that is asked.

Researchers, including Charmaz (1991, 1995), have questioned the role of biographical disruption in chronic illness. Some have argued that biographical disruption is not necessarily associated with all chronic illnesses (e.g., Williams, 2000). Williams considered that if illness is expected in one's life, then Bury's theory of disruption does not apply to the same degree. Factors such as previous traumas, beliefs that illness is inevitable, and negative cognitions about one's life could mean that illness is anticipated and thus less disruptive. Individuals who are diagnosed at a young age may experience illness as more disruptive given that illness is often expected for older individuals as part of an assumed biography (Faircloth, Boylstein, Rittman, Young, & Gubrium, 2004). Individuals with IBD have expressed both expected and disruptive experiences of the illness. Chloe described IBD as somewhat anticipated in her life story, given her self-concept prior to her IBD diagnosis:

> I think I always felt like the sick duckling in the family. So when this happened I [thought] of course, I'm sick again. I just think of the disease as just another thing that I'm going through. . .my body's never liked me. . .and so this is just part of my body rejecting itself again.

Chloe's diagnosis of IBD supported her established identity as a "sick duckling," thus, the IBD was experienced as more normal than disruptive. However, for young individuals who identify as previously healthy, IBD can be highly disruptive. Violet shared, "I was this young active person. It's weird, I don't really think of it being me, but being sort of a separate person." As a young and healthy woman before her diagnosis, Violet explained that the diagnosis changed her self-concept so much that she now understands herself as a separate person postdiagnosis.

Recently, researchers have searched for more nuance in the categorization of chronic illness as either expected and normal, or unexpected and disruptive. Sanders, Donovan, and Dieppe (2002) found that osteoarthritis can be experienced as disruptive and normal. Others have argued that while illness is anticipated in older adults, it does not preclude the existence of biographical disruption (Larsson & Grassman, 2012). The idea of *biographical contingency* has also been put forth to describe the experience of illness as sometimes disruptive, and sometimes in the background of lived experience (Monaghan & Gabe, 2015). Recent studies advocate for a more nuanced understanding of illness's impact on biography, and resonate with illness narratives of IBD. With its relapse-remission structure, IBD can be an all-consuming, disruptive experience and yet in remission it can also exist as a normalized dimension of health maintenance. Given IBD's nonlinear trajectory, Saunders (2017) asserted that biographical disruption is highly influenced by this disease pattern, and more aptly is experienced as *recurrent* biographical disruption. For illnesses with this disease pattern, Bury's *mobilization of resources* in the wake of illness onset is not a one-time event or adjustment; it must be understood more fluidly or even cyclically (Sanders, Ong, Roberts, & Corbett, 2015).

Loss of self

Bury and Charmaz pioneered studying how loss and uncertainty affect individuals with chronic illness. Charmaz reported that physical pain, psychological distress, and the effects of medical procedures are forms of suffering that are linked to the loss of self. Loss of self, she asserted, is the most fundamental form of suffering for individuals with chronic illness, as it prompts self-image to crumble without simultaneously developing new, valued self-images (Charmaz, 1983). This disjunction between the body and the self "reemerge[s] with each disruptive episode" (Charmaz, 1995, p. 659). Chronic illness disrupts previously relied upon meanings, without which individuals may suffer a loss of self, as their illness forces them to build new meanings and new images of self.

Charmaz (1983) details four ways that individuals with chronic illness feel a loss of self and loss of previous life meanings, through the ill person's (1) restricted life, (2) social isolation, (3) being discredited, and (4) burdening others. While these can appear more prominent during times of severe or active symptoms, over time there is a cumulative effect of the many losses that change previous self-images and identities. Losing these meanings can result in secondary consequences such as a loss of financial security, family strains, stigma, and restrictions on lifestyle. Given the uncertainty that characterizes so many chronic illnesses, many individuals voluntarily restrict their lives more than may be needed, causing even greater damage to previous self-image and meanings held (Charmaz, 1983).

The social isolation of illness, prompted by decreased activity in various settings, can lead to a loss of previous meanings. According to Charmaz (1983), isolation can also occur insidiously, through friendships that become more distant due to inattentive friends and/or the individual's limited resources (i.e., time and energy are less available to maintain relationships). Time-consuming medical routines completed at home and a focus on one's self-care activities (e.g., meal planning) reduce time for social interactions. Finally, the visibility of obvious suffering has been shown to be challenging for partners and caretakers.

Feeling discredited by others is another way an ill individual's previous identity and sense of self may be minimized, leaving them without previous meanings or new meanings. Others may assume that the ill individual is limited and precluded from doing work or social activities. Ill individuals may discredit themselves when some attribute that was previously valued as key to self-image can no longer be relied upon. Finally, becoming a burden is a subjective experience of individuals with chronic illness that often stems from never before having to be physically or financially dependent.

Temporal aspects of meaning-making

Time is an important dimension of meaning-making through narrative. Bury, Charmaz, and those who have written in the intervening years, give nod to how individuals organize past, present, and future around the onset of a chronic illness. Still, some scholars have recently called for greater attention to the temporal aspects of biographical disruption (Morden, Jinks, & Ong, 2015). Temporal aspects of disease (e.g., challenges of daily life, memorializing key events, altered sense of self in time, and mapping illness timelines onto biographical timelines) are a key organizing structure for how narrative repair and meaning-making occur.

The challenges of living with symptoms has been explored at length by Charmaz (1991, 1995). This sentiment was echoed by many study participants and expressed with poignant honesty by Liz, who shared her attempts to stay in the present tense during a flare up: "I would think, 'This is like torture.' I would think, 'Oh, where am I going to be in a year? Will I be better?' And, 'you shouldn't think that way. You should just take it day by day,' I think. But I couldn't help but think, 'Where will I be in a year?'" Another participant, Ivy, caught herself often attempting to predict an uncertain future. For many, the timeline of life beyond illness became dotted with memorialized events associated with the illness, which for some is a source of meaning. Three years after a major surgery, Violet reflected that time of pain is an important anniversary and a sign of her personal strength: "I just had the anniversary last month, the 3-year anniversary of my surgery…and I feel really empowered. I look back and say, 'Wow…I've come so far since then.' So that anniversary feels empowering but my birthday still feels, um, painful." Reflecting on the anniversary of her surgery (colectomy) became for Violet a source of meaning-making, choosing to recognize her strength, perseverance, and progress, while recognizing that it is not free from distress given its proximity to her birthday.

In line with Bury's concept of biographical disruption and Charmaz's discussion of loss of self, Violet's experience shows a sharp division of time into before and after illness onset. Violet described her conception of her illness, and presented it in three disparate, well-bounded time periods: "I sort of have these three time points in my life: before I was sick, during, and now, after. I compartmentalize them in that way." Violet has made sense of her changing self by defining these distinct selves, each associated with a different stage of her illness (prediagnosis, flare up, and remission, respectively). Nearly all participants shared a similar sentiment of a different "self" before diagnosis. Saunders (2017) examined temporal experiences of young adults with IBD and argued that the relapse-remission structure of IBD results in a unique biographical disruption that recurs and is constructed in narrative through organizations of past, present, and anticipated future experiences.

The physical toll of symptoms of chronic illness can additionally disrupt one's expectations for the physical experience at one's given age. Many participants shared that the physical symptoms of IBD made them feel displaced in time, as if they were experiencing being a young child or an elderly person. Jean-Paul shared: "I experienced what it's like to be really old. When you get down to 45 kgs [99lbs], climbing the stairs feels like running a marathon. I really felt like an old person, and it's very hard because you know with your [prior] body you could do that, but now you can't do it." Another participant expressed that her experience of a flare up transported her to old age: "There is a loss of control over basic functions that most people don't confront until very old age." Audrey expressed feeling like she returned to helplessness of being a child: "I feel like a little kid with the accidents. I go to Target and buy diapers for days when it's really bad. I feel like I'm back to being 2 or 3-years-old, where I need my parents to help me with the simplest things." This sense of temporal displacement shows how meaning in illness can be a nonlinear, dynamic experience.

Meaning reconstruction has also been conceptualized as a constellation of spaces of liminality and has been studied in the context of chronic illness (Molzahn, Bruce, & Sheilds, 2008). Liminality is a process of biographical reconstruction characterized by a constant tension between feeling that life continues as normal and feeling that the illness is present in one's life (Molzahn et al., 2008). Tied to the concept of biographical disruption, liminality is understood as an initial attempt to make sense of the disruption of the illness, and then persists as a "continual adaptation to illness by constructing its meaning through narrative" (Koutri & Avdi, 2016, p. 81).

For IBD patients, liminality can be heightened between the first and second flare of symptoms. After a first flare up, many individuals with IBD can regain a sense of previous health or vitality, making the flare seem more like a one-time episode of poor health than the first of many episodes. While they intellectually know that a future flare will occur, their illness experience still mimics other experiences of nonchronic illness. As Ivy shared: "luckily I haven't had another flare since, but I'm sure that once that happens, um, I will definitely measure time in flares [versus] in good times." The lack of multiple flares keeps her suspended in a liminal space of how she understands the timeline of her illness, not allowing her illness narrative to be chronologically ordered by alternating flares and remission. In the meantime, she waits. Jean-Paul reiterates this suspension after his first flare: "I've only had one flare up, so for now it still feels like a one-time disease than a chronic disease. So I don't know if I've accepted that fact." Experiencing liminality between flares may reflect a subtle reluctance to accept the chronicity of the illness; between the first and second flare up, the chronic part of the disease, and thus disease acceptance and meaning-making, are thwarted. Amina's experience confirms this effect of multiple flare ups over time:

> If I'd had one flare and been able to go into remission, it would have been easier for me to chalk it up as a one-time thing. But when you go into your second, third, fourth, fifth flare, it's just never ending. I really started to come to terms that this is what the rest of my life looks like.

Amina described the multiple flares as a release from the liminality and suspension before her second flare. Just as there is stress in the uncertainty of the illness, Amina seems to express future flares as a relief that allowed her to come to terms with the chronic nature of IBD.

Reconstruction of meaning

As shown in early research on biographical disruption and loss of self, chronic illness often leaves a chasm of meaning that needs to be reconstructed to incorporate the illness. The self can be challenged by illness, but with this challenge comes an opportunity for growth and new meaning (Frank, 1995). Meaning can be constructed in the wake of a chronic illness, both individually and socially. Individually, this can occur through narrative reconstruction, such as searching for the cause of the illness, building a new relationship with one's body and self, and reconstruction of habits. Socially, meaning can be thought of as being coconstructed with caregivers, family, significant others, and medical providers, all of whom can play important roles in reconstructing a narrative with the ill individual. One of our participants, Chloe, summarized this well: "So I wouldn't necessarily say that there's meaning in any illness, but you can bring things to it. You can learn things about yourself and about the other people around you, and how to relate to people, how to relate to your body, how everything in your body affects [you]".

Individual process of meaning reconstruction

The concept of *narrative reconstruction* was introduced by Williams (1984) in a study of individuals with rheumatoid arthritis. Across participants, Williams found an iterative process of integrating the cause of an illness into the individual's life story as a way to understand the present through one's past. Individuals narrated their experiences in a way that imposed a sense of order. Throughout their illness narratives, years after diagnosis, they were able to provide order, explanation, and a sense of coherence about the causes and impact of their illness.

Searching for the cause of an illness is one avenue through which individuals try to regain control over their narrative and make sense of chronic illness. Many hypotheses may be put forth by individuals about the cause of their disease, including viral, genetic, and environmental factors that integrate their personal history and experiences (Williams, 1984). Further, it has been shown that individuals who identify stress as a possible illness etiology may carefully trace through a multitude of events that caused enough stress to warrant its physical manifestation as a disease. This appraisal was echoed by Amina, who believes stress is the main cause for flares: "Life events can sometimes trigger your first symptoms. In my mind I think, 'Okay, I got so worked up about planning my wedding that I made myself sick.' My doctor assures me that's not the case, but that's how I've made sense of it." Amina's story functions as a coherent narrative of how she became sick. Williams (1984) noted that these types of explanations have functional and causal components and "represent not only explanations for the onset of a given disease, but also acts of interpretation, narrative reconstructions of profound discontinuities in the social processes of their daily lives" (p. 179).

Redefining one's relationship with one's body is another important avenue for meaning-making in chronic illness. Many individuals attempt to deem the illness as something separate and external from their self-concept, and in doing so, they alienate their body. This process shows that an attachment to a narrative of past health, untouched by chronic illness, impedes acceptance of the illness and meaning-making. Accepting one's body as ill and the illness's chronic nature allows for a closeness with one's body that is not hindered by hopes for recovery. Struggling with illness allows it to be integrated into one's life narrative and to become integrated with one's self-concept (Corbin & Strauss, 1987). In turn, this allows individuals to reunite with their body in a new meaning in the context of chronic illness. Frank (1995), discussing his own illness experience, reflected:

> I wondered at what the body could still do for me, as diseased as I knew it must be. That day I stopped resenting 'it' for the pain I had felt and began to appreciate my body, in some ways for the first time in my life. I stopped evaluating my body and began to draw strength from it. And I recognized that this body was me. (p. 60–61)

Frank experienced newfound connection to his changed, chronically ill body. Only with acceptance of how the illness disrupted self-concept could he create new meaning. This has been conceptualized as *surrendering* to one's ill body (Charmaz, 1991). The result of the struggle with one's body is a surrender to its limitations, which Charmaz outlines as (1) ceasing trying to control one's body, (2) stopping trying to conquer one's illness, and (c3) recognizing that one's ill body is an inextricable part of oneself. "Surrendering differs from being overtaken by illness...or giving up...being overtaken occurs without choice; surrendering is an active, intentional process" (Charmaz, 1991, p. 672). This process of surrendering is a necessary part of being able to fully experience the ill body, in a "newly authentic" way (Charmaz, 1991, p. 672).

Another avenue through which individual meaning-making can occur is through changed habits. Chronic illness often forces individuals to change daily behavioral patterns. It has been found that reconstruction of the self can thus take place, even incidentally, through habit changes (Charmaz, 2002). One participant in Charmaz's study maintained a continuity of self by making necessary dietary adaptations for living with IBD. For others, habit change was a profound reconstruction of the self as they abandoned old habits and constructed new ones that fit their limitations. Charmaz (2002) asserted:

> Reconstruction of self emerges through experiential meanings and is given form and definition through stories. The self is continually reconstructed-but it may become a shell of a former self as the tasks of care consume time and consciousness. Reconstruction does not necessarily mean a better self; it does mean a modified, revised, and perhaps re-envisioned self. (p. 38S)

For many individuals, being diagnosed with IBD and experiencing an initial flare changes how they relate to themselves. This change may be facing a fear of medical procedures, or it could be recognizing, in the wake of sickness, that they and their bodies are strong. Many of our participants expressed gratitude toward their IBD, feeling that it helped them mature and develop a habit of relating to themselves as strong.

In addition, research has identified work as a dimension of life in which individuals can construct meaning. How people experience and find meaning through work has been extensively studied in psychology (Dik & Duffy, 2015). Meaning in work has been defined as having the sense that one's effort is personally meaningful and aligned with one's values or goals (Dik, Byrne, & Steger, 2011). Steger, Dik, and Duffy (2012) introduced a multidimensional model of meaningful work that transcends simple job execution; it posits that meaningful work provides synergy with one's meaning in life. Individuals whose identity has been shaken by chronic illness might find meaning by integrating their illness experience into their work. While few studies address meaning-making through work for individuals with chronic illness, many psychologists have explored individuals' desire to help others through their work, a drive referred to as prosocial behavior (Blustein, 2006).

Young individuals may need to reevaluate their chosen career due to the demands of IBD. For some, meaning in work can be found by integrating illness experience with career. For others, this adjustment occurs through changing their field or position to honor a new meaning of work–life balance and "slowing down." In this process, many find greater meaning in their work, whether their prediagnosis plan for work is reaffirmed or readjusted due to the onset of IBD. Violet shared her experience with IBD was instrumental in her decision to choose medicine as a career:

> After my diagnosis, I was really exposed to the medical field...that opened my eyes...I loved learning about the relationship between clinicians and patients and communication barriers to understanding disease...I made the decision to pursue PA [physical assistant] school to focus on health literacy. That's all stemming from being sick and feeling lost, and feeling like I didn't have any agency or control. Improving health literacy gives control to patients...so that's my personal focus.

Violet engaged in two core processes of finding meaning in work: being part of something bigger than oneself, and contributing to the social good (Blustein, 2019). Others found meaning by adjusting their work experience to allow for a better work–life balance, or by changing jobs entirely in hopes of supporting a new meaning. Jean-Paul, who was in an advanced engineering program when diagnosed, reprioritized how he spent his time: "I spend more time with the people I cherish. I try to enjoy my life more... I try to enjoy it outside of my [work]". He reported that he was grateful for this reprioritizing, feeling that it invigorated other dimensions of his life that had been previously sidelined by his career ambition. Research has not sufficiently explored avenues for meaning-making through work for individuals with chronic illness. Given the vast literature on meaning in work, and the importance of meaning-making for individuals with chronic illness, future research would further benefit this area of study.

Social process of meaning reconstruction

Constructing meaning in the wake of chronic illness is also a social process. Individual meaning-making cannot be examined in isolation, as it is inevitably reciprocally linked to one's social world. Frank (2001) reflected on his own experience of illness: "everyone who touches you affects your healing" (p. 361). If we consider meaning-making part of Frank's idea of healing, then it follows that meaning can be coconstructed with a constellation of individuals including (1) medical providers, (2) family, partners, caretakers, and (3) patient, work, or school communities.

When managing chronic illness, medical professionals take on a central role for patients. There is often an increased sense of intimacy with doctors as they witness their patients' major adjustment and transformation. As such, medical providers can coconstruct illness meaning with the patient. Not only are medical providers often a primary, early source of information, but they also can be pivotal in integrating this new medical reality into the life story of the patient. The importance of the coconstruction of patient narratives in the medical encounter is widely recognized in the medical literature (Eggly, 2002; Lipkin, 1995). In fact, the literature recognizes the role of the medical provider in "shaping the storytelling" of the patient's narrative (Lipkin, 1995, p. 71). As patients with IBD try to navigate the idiosyncratic constellation of symptoms and uncertain disease progression, this medical encounter can take on a lot of meaning. Amina reflected on the importance of this encounter for her overall healing:

> [This doctor] listened to me more than any other doctor ever had. He let me cry and talk about my fears...I felt heard by somebody who I knew understood. It's invaluable when you're diagnosed-with-ulcerative-colitis sick to have medical providers that make [you] feel like they [care]. When you have this disease and you struggle so hard to get others to understand what you're going through, to have two people on your side makes all the difference.

New relationships ripe for coconstruction of meaning exist beyond medical providers. These can occur from meeting others in treatment settings, online forums, personal networks, or via structured in-person support networks. More and more, these communities, especially patient communities, are being built through online platforms. Many individuals have cited these communities as a place to learn to develop and share their illness experience and narrative. Facebook support groups were one avenue for Amina to construct her illness narrative and share it with others:

> I was very reserved at first. I was a lurker. I just read other people's stories. I finally grew the courage to comment on posts...the more comfortable I became talking about my experiences and my personal life, the more comfortable I became talking about it outside of that Facebook group. I was able to start to articulate all these thoughts that had been swirling around in my head for months, or years...If you can verbalize it and get it out, then it really helps you come to terms with your illness and start to process, 'Okay, how am I going to deal with this?'

The online community provided Amina a forum in which she could begin to build a narrative of her experiences of IBD. She learned to tell her story in the group, which gave her the courage and strength to begin sharing it with people in her life.

Many extant relationships become avenues for social reconstruction of meaning. Bury's (1982) *mobilization of resources* is one response to the biographical disruption and a way to make meaning out of the illness. This can take the form of ending or creating more distance in some relationships, and/or strengthening relationships that are mutually supportive. The presence of a supportive social network in the face of chronic illness can make a big difference in the course of the illness; in relationships that successfully navigate the biographical disruption of illness, there is an opportunity to coconstruct meaning.

Indeed, learning to talk about one's illness can be an important process for individuals with IBD. Julia describes her initial reluctance to open up about IBD and then her growing comfort with disclosure. "At first I didn't share it, and I'm not really sure why...It's evolved as I've gotten more comfortable with it. I've just been able to tell people more. I don't think I ever was afraid to tell people, I just didn't. But now I definitely express it more". This was an experience that also minimized Chloe's social isolation. After receiving waves of support following a Facebook post about her illness experience, Chloe was left with one resounding sentiment: "Oh wow. I'm not alone."

Future research may consider how becoming more vocal about one's illness is connected to developing one's illness narrative and finding meaning in the illness. Not unsurprisingly, many participants expressed that their illness taught them how to advocate for their physical needs, process their emotions, and relinquish long-held roles of the "silent sufferer."

Implications

The study of meaning-making through illness narratives has many potential benefits to patients and the development of health care initiatives. Patient stories of encounters with doctors, psychologists, and other health care providers and adjustments to identity required by chronic illnesses are important to understand. Health professionals can benefit from awareness of the uncertainties of living with IBD and other unpredictable chronic illnesses. In counseling and psychotherapy, there are opportunities for purposeful meaning-making. Therapists may be unaware of how they influence the construction of patient narratives. Being attuned to the patient's narrative and meaning-making processes can allow providers to better understand where an individual is on the spectrum from isolation to community and how their support system impacts their treatment and disease course. These narratives allow providers to understand the heightened vulnerability to isolation in earlier stages of the illness, and the toll of the physical symptoms and the limitations they impose. Finally, finding meaning in illness has been identified as a key process in readiness for self-care for individuals with chronic illness (Baker & Stern, 1993).

A greater understanding of illness narratives and meaning-making has well-documented benefits to the ill person's mental and physical health. Many recent studies have shown that having a sense of meaning in life is associated with better psychological and physical health (Haugan, 2014), and those with a greater sense of purpose in life live longer (Cohen, Bavishi, & Rozanski, 2016). Patients with chronic illness therefore, who are vulnerable to ruptured sense of meaning, could benefit greatly from attunement to their sense of meaning before and after their diagnosis.

We have tried to balance the importance of sharing patients' voices with the importance of synthesizing their voices with the literature. We applaud Frank's (2001) call to strive for a deep understanding of patient narratives without simply forcing them into themes and subthemes. Attuning to illness narratives and meaning-making processes in illness can promote psychological and physical health. It is important to consider the whole narrative, particularly the parts of the patient experiences that they may resist telling, that fall out of words and instead into silences, lack of eye contact, or tears. The parts of the narrative that struggle to be told can hold as much meaning as the key events and emotions that *can* be vocalized. Isolation, denial of illness, and biographical disruption can all live as untold parts of the narrative—what the individual cannot yet make sense of. Both qualitative research and narrative analysis have begun to make room for the expression of story and experience. Building space for it with caretakers, health care providers, within patient communities, and within the individual is an important part of helping people with chronic illness to build a coherent sense of self and life story that incorporates the illness.

Conclusion

The experience of living with a chronic illness can disrupt many aspects of one's life and self-concept. While individuals are challenged by illness, there are opportunities for growth and new meaning in life. Narrative structures can help individuals organize and integrate their experience to make meaning of the illness. This chapter examined prior literature on illness narratives and a recent qualitative study of individuals with moderate to severe IBD.

Loss of self and biographical disruption contribute to suffering from chronic illness. When individuals build new meanings and develop self-concepts that incorporate illness, without letting the illness define them, growth occurs. There are many avenues through which this growth can occur. Renegotiating who one is and how one sees oneself (physically and mentally), readjusting goals and ambitions, and generally finding a new relationship with one's body are critical aspects of healing. Redefining one's relationship with one's body is important in making meaning, and accepting one's illness can facilitate greater authenticity. Changing habits and reprioritizing, beyond their importance for illness adjustment, can also lead to finding meaning in the illness.

Social aspects of one's life can also be powerful avenues for finding meaning in chronic illness. Extant relationships with family and friends, as well as new relationships with fellow patients and medical providers are all areas ripe for the coconstruction of meaning. Collaborating on an illness narrative with one's doctor, where the patient brings the personal experience of illness and the provider brings knowledge of the illness, allows for a mutually agreeable interpretation of key events. Support groups and social support networks also contribute to a patient's understanding of the impact of the illness and inform the search for meaning. Learning how to manage one's illness in the context of work and engaging in meaningful work can also help one find purpose. All of these help in the transition to accepting one's chronic illness and potentially finding meaning.

References

Baker, C. E., & Stern, P. N. (1993). Finding meaning in chronic illness as the key to self-care. *Canadian Journal of Nursing Research*, *25*(2), 23–36.

The psychology of working: A new perspective for career development, counseling, and public policy. New York: Routledge. .

Blustein, D. L. (2019). *The impact of work in an age of uncertainty*. New York: Oxford University Press.

Bury, M. R. (1982). Chronic illness as biographical disruption. *Sociology of Health and Illness*, *18*, 220–240.

Bury, M. R. (1988). Meaning at risk: The experience of arthritis. In R. Anderson, & M. Bury (Eds.), *Living with chronic illness. The experience of patients and their families*. London: Unwin Hyman.

Bury, M. R. (2001). Illness narratives: Fact or fiction? *Sociology of Health and Illness*, *23*, 263–285.

Byrne, G., Rosenfeld, G., Leung, Y., Qian, H., Raudzus, J., Nunez, C., et al. (2017). Prevalence of anxiety and depression in patients with inflammatory bowel disease. *Canadian Journal of Gastroenterology & Hepatology*, 6496727.

Charmaz, K. (1983). Loss of self: A fundamental form of suffering in the chronically ill. *Sociology of Health and Illness*, *5*(2), 168–195.

Charmaz, K. (1991). *Good days, bad days: The self in chronic illness and time*. New Brunswick, NJ: Rutgers.

Charmaz, K. (1995). The body, identity, and self: Adapting to impairment. *The Sociological Quarterly*, *36*(4), 657–680.

Charmaz, K. (2002). The self as habit: The reconstruction of self in chronic illness. *OTJR: Occupation, Participation and Health, 22*(1_suppl).

Charon, R. (2008). *Narrative medicine: Honoring the stories of illness*. New York: Oxford University Press.

Cohen, R., Bavishi, C., & Rozanski, A. (2016). Purpose in life and its relationship to all-cause mortality and cardiovascular events: A meta-analysis. *Psychosomatic Medicine, 78*, 122–133.

Corbin, J., & Strauss, A. L. (1987). Accompaniments of chronic illness: Changes in body, self, biography, and biographical time. In J. A. Roth, & P. Conrad (Eds.), *Research in the sociology of health care: The experience and management of chronic illness* (pp. 249–281). Greenwich, CT: JAI Press.

Crohn's and Colitis Foundation. (2019). What is IBD? Retrieved from <https://www.crohnscolitisfoundation.org/>.

Dik, B. J., Byrne, Z. S., & Steger, M. F. (Eds.), (2011). *Purpose and meaning in the workplace*. Washington, DC: American Psychological Association.

Dik, B. J., & Duffy, R. D. (2015). Strategies for discerning and living a calling. In P. Hartung, M. Savickas, & B. Walsh (Eds.), *APA handbook of career intervention* (pp. 305–317). Washington, DC: American Psychological Association.

Early, E. A. (1982). The logic of well-being: Therapeutic narratives in Cairo, Egypt. *Social Science and Medicine, 16*, 242–261.

Eggly, S. (2002). Physician-patient co-construction of illness narratives in the medical interview. *Health Communication, 14*(3), 339–360.

Faircloth, C. A., Boylstein, C., Rittman, M., Young, M. E., & Gubrium, J. (2004). Sudden illness and biographical flow in narratives of stroke recovery. *Sociology of Health & Illness, 26*(2), 242–261.

Frank, A. (1995). *The wounded storyteller: Body, illness, and ethics*. Chicago: University of Chicago Press.

Frank, A. (2001). Can we research suffering? *Qualitative Health Research, 11*(3), 353–362.

Gellner, E. A. (1992). *Reason and culture: The historic role of rationality and rationalism*. Oxford: Blackwell.

Good, B. J., Del Vecchio Good, M. J., Togan, I., Ilbar, Z., Guvener, A., & Gelizen, I. (1994). In the subjunctive mode: Epilepsy narratives in Turkey. *Social Science and Medicine, 38* (6), 835–842.

Haidet, P., Kroll, T. L., & Sharf, B. F. (2006). The complexity of patient participation: Lessons learned from patients' illness narratives. *Patient Education and Counseling, 62*(3), 323–329.

Haugan, G. (2014). Meaning-in-life in nursing-home patients: A valuable approach for enhancing psychological and physical well-being? *Journal of Clinical Nursing, 23*, 1830–1844.

Hill, C. E., Thompson, B. J., & Williams, E. N. (1997). A guide to conducting consensual qualitative research. *The Counseling Psychologist, 25*(4), 517–572.

Jordan, C., Sin, J., Fear, N. T., & Chalder, T. (2016). A systematic review of the psychological correlates of adjustment outcomes in adults with inflammatory bowel disease. *Clinical Psychology Review, 47*, 28–40.

Koutri, I., & Avdi, E. (2016). The suspended self: Liminality in breast cancer narratives and implications for counselling. *The European Journal of Counselling Psychology, 5*(1), 78–96.

Larsson, A. T., & Grassman, E. J. (2012). Bodily changes among people living with physical impairments and chronic illnesses: Biographical disruption or normal illness? *Sociology of Health & Illness, 34*(8), 1156–1169.

Leventhal, H., Meyer, D., & Nerenz, D. (1980). The common sense model of illness danger. In S. Rachman (Ed.), *Medical psychology* (2, pp. 7–30). New York: Pergamon.

Leventhal, H., Phillips, L. A., & Burns, E. (2016). The Common-Sense Model of Self-Regulation (CSM): A dynamic framework for understanding illness self-management. *Journal of Behavioral Medicine*, *39*(6), 935–946.

Lipkin, M. (1995). Personal narratives: Performing the medical interview. In M. Lipkin, Jr., S. Putnam, & A. Lazare (Eds.), *The medical interview* (pp. 65–82). New York: Springer-Verlag.

Lönnfors, S., Vermeire, S., Greco, M., Hommes, D., Bell, C., & Avedano, L. (2014). IBD and health-related quality of life—Discovering the true impact. *Journal of Crohns and Colitis*, *8*(10), 1281–1286.

Molzahn, A. E., Bruce, A., & Sheilds, L. (2008). Learning from stories of people with chronic kidney disease. *Nephrology Nursing Journal*, *35*(1), 13–20, Retrieved July 30, 2019.

Monaghan, L. F., & Gabe, J. (2015). Chronic illness as biographical contingency? Young peoples experiences of asthma. *Sociology of Health & Illness*, *37*(8), 1236–1253.

Morden, A., Jinks, C., & Ong, B. N. (2015). Temporally divergent significant meanings, biographical disruption and self-management for chronic joint pain. *Health: An Interdisciplinary Journal for the Social Study of Health, Illness and Medicine*, *21*(4), 357–374.

Neimeyer, R. A. (2004). Fostering posttraumatic growth: A narrative elaboration. *Psychological Inquiry*, *15*, 53–60.

Neuendorf, R., Harding, A., Stello, N., Hanes, D., & Wahbeh, H. (2016). Depression and anxiety in patients with inflammatory bowel disease: A systematic review. *Journal of Psychosomatic Research*, *87*, 70–80.

Park, C. L. (2010). Making sense of the meaning literature: An integrative review of meaning making and its effects on adjustment to stressful life events. *Psychological Bulletin*, *136*(2), 257–301.

Roussi, P., & Avdi, E. (2008). Meaning-making and chronic illness: Cognitive and narrative approaches. *Hellenic Journal of Psychology*, *5*(2), 147–178.

Sanders, C., Donovan, J., & Dieppe, P. (2002). The significance and consequences of having painful and disabled joints in older age: co-existing accounts of normal and disrupted biographies. *Sociology of Health & Illness*, *24*(2), 227–253.

Sanders, T., Ong, B. N., Roberts, D., & Corbett, M. (2015). Health maintenance, meaning, and disrupted illness trajectories in people with low back pain: A qualitative study. *Health Sociology Review*, *24*(1), 1–14.

Saunders, B. (2017). 'It seems like you're going around in circles': Recurrent biographical disruption constructed through the past, present and anticipated future in the narratives of young adults with inflammatory bowel disease. *Sociology of Health & Illness*, *39*(5), 726–740.

Sears, S. R., Stanton, A. L., & Danoff-Burg, S. (2003). The yellow brick road and the women with early-stage breast cancer. *Health Psychology*, *22*, 487–497.

Singh, S., Blanchard, A., Walker, J. R., Graff, L. A., Miller, N., & Bernstein, C. N. (2011). Common symptoms and stressors among individuals with inflammatory bowel diseases. *Clinical Gastroenterology and Hepatology*, *9*(9), 769–775.

Steger, M. F., Dik, B. J., & Duffy, R. D. (2012). Measuring meaningful work. *Journal of Career Assessment*, *20*(3), 322–337.

Tedeschi, R. G., & Calhoun, L. G. (2004). Target article: Posttraumatic growth: Conceptual foundations and empirical evidence. *Psychological Inquiry*, *15*(1), 1–18.

Wiener, C. L. (1982). The burden of rheumatoid arthritis: Tolerating the uncertainty. *Deciphering Sociological Research*, 286–297.

Williams, G. (1984). The genesis of chronic illness: narrative reconstruction. *Sociology of Health & Illness*, *6*, 175–200.

Williams, S. (2000). Chronic illness as biographical disruption or biographical disruption as chronic illness? Reflections on a core concept. *Sociology of Health & Illness*, *22*(1), 40–67.

CHAPTER

8

Resilience trajectories of cancer survivors: a meaning-making perspective

Crystal L. Park[1], *Kate E. Dibble*[2], *Sinead Sinnott*[1], *Tara Sanft*[3] *and Keith M. Bellizzi*[2]

[1]Department of Psychological Sciences, University of Connecticut, CT, United States, [2]Department of Human Development and Family Studies, University of Connecticut, CT, United States, [3]Medical Oncology, Yale University School of Medicine, New Haven, CT, United States

While in treatment, I had been surrounded by the world's best army: My supportive family and friends and a brilliant medical team who had worked tirelessly to keep me alive... Now that I had survived the "cut, poison, burn" of this disease, I no longer had the cavalry running after me. Suddenly I found myself standing dazed and alone in the rubble, wondering what had happened and where everyone had gone. **Suleika Jaouad, Cancer Survivor, New York Times, March 16, 2015**

Transition from active treatment to longer-term survivorship

The number of cancer survivors in the United States is large and increasing; there are currently over 16.9 million survivors, and it is estimated that there will be 21.7 million by 2029 (NCI, 2019). Cancer diagnosis and treatment constitute a constellation of stressors for patients and their loved ones. Active/primary treatment can last several years and brings with it challenges that persist and evolve well beyond the point at which treatment concludes (Costanza, Ryff, & Singer, 2009;

Navigating Life Transitions for Meaning
DOI: https://doi.org/10.1016/B978-0-12-818849-1.00008-4

Elliott et al., 2011; Santin, Mills, Treanor, & Donnelly, 2012). Indeed, the results of several large-scale surveys have documented high levels of clinically significant symptoms of depression and anxiety following treatment (Champagne et al., 2016; Deimling, Kahana, Bowman, & Schaefer, 2002), with most survivors reporting being significantly concerned about recurrence (Baker, Denniston, Smith, & West, 2005; Bellizzi et al., 2008). Further, a large, nationally representative study indicated that cancer survivors, relative to matched noncancer controls, reported significantly lower levels of physical and mental health as well as greater role limitations and social functioning (Santin et al., 2012). Another large nationally representative sample drawn from the MIDUS Study assessed prediagnosis to postdiagnosis changes in survivors and found that most cancer survivors experienced reductions in mental health following diagnosis, although many demonstrated resilience in social well-being relative to matched controls (Costanza et al., 2009). Further, many cancer survivors experience a significant decrease in existential confidence relating to identity, uncertainty, and worry concerning their future (Hullman, Robb, & Rand, 2016).

In addition to these studies of people in survivorship, there is some evidence that the *transition* from active treatment to survivorship remains a highly stressful and potentially critical juncture in determining their long-term postactive treatment well-being. At treatment end, patients' frequent interactions with their medical team, and the accompanying sense of protection, abruptly ceases. At this point, cancer patients also often experience decreased social and emotional support, face fears of cancer recurrence, and experience lingering or emerging physical and psychological effects of diagnosis and treatment (Stanton, Rowland, & Ganz, 2015). At this time, survivors may also make efforts to make sense of their cancer experience and its ultimate impact on their lives (Stanton, 2012).

This reentry period (Mullan, 1985), wherein one marks the psychosocial transition from "cancer patient" to "person with a history of cancer," typically spans the point from completion of major cancer treatments, which can vary from a few weeks to more than a year, through the next several months to their first follow-up or beyond. Health care professionals are often ill-equipped to prepare patients for this reentry period, which can contribute to cancer survivors and their family and friends holding unrealistic expectations for survivors' rapid recovery and "return to normal" (IOM, 2006); survivors are often surprised by their feelings as treatment ends. As physician Elizabeth McKinley (2000) wrote, "I thought I would feel happy about finally reaching the end of treatment, but instead, I was sobbing... Instead of joyous, I felt lonely, abandoned, and terrified. This was the rocky beginning of cancer survivorship for me" (p. 479).

As described in clinical accounts and research reports, the months after treatment typically involve loss of the emotional safety net that patients often experience during active treatment and the accompanying supportive milieu offered by frequent visits to health care providers, resumption or alteration of former roles within and outside the home, a decline in social support, and experiences of lingering or emerging physical and psychological effects of diagnosis and treatment (e.g., IOM, 2006; Stanton, 2012; Talcott et al., 2003).

Research on psychological trajectories suggests that some survivors experience an increase in psychological distress following the completion of medical treatment (15% of 171 breast cancer survivors in Henselmans et al., 2010). The boundaries of the reentry period are variable; we suggest that reentry can span more than a year after medical treatment completion, depending on the length and intensity of treatment as well as other contextual factors. The reentry period might be truncated when only brief, local treatment is used (i.e., no chemotherapy or targeted therapies following surgery or radiation). Reentry may be prolonged and more challenging when treatment is onerous, or the cancer experience prompts a profound shift in core beliefs, activities, or relationships. When cancer is diagnosed in young adulthood, for example, survivors often face unique demands at reentry. Cancer can represent an abrupt transition into the responsible world of adulthood while also necessitating at least temporary dependence on parents and others for support. The classic tasks of this developmental period—creating intimacy, establishing a niche in society, starting families, and building careers (Erikson, 1968)—can be uniquely jeopardized by life-threatening illness such as cancer. Issues related to childbearing and fertility preservation can compound the complexity of treatment decisions (Lee, Cohen, Edgar, Laizner, & Gagnon, 2006) and present challenges after treatment. Although fertility preservation is often discussed along with treatment decisions (Forman, Anders, & Behera, 2010), some survivors become aware of these issues only as they begin to consider childbearing. Additionally, the financial toxicity of cancer care can leave a young person without savings, bankrupt, or dependent on employment to maintain existing health insurance.

The reentry phase following cancer treatment has been observed to follow a fairly predictable course in many studies of cancer patients currently undergoing treatment(s) (Henselmans et al., 2010; Hou et al., 2010; Lazovich, Robien, Cutler, Virnig, & Sweeney, 2009; Michael, Kawachi, Berkman, Holmes, & Colditz, 2000) and qualitative researchers have added to our understanding of this phenomenon (Ahles & Saykin, 2007; Armes et al., 2009; Polsky et al., 2005; Talcott et al., 2003). After completion of active cancer treatment, patients are moved to follow-up care and surveillance to monitor the status of remission, lessening those interactions that patients experienced with their oncologists during active treatment. When this occurs, cancer survivors have reported a significant decrease in their sense of being protected (Henselmans et al., 2010) as well as the amount of emotional support available to them (Bower, 2008; Talcott et al., 2003). In conjunction with the loss in consistent support immediately after active treatment concludes, fears of recurrence (Bellizzi et al., 2008; Bower et al., 2011; Ganz et al., 2004; Luker, Beaver, Lemster, & Owens, 1996) and issues with physical functioning remain (Arora et al., 2002; Bower et al., 2011), but usually subside with time. In a sample of 223 recent breast cancer survivors, many reported worries related to recurrence, pain, death, harm from chemotherapy, and medical bills (Ganz et al., 2004).

Several characteristics of survivors such as demographic, cancer-related, and psychosocial factors have been noted to longitudinally predict reductions in health-related quality of life (HRQoL) and overall health in cancer patients transitioning into the reentry phase. For instance, survivors of younger age have been found to exhibit poorer HRQoL scores and higher unmet needs compared with adults (Beckjord et al., 2008; Bloom, Petersen, & Kang, 2007; Burgess et al., 2005; Costanza et al., 2009; Helgeson, Snyder, & Seltman, 2004; Jansen et al., 2011; Kroenke et al., 2004). Interestingly, completion of cancer treatment (s) such as chemotherapy and endocrine therapies (Armes et al., 2009; Thornton, Carson, Shapiro, Farrar, & Andersen, 2008) or the diagnosis of comorbid conditions (Beckjord et al., 2008; Bower, 2008; Lynch, Steginga, Hawkes, Pakenham, & Dunn, 2008) appear to increase problems during reentry and into survivorship. Highly dependent on developmental stage and explicit treatment(s) undergone, short-term threats to successful reentry and survivorship for pediatric, adolescent and young adult cancer survivors range from sexual and reproductive issues (e.g., fertility, premature menopause), depressive/anxiety symptomology, and experiencing issues in their careers and relationships (Zebrack, 2011). While research into racial and ethnic differences remains in its early stages, the evidence that has accumulated to date suggests that HRQoL is decreased among ethnic minority groups diagnosed with cancer in comparison to their Caucasian counterparts (Hao et al., 2011; Janz et al., 2009; Yanez, Thompson, & Stanton, 2011), and current research is ongoing to better understand why these disparities exist (Hao et al., 2011).

Individuals vary in their recovery following cancer

Myriad studies of health and well-being in survivorship have demonstrated that while decrements in well-being are often observed *on average*, there is tremendous variation across survivors on many different indices of well-being (e.g., Costanza et al., 2009). As we noted, many individuals report significant difficulties returning to normal daily life following cancer treatment, with elevated rates of anxiety, depression, and PTSD symptoms, such as intrusive and avoidance symptoms (Bellizzi & Blank, 2011). Importantly, however, thriving and perceptions of posttraumatic growth are also commonly reported coexisting outcomes (Bellizzi et al., 2012). Although researchers have called into question the extent to which reports of positive outcomes reflect well-being as standardly measured (e.g., Frazier et al., 2009), it is clear that individuals vary widely in their psychosocial adjustment, which has important implications for quality of life among cancer survivors. One promising way to understand individuals' courses of recovery is through trajectories over time.

In the broader trauma and coping literature, an analytic approach to modeling posttrauma adjustment has identified four basic posttrauma trajectories: resilience, recovery (sometimes called "emerging resilience"; Bonanno & Diminich, 2013), chronic distress, and impairment (Bonanno, 2004). From this trajectories perspective, resilience is defined as continued well-being across the challenge or stressor ("minimal impact resilience"). By considering individuals' trajectories of adjustment, we can go beyond average tendencies to model individual variations in resilience and recovery. Several studies of cancer survivorship have examined adjustment postcancer, reporting the same four trajectories as proposed in Bonanno's (2004) original model of trauma (e.g., Helgeson et al., 2004). However, studies of trajectories in cancer have not focused on end of primary treatment as an important point of stress; the majority of work in this area has primarily captured data on the experience of individuals as they adjust to a cancer *diagnosis*, rather than as they adjust to the changes inherent in completing treatment (reentry). With just one exception, extant studies of cancer adjustment trajectories have measured uniform times from diagnosis for convenience (e.g., 3, 6, 9 months; Manne et al., 2008) rather than assessing adjustment relative to the milestone of ending treatment and beginning "survivorship." The one study that did identify and assess survivors at this critical point then examined only one later point, concluding the entire study within a year of diagnosis (Henselmans et al., 2010), rather than focusing on posttreatment trajectories. We propose that within cancer survivorship, there are three types of trajectories that occur across the transition to survivorship: continued distress, recovery, and resilience (see Fig. 8.1).

It is worth noting that nearly all existing studies of cancer adjustment trajectories focus on quality of life or psychological distress, which comprise a rather narrow subset of domains of well-being and capture only

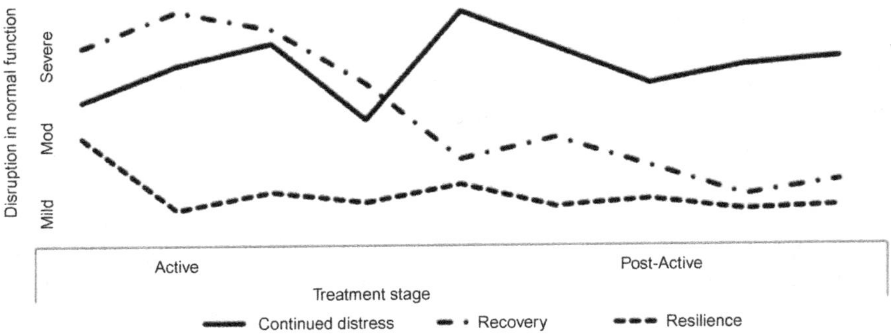

FIGURE 8.1 Hypothetical trajectories of adjustment from active treatment through survivorship. Source: *Based on Bonanno, G. A. (2004). Loss, trauma, and human resilience: Have we underestimated the human capacity to thrive after extremely aversive events? American Psychologist, 59, 20–28.*

one piece of the posttreatment experience. It may be that survivors are resilient in some domains and struggle to recover in others, although there is little data on this point at this time (Bellizzi et al., 2012). Further, we know little about why individual survivors exhibit such different patterns of adjustment. Only one existing study of trajectories of adjustment, that of women with gynecological cancer, identified any distinct coping processes as predictors of well-being (Manne et al., 2008). The introduction of coping into the study of resilience is key, as it provides information about both psychological well-being and environmental and intrapersonal resources for adjustment and is an actionable focus of interventions.

While many factors that impede or facilitate recovery and resilience following cancer treatment have been identified, these factors have rarely been examined from and integrated within a strong theoretical base. Further, because of the relevance of appraisals and coping *to* well-being over time, it remains important to identify individual- and environmental-level factors that guide these processes, which are outlined below. Using a trajectories approach allows the identification of distinct sets of predictors of these processes for each individual rather than simply predicting group trajectories. In doing so, a deeper understanding of survivors' *processes* of drawing on their resources and *coping* with the stressors they confront as a part of daily life is necessary to characterize recovery and resilience, as well as informing interventions to promote resilience.

Pretransition factors

A number of predictive factors about the conditions of cancer predict individual well-being during the transition to survivorship once in remission. Type of cancer, amount of time since diagnosis, age, and comorbidities all contribute to individual distress or adjustment during the stressful period following cancer treatment. For example, one study found that pancreatic cancer survivors are more likely to have depression alone, while uterine cancer survivors are least likely (Brintzenhofe-Szoc, Levin, Li, Kissane, & Zabora, 2009). Breast cancer survivors are most likely to have anxiety alone, while brain cancer survivors are least likely (Brintzenhofe-Szoc et al., 2009). A combination of both depression and anxiety symptoms are most likely among stomach cancer survivors and least likely among ovarian cancer survivors (Brintzenhofe-Szoc et al., 2009). Previous studies have found that lung, breast, pancreatic, and oropharyngeal cancer survivors are at increased risk of depression compared to survivors of other cancer types (Carney, Jones, Woolson, Noyes, & Doebbeling, 2003; Massie, 2004). It is posited that there may be increased risk of depression among certain types of cancer due to increased concentrations of interleukin-6 (Musselman, Miller, Porter, Manatunga, & Nemeroff, 2001). These differences in psychopathology could also be due to a range of different psychosocial factors, such as support services available to certain types of cancer, the prognosis of certain cancer types, or treatments available for each treatment type.

Studies have found that higher levels of symptoms are associated with younger age and less time since diagnosis. Anxiety and depression symptoms generally decrease as time since diagnosis increases and as survivors get older (Arden-Close, Gidron, & Moss-Morris, 2008; Maass, Roorda, Berendsen, Verhaak, & de Bock, 2015; Park et al., 2018), and there is also evidence of decreased fears of cancer recurrence with increased age and time since diagnosis among breast cancer survivors (Taylor et al., 2012). Interestingly, in a sample of Latina cancer patients who had not yet started chemotherapy, longer time since diagnosis was associated with higher depression and anxiety (Lee et al., 2018). It may be that these symptoms increase as the beginning of treatment gets closer, but then decrease throughout or after treatment. Or it could be that the time spent waiting for treatment to start is correlated with high anxiety, as the fear of the "unknown" is very high during this period (i.e., patients are not sure what side effects they will experience during chemotherapy and the anticipation of these side effects can be worse than those actually experienced).

Appraised meaning of the cancer

Appraisals refer to the individuals' understanding of the stressor and their ability to respond to it; as such, appraisals are the central drivers of coping and adjustment (Lazarus & Folkman, 1984; Lent, 2007). Given their central role, it is surprising that so little research has been conducted on survivors' appraisals and changes in appraisals over time (Hoffman, Lent, & Raque-Bogdan, 2013); the available work suggests that survivors' appraisals are strong predictors of their adjustment (Park, Edmondson, Fenster, & Blank, 2008a). How individuals appraise the meaning or threat related to the cancer may impact how they respond to it on a behavioral and psychological level.

Lazarus and Folkman (1984) posited that differences in appraisals of stressor as threatening, harmful, or challenging predict differential response and outcome. A meta-analysis demonstrated differences in coping responses based on threat appraisals in the context of cancer (Franks & Roesch, 2006). Higher appraisals of harm or threat of cancer predict increased distress over time (Bigatti, Steiner, & Miller, 2012; Mazanec, Daly, Douglas, & Musil, 2011), with evidence that appraisals of cancer harm may result in increased anxiety (Bjorck, Hopp, & Jones, 1999) while increased appraisals of cancer threat may result in increased anxiety, depression, general distress, and cancer-related distress (Bjorck et al., 1999; Hamama-Raz, Solomon, Schachter, & Azizi, 2007; Lynch et al., 2008).

Appraisals of cancer as a threat, harm, or challenge may determine how much control individuals feel they have over the cancer and the survivorship process. Those who perceive a cancer as a challenge to be met may experience increased perceptions of control (Gabrys, Tabri, Anisman, & Matheson, 2018). Increased internal locus of control of the process of dealing with cancer can result in decreased distress (Norton et al., 2005), and may buffer stress responses after chemotherapy (Henselmans, Sanderman, Baas, Smink, & Ranchor, 2009). A lack of a sense of control may prompt feelings of uncertainty about the future, although survivors sometimes report coping with these feelings of uncertainty and lack of control by focusing on engagement with their lives, such as continuing to go to work, reaching out to social supports, and caring for their families (Warren, 2010). These strategies can be utilized as a means of connecting with meaningful aspects of one's life and allowing survivors to behave proactively in their lives rather than ruminating on their uncertainty about their cancer diagnosis. Engaging in strategies that may give one a sense of meaning can be adaptive, as a sense of meaning in life is inversely associated with distress among cancer patients and survivors (Winger, Adams, & Mosher, 2016).

Psychosocial resources

Environmental and intrapersonal resources coupled with individuals' efforts to adjust to reentry and survivorship also influence trajectories of adjustment. Studies of survivors of a variety of types of cancer have highlighted consistent relations between social support, self-efficacy, and optimism with increased HRQoL and healthier adjustment to survivorship (e.g., Blank & Bellizzi, 2006; Fong, Scarapicchia, McDonough, Wrosch, & Sabiston, 2016; Park, Cho, Blank, & Wortmann, 2013). More specifically, research has shown that survivors who received higher levels of emotional support immediately after a cancer diagnosis noted more positive experiences relating to their cancer during survivorship (Schroevers, Helgeson, Sanderman, & Ranchor, 2009). Similarly, optimism, combined with stable social support, has been found to moderate negative impacts of cancer diagnosis and survivorship (Friedman et al., 2005), attenuate cancer symptom distress, promote higher HRQoL (Manning-Walsh, 2006), and facilitate higher levels of social support (Sammarco, 2009). Although emotion regulation has seldom been studied in cancer survivors, it has been theorized to promote resilience in survivorship (Wills & Bantum, 2012) and in the broader literature in coping with highly stressful events, emotion regulation has been shown to promote well-being in many important life domains (Heatherton, 2011). Further, emotion regulation skills are highly amenable to improvement and may be a useful target in interventions for cancer survivors (Cameron, Booth, Schlatter, Ziginskas, & Harman, 2007). For example, survivors may benefit from interventions that promote reappraisal skills or mindfulness to promote higher levels of positive emotions and tamp down distress (Boyle, Stanton, Ganz, Crespi, & Bower, 2017).

Coping

The updated model portrayed in Fig. 8.2 also highlights the critical roles of coping, in conjunction with appraisal (outlined above), in

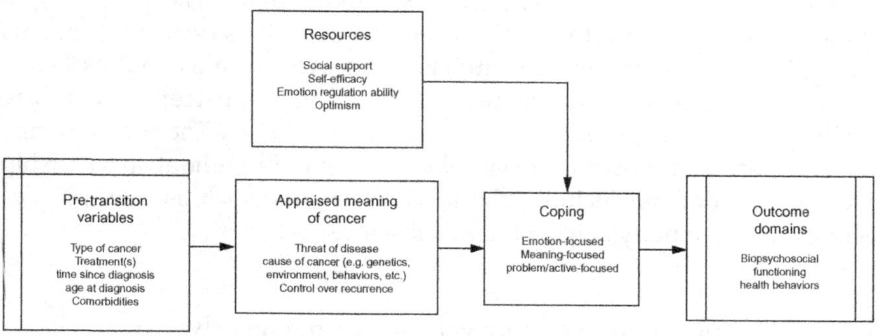

FIGURE 8.2 Updated biopsychosocial model of determinants of survivors' trajectories of recovery following completion of primary treatment. Source: *From Lent, R. W. (2007). Restoring emotional well-being: A theoretical model. In M. Feuerstein (Ed.), Handbook of cancer survivorship (pp. 231–247). New York: Springer.*

predicting adjustment or resilience during reentry and survivorship. Coping refers to the responses individuals make to the demands of the stressful situation and are often divided into strategies that focus on taking direct action to solve the problem (problem/active-focused coping), strategies that focus on managing distressing emotions because of such problem (emotion-focused coping), and strategies that focus on understanding the situation in a different way (meaning-focused coping) (Park, 2010). Regulating emotional distress through problem-focused avenues (e.g., problem solving, cognitive reappraisal) has been shown to lessen depressive symptoms in breast cancer survivors, and only those who had less positive emotional expression had more depressive symptoms (Marroquin, Czamanski-Cohen, Weihs, & Stanton, 2016). Meaning-focused coping has consistently been found to lead to positive outcomes in cancer survivors as well (Kvillemo & Bränström, 2014). Overall, survivors' coping efforts have been demonstrated to predict well-being in many domains across many studies.

Outcome domains

The four domains that collectively comprise survivors' well-being (Costanza et al., 2009; Stanton et al., 2005) are outlined in Fig. 8.2. Although other domains exist, these four domains—physical, psychological, and social functioning, and health behaviors—appear to be the most commonly affected by cancer and those most commonly studied (Stanton et al., 2015). Together, these domains provide a comprehensive view of survivors' well-being. Physical functioning includes self-reported general physical functioning and cancer-specific physical functioning such as fatigue. Sleep disturbances are also common among this population, and are associated with mood disturbances, decreased HRQoL, fatigue, immune functioning, and mortality (Palesh et al., 2014; Savard & Morin, 2001). The psychological domain includes general mental functioning as well as cancer-specific distress (PTSD-like symptoms of intrusion and avoidance as well as fear of recurrence). Positive psychological constructs, such as perceptions of thriving or posttraumatic growth, are also be included here. The social domain includes satisfaction within social roles over time throughout survivorship. The lifestyle domain includes the usual behaviors, such as diet, physical activity and sedentary behavior, and substance use.

Using a comprehensive biopsychosocial perspective to understand survivors' trajectories

Cancer-related adjustment may be best understood through a biopsychosocial approach, such as the Biopsychosocial Restorative Model of

Well-Being (Lent, 2007), an illness-specific adaptation of Lazarus and Folkman's (1984) transactional model of stress and coping applied to cancer survivorship (see Fig. 8.2). This model includes cancer- and treatment-related factors, personal and social resources, and appraisal and coping processes that occur throughout the adaptation process and that may influence the path of survivors' trajectories. Importantly, the model emphasizes each survivor's unique circumstances and appraised meaning of their illness as well as the meaning making and other types of coping in which they engage. Survivors' coping has been demonstrated to predict well-being in many domains across many studies (see Franks & Roesch, 2006; Park et al., 2008a), although studies of survivors' coping and health behavior change are rare (Park, Edmondson, Fenster, & Blank, 2008b).

As research on resilience trajectories evolves, we encourage integration of theoretically driven research questions, including consideration of the proposed model of resilience presented in this chapter. Using theoretically based approaches allows for identification, assessment, and targeted approaches to research and clinical practice in the growing population of cancer survivors in the United States and beyond.

References

Ahles, T. A., & Saykin, A. J. (2007). Candidate mechanisms for chemotherapy-induced cognitive changes. *Nature Reviews Cancer, 7*, 192–201.

Arden-Close, E., Gidron, Y., & Moss-Morris, R. (2008). Psychological distress and its correlates in ovarian cancer: A systematic review. *Psycho-Oncology, 17*, 1061–1072.

Armes, J., Crowe, M., Colbourne, L., Morgan, H., Murrells, T., Oakley, C., ... Richardson, A. (2009). Patients' supportive care needs beyond the end of cancer treatment: A prospective, longitudinal survey. *Journal of Clinical Oncology, 27*, 6172–6179.

Arora, N. K., Johnson, P., Gustafson, D. H., McTavish, F., Hawkins, R. P., & Pingree, S. (2002). Barriers to information access, perceived health competence, and psychosocial health outcomes: Test of a mediation model in a breast cancer sample. *Patient Education and Counseling, 47*, 37–46.

Baker, F., Denniston, M., Smith, T., & West, M. M. (2005). Adult cancer survivors: How are they faring? *Cancer, 104*, 2565–2576.

Beckjord, E. B., Arora, N. K., McLaughlin, W., Oakley-Girvan, I., Hamilton, A. S., & Hesse, B. W. (2008). Health-related information needs in a large and diverse sample of adult cancer survivors: Implications for cancer care. *Journal of Cancer Survivorship, 2*, 179–189.

Bellizzi, K. M., & Blank, T. O. (2011). Posttraumatic stress and posttraumatic growth. In J. Lester, & P. Schmitt (Eds.), *Personalized approach to rehabilitation and survivorship care* (pp. 175–183). Pittsburgh, PA: Oncology Nursing Society.

Bellizzi, K. M., Latini, D. M., Cowan, J. E., DuChane, J., Carroll, P. R., & the CaPSURE Investigators. (2008). Fear of recurrence, symptom burden and health-related quality of life in men with prostate cancer. *Urology, 72*, 1269–1273.

Bellizzi, K. M., Smith, A., Schmidt, S., Keegan, T. H., Zebrack, B., Lynch, C. F., ... Simon, M. (2012). Positive and negative psychosocial impact of being diagnosed with cancer as an adolescent or young adult. *Cancer, 118*, 5155–5162.

Bigatti, S. M., Steiner, J. L., & Miller, K. D. (2012). Cognitive appraisals, coping and depressive symptoms in breast cancer patients. *Stress & Health, 28*, 355–361.

Bjorck, J. P., Hopp, D. P., & Jones, L. W. (1999). Prostate cancer and emotional functioning: Effects of mental adjustment, optimism, and appraisal. *Journal of Psychosocial Oncology, 17*, 71–85.

Blank, T. O., & Bellizzi, K. M. (2006). After prostate cancer: Predictors of well-being among long-term prostate cancer survivors. *Cancer, 106*, 2128–2135.

Bloom, J. R., Petersen, D. M., & Kang, S. H. (2007). Multi-dimensional quality of life among long-term (5+ years) adult cancer survivors. *Psycho-Oncology: Journal of the Psychological, Social, and Behavioral Dimensions of Cancer, 16*, 691–706.

Bonanno, G. A. (2004). Loss, trauma, and human resilience: Have we underestimated the human capacity to thrive after extremely aversive events? *American Psychologist, 59*, 20–28.

Bonanno, G. A., & Diminich, E. D. (2013). Positive adjustment to adversity–trajectories of minimal–impact resilience and emergent resilience. *Journal of Child Psychology and Psychiatry, 54*, 378–401.

Bower, J. E. (2008). Behavioral symptoms in patients with breast cancer and survivors. *Journal of Clinical Oncology, 26*, 768–777.

Bower, J. E., Ganz, P. A., Irwin, M. R., Kwan, L., Breen, E. C., & Cole, S. W. (2011). Inflammation and behavioral symptoms after breast cancer treatment: Do fatigue, depression, and sleep disturbance share a common underlying mechanism? *Journal of Clinical Oncology, 29*, 3517–3522.

Boyle, C. C., Stanton, A. L., Ganz, P. A., Crespi, C. M., & Bower, J. E. (2017). Improvements in emotion regulation following mindfulness meditation: Effects on depressive symptoms and perceived stress in younger breast cancer survivors. *Journal of Consulting and Clinical Psychology, 85*, 397–402.

Brintzenhofe-Szoc, K. M., Levin, T. T., Li, Y., Kissane, D. W., & Zabora, J. R. (2009). Mixed anxiety/depression symptoms in a large cancer cohort: Prevalence by cancer type. *Psychosomatics, 50*, 383–391.

Burgess, C., Cornelius, V., Love, S., Graham, J., Richards, M., & Ramirez, A. (2005). Depression and anxiety in women with early breast cancer: Five year observational cohort study. *BMJ, 330*, 702.

Cameron, L. D., Booth, R. J., Schlatter, M., Ziginskas, D., & Harman, J. E. (2007). Changes in emotion regulation and psychological adjustment following use of a group psychosocial support program for women recently diagnosed with breast cancer. *Psycho-Oncology, 16*, 171–180.

Carney, C. P., Jones, L., Woolson, R. F., Noyes, R., Jr., & Doebbeling, B. N. (2003). Relationship between depression and pancreatic cancer in the general population. *Psychosomatic Medicine, 65*, 884–888.

Champagne, A. L., Brunault, P., Huguet, G., Suzanne, I., Senon, J. L., Body, G., ... Camus, V. (2016). Personality disorders, but not cancer severity or treatment type, are risk factors for later generalised anxiety disorder and major depressive disorder in non metastatic breast cancer patients. *Psychiatry Research, 236*, 64–70.

Costanza, E. S., Ryff, C. D., & Singer, B. H. (2009). Psychosocial adjustment among cancer survivors: Findings from a national survey of health and well-being. *Health Psychology, 28*, 147–156.

Deimling, G., Kahana, B., Bowman, K., & Schaefer, M. (2002). Cancer survivorship and psychological distress in later life. *Psycho-Oncology, 11*, 479–494.

Elliott, J., Fallows, A., Staetsky, L., Smith, P. W. F., Foster, C. L., Maher, E., & Corner, J. (2011). The health and well-being of cancer survivors in the UK: Findings from a population-based survey. *British Journal of Cancer, 105*, 11–20.

Erikson, E. H. (1968). *Identity: Youth and crisis*. New York: W. W. Norton Company.

Fong, A. J., Scarapicchia, T. M., McDonough, M. H., Wrosch, C., & Sabiston, C. M. (2016). Changes in social support predict emotional well-being in breast cancer survivors. *Psycho-Oncology, 26*, 664–671.

Forman, E. J., Anders, C. K., & Behera, M. A. (2010). A nationwide survey of oncologists regarding treatment-related infertility and fertility preservation in female cancer patients. *Fertility & Sterility, 94*, 1652–1656.

Franks, H. M., & Roesch, S. C. (2006). Appraisals and coping in people living with cancer: A meta -analysis. *Psycho-Oncology, 15*, 1027–1037.

Frazier, P., Tennen, H., Gavian, M., Park, C. L., Tomich, P., & Tashiro, T. (2009). Does self-reported posttraumatic growth reflect genuine positive gains? *Psychological Science, 20*, 912–919.

Friedman, L. C., Kalidas, M., Elledge, R., Chang, J., Romero, C., ... Liscum, K. R. (2005). Optimism, social support and psychosocial functioning among women with breast cancer. *Psycho-Oncology, 15*, 595–603.

Gabrys, R. L., Tabri, N., Anisman, H., & Matheson, K. (2018). Cognitive control and flexibility in the context of stress and depressive symptoms: The cognitive control and flexibility questionnaire. *Frontiers in Psychology, 9*.

Ganz, P. A., Kwan, L., Stanton, A. L., Krupnick, J. L., Rowland, J. H., Meyerowitz, B. E., ... Belin, T. R. (2004). Quality of life at the end of primary treatment of breast cancer: First results from the moving beyond cancer randomized trial. *Journal of the National Cancer Institute, 96*, 376–387.

Hamama-Raz, Y., Solomon, Z., Schachter, J., & Azizi, E. (2007). Objective and subjective stressors and the psychological adjustment of melanoma survivors. *Psycho-Oncology, 16*, 287–294.

Hao, Y., Landrine, H., Smith, T., Kaw, C., Corral, I., & Stein, K. (2011). Residential segregation and disparities in health-related quality of life among Black and White cancer survivors. *Health Psychology, 30*, 137–144.

Heatherton, T. F. (2011). Neuroscience of self and self-regulation. *Annual Review of Psychology, 62*, 363–390.

Helgeson, V. S., Snyder, P. R., & Seltman, H. (2004). Psychological and physical adjustment to breast cancer over 4 years: Identifying distinct trajectories of change. *Health Psychology, 23*, 3–15.

Henselmans, I., Helgeson, V. S., Seltman, H., de Vries, J., Sanderman, R., & Ranchor, A. V. (2010). Identification and prediction of distress trajectories in the first year after a breast cancer diagnosis. *Health Psychology, 29*, 160–168.

Henselmans, I., Sanderman, R., Baas, P. C., Smink, A., & Ranchor, A. V. (2009). Personal control after a breast cancer diagnosis: Stability and adaptive value. *Psycho-Oncology, 18*, 104–108.

Hoffman, M. A., Lent, R. W., & Raque-Bogdan, T. L. (2013). A social cognitive perspective on coping with cancer theory, research, and Intervention. *The Counseling Psychologist, 41*, 240–267.

Hou, W. K., Law, C. C., Law, J., & Fu, Y. T. (2010). Resource loss, resource gain, and psychological resilience and dysfunction following cancer diagnosis: a growth mixture modeling approach. *Health Psychol., 29*(5), 484–495.

Hullman, S. E., Robb, S. L., & Rand, K. L. (2016). Life goals in patients with cancer: A systematic review of the literature. *Psycho-Oncology, 25*, 387–399.

Institute of Medicine. (2006). *From cancer patient to cancer survivor: Lost in transition*. Washington, DC: National Academies Press.

Jansen, L., Herrmann, A., Stegmaier, C., Singer, S., Brenner, H., & Arndt, V. (2011). Health-related quality of life during the 10 years after diagnosis of colorectal cancer: A population-based study. *Journal of Clinical Oncology, 29*, 3263–3269.

Janz, N. K., Mujahid, M. S., Hawley, S. T., Griggs, J. J., Alderman, A., Hamilton, A. S., & Katz, S. J. (2009). Racial/ethnic differences in quality of life after diagnosis of breast cancer. *J. Cancer Survivor.*, *3*(4), 212–222.

Kroenke, C. H., Rosner, B., Chen, W. Y., Kawachi, I., Colditz, G. A., & Holmes, M. D. (2004). Functional impact of breast cancer by age at diagnosis. *Journal of Clinical Oncology*, *22*, 1849–1856.

Kvillemo, P., & Bränström, R. (2014). Coping with breast cancer: A meta-analysis. *PLoS One*, *9*, e112733.

Lazarus, R. S., & Folkman, S. (1984). *Stress, appraisal and coping*. New York: Springer.

Lazovich, D., Robien, K., Cutler, G., Virnig, B., & Sweeney, C. (2009). Quality of life in a prospective cohort of elderly women with and without cancer. *Cancer*, *115*, 4283–4297.

Lee, V., Cohen, S. R., Edgar, L., Laizner, A. M., & Gagnon, A. J. (2006). Meaning-making intervention during breast or colorectal cancer treatment improves self-esteem, optimism, and self-efficacy. *Social Science & Medicine*, *62*, 3133–3145.

Lee, M. S., Tyson, D. M., Gonzalez, B. D., Small, B. J., Lechner, S. C., Antoni, M. H., … Jacobsen, P. B. (2018). Anxiety and depression in Spanish-speaking Latina cancer patients prior to starting chemotherapy. *Psycho-Oncology*, *27*, 333–338.

Lent, R. W. (2007). Restoring emotional well-being: A theoretical model. In M. Feuerstein (Ed.), *Handbook of cancer survivorship* (pp. 231–247). New York: Springer.

Luker, K. A., Beaver, K., Lemster, S. J., & Owens, R. G. (1996). Information needs and sources of information for women with breast cancer: A follow-up study. *Journal of Advanced Nursing*, *23*, 487–495.

Lynch, B. M., Steginga, S. K., Hawkes, A. L., Pakenham, K. I., & Dunn, J. (2008). Describing and predicting psychological distress after colorectal cancer. *Cancer*, *112*, 1363–1370.

Maass, S. W. M. C., Roorda, C., Berendsen, A. J., Verhaak, P. F. M., & de Bock, G. H. (2015). The prevalence of long-term symptoms of depression and anxiety after breast cancer treatment: A systematic review. *Maturitas*, *82*, 100–108.

Manne, S., Rini, C., Rubin, S., Rosenblum, N., Bergman, C., Edelson, M., … Rocereto, T. (2008). Long-term trajectories of psychological adaptation among women diagnosed with gynecological cancers. *Psychosomatic Medicine*, *70*, 677–687.

Manning-Walsh, J. (2006). Social support as a mediator between symptom distress and quality of life in women with breast cancer. *Journal of Obstetric, Gynecologic, & Neonatal Nursing*, *34*, 482–493.

Marroquin, B., Czamanski-Cohen, J., Weihs, K. L., & Stanton, A. L. (2016). Implicit loneliness, emotion regulation, and depressive symptoms in breast cancer survivors. *Journal of Behavioral Medicine*, *39*, 832–844.

Massie, M. J. (2004). Prevalence of depression in patients with cancer. *JNCI Monographs*, *2004*, 57–71.

Mazanec, S. R., Daly, B. J., Douglas, S., & Musil, C. (2011). Predictors of psychosocial adjustment during the post-radiation treatment transition. *Western Journal of Nursing Research*, *33*, 540–559.

McKinley, E. D. (2000). Under Toad days: Surviving the uncertainty of cancer recurrence. *Annals of Internal Medicine*, *133*, 479–480.

Michael, Y. L., Kawachi, I., Berkman, L. F., Holmes, M. D., & Colditz, G. A. (2000). The persistent impact of breast carcinoma on functional health status: Prospective evidence from the Nurses' Health Study. *Cancer*, *89*, 2176–2186.

Mullan, F. (1985). Seasons of survival: Reflections of a physician with cancer. *New England Journal of Medicine*, *313*, 270–273.

Musselman, D. L., Miller, A. H., Porter, M. R., Manatunga, A., … Nemeroff, C. B. (2001). Higher than normal plasma interleukin-6 concentrations in cancer patients with depression: Preliminary findings. *American Journal of Psychiatry*, *158*, 1252–1257.

National Cancer Institute (2019). <https://cancercontrol.cancer.gov/ocs/statistics/statistics.html#ref1>.

Norton, T. R., Manne, S. L., Rubin, S., Hernandez, E., Carlson, J., Bergman, C., & Rosenblum, N. (2005). Ovarian cancer patients' psychological distress: The role of physical impairment, perceived unsupportive family and friend behaviors, perceived control, and self-esteem. *Health Psychology, 24*, 143–152.

Palesh, O., Aldridge-Gerry, A., Zeitzer, J. M., Koopman, C., Neri, E., Giese-Davis, J., ... Spiegel, D. (2014). Actigraphy-measured sleep disruption as a predictor of survival among women with advanced breast cancer. *Sleep, 37*, 837–842.

Park, C. L. (2010). Making sense of the meaning literature: An integrative review of meaning making and its effects on adjustment to stressful life events. *Psychological Bulletin, 136*, 257–301.

Park, J. L., Brandelli, Y., Russell, K. B., Reynolds, K., Li, Y., Ruether, D., & Giese-Davis, J. (2018). Unmet needs of adult survivors of childhood cancers: Associations with developmental stage at diagnosis, cognitive impairment, and time from diagnosis. *Journal of Adolescent and Young Adult Oncology, 7*, 61–71.

Park, C. L., Cho, D., Blank, T. O., & Wortmann, J. H. (2013). Cognitive and emotional aspects of fear of recurrence: Predictors and relations with adjustment in young to middle-aged cancer survivors. *Psycho-Oncology, 22*, 1630–1638.

Park, C. L., Edmondson, D., Fenster, J. R., & Blank, T. O. (2008a). Meaning making and psychological adjustment following cancer: The mediating roles of growth, life meaning, and restored just-world beliefs. *Journal of Consulting and Clinical Psychology, 76*, 863–875.

Park, C. L., Edmondson, D., Fenster, J. R., & Blank, T. O. (2008b). Positive and negative health behavior changes in cancer survivors: A stress and coping perspective. *Journal of Health Psychology, 13*, 1198–1206.

Polsky, D., Doshi, J. A., Marcus, S., Oslin, D., Rothbard, A., ... Thompson, C. L. (2005). Long-term risk for depressive symptoms after a medical diagnosis. *Archives of Internal Medicine, 165*, 1260–1266.

Sammarco, A. (2009). Quality of life of breast cancer survivors: A comparative study of age cohorts. *Cancer Nursing, 32*, 347–356.

Santin, O., Mills, M., Treanor, C., & Donnelly, M. (2012). A comparative analysis of the health and wellbeing of cancer survivors to the general population. *Supportive Care in Cancer, 20*, 2545–2552.

Savard, J., & Morin, C. M. (2001). Insomnia in the context of cancer: A review of a neglected problem. *Journal of Clinical Oncology, 19*, 895–908.

Schroevers, M. J., Helgeson, V. S., Sanderman, R., & Ranchor, A. V. (2009). Type of social support matters for prediction of posttraumatic growth among cancer survivors. *Psycho-Oncology, 19*, 46–53.

Stanton, A. L. (2012). What happens now? Psychosocial care for cancer survivors after medical treatment completion. *Journal of Clinical Oncology, 30*, 1215–1220.

Stanton, A. L., Ganz, P. A., Rowland, J. H., Meyerowitz, B. E., Krupnick, J. L., & Sears, S. R. (2005). Promoting adjustment after treatment for cancer. *Cancer, 104*, 2608–2613.

Stanton, A. L., Rowland, J. H., & Ganz, P. A. (2015). Life after diagnosis and treatment of cancer in adulthood: Contributions from psychosocial oncology research. *American Psychologist, 70*, 159–174.

Talcott, J. A., Manola, J., Clark, J. A., Kaplan, I., Beard, C. J., ... D'Amico, A. V. (2003). Time course and predictors of symptoms after primary prostate cancer therapy. *Journal of Clinical Oncology, 21*, 3979–3986.

Taylor, T. R., Huntley, E. D., Sween, J., Makambi, K., Mellman, T. A., Williams, C. D., ... Frederick, W. (2012). An exploratory analysis of fear of recurrence among African-American breast cancer survivors. *International Journal of Behavioral Medicine, 19*, 280–287.

Thornton, L. M., Carson, W. E., III, Shapiro, C. L., Farrar, W. B., & Andersen, B. L. (2008). Delayed emotional recovery after taxane-based chemotherapy. *Cancer: Interdisciplinary International Journal of the American Cancer Society, 113*, 638–647.

Warren, M. (2010). Uncertainty, lack of control and emotional functioning in women with metastatic breast cancer: A review and secondary analysis of the literature using the critical appraisal technique. *European Journal of Cancer Care, 19*, 564–574.

Wills, T. A., & Bantum, E. O. C. (2012). Social support, self-regulation, and resilience in two populations: General-population adolescents and adult cancer survivors. *Journal of Social and Clinical Psychology, 31*, 568–592.

Winger, J. G., Adams, R. N., & Mosher, C. E. (2016). Relations of meaning in life and sense of coherence to distress in cancer patients: A meta-analysis. *Psycho-Oncology, 25*, 2–10.

Yanez, B., Thompson, E. H., & Stanton, A. L. (2011). Quality of life among Latina breast cancer patients: A systematic review of the literature. *Journal of Cancer Survivorship, 5*, 191–207.

Zebrack, B. J. (2011). Psychological, social, and behavioral issues for young adults with cancer. *Cancer, 117*, 2289-229.

CHAPTER

9

At the heart of meaning-making: an acceptance and commitment approach to developing adaptive meaning following acute cardiac events

Maja Bergman and Merle A. Keitel

Division of Psychological and Educational Services, Graduate School of Education, Fordham University at Lincoln Center, New York, NY, United States

With nearly 650,000 deaths annually, cardiovascular disease is the leading cause of death in the United States for both men and women. Each year, approximately 28 million Americans are diagnosed with heart disease and about one and a half million patients are discharged following an acute cardiac event such as myocardial infarction, unstable angina, or sudden cardiac arrest (Benjamin et al., 2018). While most investigative efforts concerning survivors of acute cardiac events have focused on physical outcomes and cognitive functioning, there is a growing body of research to suggest that these events greatly impact quality of life and well-being (e.g., Kronish, Edmondson, Goldfinger, Fei, & Horowitz, 2012; Vilchinsky, Ginzburg, Fait, & Foa, 2017).

Navigating Life Transitions for Meaning
DOI: https://doi.org/10.1016/B978-0-12-818849-1.00009-6

Adjustment after experiencing an acute cardiac event

Psychological distress

Since the inclusion of life-threatening illness as a traumatic event in the fourth edition of *The Diagnostic and Statistical Manual of Mental Disorders* (DSM; American Psychiatric Association, 2000), acute cardiac events have been identified as a potential trigger for posttraumatic stress disorder (PTSD). Following the fifth edition of the DSM (American Psychiatric Association, 2013) and its added qualifier that experiencing life-threatening illness is not necessarily considered a traumatic event that satisfies the criteria for a PTSD diagnosis, there has been much debate about whether symptoms of distress following acute cardiac events should be classified as adjustment disorder or PTSD. Although the authors of a recent review of the research concluded that the high rates of posttraumatic stress following acute cardiac events lent validity to cardiac-induced PTSD (CDI-PTSD) as a diagnosis (Vilchinsky et al., 2017), it has also been suggested that this disorder might have a specific presentation. While CDI-PTSD shares most of the characteristics of PTSD developed from other types of traumatic events, there also appear to be some unique features.

An Enduring Somatic Threat model of posttraumatic stress reactions following acute medical events has been proposed to describe differences between PTSD due to past discrete and external traumatic events (e.g., combat trauma) and PTSD derived from life-threatening medical conditions such as cardiovascular events that are internal and chronic/enduring in nature (Edmondson, 2014). Intrusive symptoms, for example, are often more future oriented, taking the form of intrusive thoughts and images about future medical procedures and feared cardiac events. Avoidance symptoms in illness-induced PTSD have been associated with poor treatment adherence as patients who are avoidant may fail to take medication or schedule follow-up visits and procedures that can remind them both of the event and the ongoing threat of their condition. Many of the reminders and cues related to the cardiac event are internal (e.g., changes in heart rate), however, and difficult to avoid. While treatments for PTSD typically focus on fear extinction and reducing hypervigilance, survivors of cardiac events are typically both required and encouraged to pay attention to somatic cues of cardiovascular activity. These internal cues can become part of a specific feedback loop as the fear responses and hyperarousal typically seen in PTSD patients include cardiovascular activation that for the CDI-PTSD patient then continue to activate threat-appraisals and further fear response/activation (Edmondson, 2014).

PTSD can be seen as the extreme end of a spectrum of posttraumatic reactions, and while most survivors of cardiac events will not go on to develop PTSD, up to a third of patients do, and many more endorse high degrees of posttraumatic stress, including symptoms of depression and anxiety (Agarwal et al., 2018; Edmondson et al., 2012). The consequences of psychological distress go beyond emotional suffering and loss of social and occupational functioning to include increased risk for future cardiac events and mortality (e.g., Edmondson et al., 2011; Kronish et al., 2012; Sumner et al., 2015).

Psychological well-being

In addition to the strong links that have been identified between psychological distress and cardiovascular risk, there is now a large body of research highlighting the relationship between psychological well-being and cardiovascular health (e.g., Boehm & Kubzansky, 2012; Kubzansky et al., 2018). How psychological well-being is defined continues to be the subject of much debate, however, and a review of psychological well-being following stressful life experiences in general as well as cardiac-specific events is somewhat complicated by two issues. For one, much of the research does not clearly make a distinction between the presence of positive outcomes and absence of negative ones, or which of these outcomes has a stronger relationship with subjective, physiological, or behavioral functioning and well-being. This presents a problem in the context of the increasing awareness that the absence of psychopathology does not equal psychological well-being (e.g., Keyes, 2005; Kubzansky et al., 2018). The second issue is that psychological well-being has been examined under a multitude of names (e.g., resilience, posttraumatic growth) within the broad framework of positive psychology. There is little consensus, however, regarding the contribution and role of these well-being factors for survivors of cardiac events.

Qualitative interviews with survivors have revealed that existential factors such as meaning and purpose are central themes (e.g., Fors, Dudas, & Ekman, 2014; Junehag, Asplund, & Svedlund, 2014), yet survivors are often left to navigate the emotional aftermath of their experience without much information or professional support (e.g., Tagney, James, & Albarran, 2003). In this chapter, we specifically examine the process of making meaning following survival of acute cardiac events. Meaning-making has been identified both as a component of psychological well-being (e.g., Kim, Sun, Park, Kubzansky, & Peterson, 2013) as well as a central aspect of transitioning into what many cardiac survivors describe as a "new normal" that, in addition to the sequelae of trauma, often includes managing symptoms of chronic health conditions and adhering to "heart-healthy" behavioral changes (e.g., Fors et al., 2014). We discuss meaning-making from a behavioral perspective, specifically acceptance and commitment therapy (ACT), and examine the role of psychological flexibility. Research has shown mixed results for psychotherapeutic interventions with respect to reduction in cardiac risk, with cognitive-behavioral approaches demonstrating greater efficacy than other approaches. It has been suggested that behavioral skills training aimed at reducing emotional reactivity might be of particular importance for the cardiovascular system (Gulliksson et al., 2011). In light of this we provide a rationale for and an illustration of ACT as applied to a case example.

Meaning-making and adjustment

Meaning in life (MIL) has a long history in the literature on psychological well-being, with aspects of meaning and meaning-making included in different models under terms such as "purpose," "sense of coherence," and "comprehension" (e.g., Antonovsky, 1987; Baumeister, 1991; Ryff, 1989; Steger, Oishi, & Kashdan, 2009). In an effort to increase cohesion in the meaning literature, an MIL model has been proposed that incorporates comprehension, purpose, and mattering to meet a definition of MIL as "the extent to which one's life is experienced as making sense, as being directed and motivated by valued goals, and as mattering in the world" (George & Park, 2016, p. 206). Investigations into the role of meaning in the adjustment and well-being of individuals following stressful events has, however, yielded mixed results. The shattering of assumptions and subsequent meaning-making following these events has been implicated as a mediator in the development and maintenance of posttraumatic stress symptoms (e.g., Janoff-Bulman, 1992; Park, 2010). However, the search for meaning has been found to not predict the presence of it (Steger, Kashdan, Sullivan, & Lorentz,2008). Whereas the presence of meaning has been linked to less distress and improved health for cardiac patients (Cohen, Mount, Tomas, & Mount, 1996; Kim et al., 2013; Motzer & Stewart, 1996), the search for meaning has been linked to increased psychological distress and neuroticism (e.g., Steger, Frazier, Oishi, & Kaler, 2006; Steger et al., 2008).

Global and situational meaning

It appears that the search for meaning is a common response to adverse events (e.g., Janoff-Bulman & Yopyk, 2004), that people engage in to various degrees, and with various rates of success in terms of meaning "found." A model of meaning-making has been proposed to explain this largely as a process of reducing discrepancies between global beliefs and goals and situational meaning through either assimilation or accommodation (Park & Folkman, 1997; Steger & Park, 2012). Global meaning refers to a person's internal organization of global beliefs, goals, and feelings into a coherent comprehension system. This global meaning is the basis for how individuals see themselves and their place in the world, as well as for how they interpret events and situations. This model suggests that the sequelae of highly stressful experiences are impacted by the degree to which they cause discrepancies between pretrauma global beliefs or "worldviews" and appraisals of a particular situation or event.

Global meaning can be disrupted following acute cardiac events as these often contradict previously held beliefs and assumptions. Not surprisingly, a sense of coherence was found to be the strongest predictor of quality of life in a sample of heart disease patients who had survived a cardiac arrest (Motzer & Stewart, 1996). Two different kinds of comprehension systems have been suggested to predict better outcomes following adverse experiences, one being a rigid but all-inclusive comprehension system such as "it's God's will." Such beliefs generally need little adjustment to new events; however, when such a broad comprehension system is shattered, it can be extremely devastating (Appel, Park, Wortmann, & van Schie, 2019; Park, 2012; Steger & Park, 2012). Furthermore, rigid pretrauma belief systems have been suggested to increase risk for PTSD, as positive ones are vulnerable to rupture and negative ones may be reinforced (e.g., Foa & Rothbaum, 2001). The second kind of comprehension system is a flexible one that supports resilience by being responsive to experience and feedback (Kashdan & Rottenberg, 2010; Steger & Park, 2012). A review of the literature concluded that meaning-making, when "resulting in adaptive made meanings," is related to better adjustment, that engagement in other forms is related to increased distress, and that "there are likely vast individual differences in these relationships" (Park, 2010, p. 293). As search for meaning is common following cardiac events (Fors et al., 2014; Fleury, Sedikides, & Lunsford, 2001; Rosenfeld & Gilkeson, 2000), interventions should target meaning-making behaviors with these findings in mind.

Meaning-making as behavior: a radical approach?

Most studies of meaning as a clinical phenomenon and target for interventions are based in humanistic and existential traditions (e.g., Frankl, 1985; Hoffman, 2009). This chapter focuses on *meaning-making* as a behavior. We are viewing behavior from the perspective of radical behaviorists who see private events such as thinking and feeling as behaviors. While this approach was pioneered by B. F. Skinner in 1961

(Schneider & Morris, 1987), it has been further developed by relational frame theory (RFT; Hayes, Barnes-Holmes, & Roche, 2001)—a comprehensive theory of language based on functional contextualism and focused on predicting and influencing verbal behavior. RFT centers around the premise that human language is learned through a particular operant conditioning process called arbitrarily applicable relational responding. Through this relational responding, which appears to be a uniquely human capacity, events and objects in our world take on verbal functions. These relational frames become the basis for how we make sense of the world and appraise the emotional significance of events and actions—which would conceptually correspond to our "global meaning system." From an RFT perspective, a sense of meaning and purpose develops from linking behavior to an overarching, inexhaustible goal that is of value for the individual (such as providing one's children with a supportive environment) within a hierarchical network of specific actions and goals (such as taking care of our own physical health). The purpose of this linking is that each action becomes reinforcing through engagement with the value it represents (Villatte, Villatte, & Hayes, 2015). For example, attending a doctor's appointment may not be considered pleasant but can be experienced as meaningful when it is clearly linked to an overarching goal of staying as healthy as possible to remain in one's children's lives. This type of meaning-making increases the likelihood that the parent will continue to engage in the behavior of attending doctor's appointments. While a full description of RFT is far beyond the scope of this chapter, we will describe its most prominent clinical application, ACT with its focus on psychological flexibility, and apply it to a case example later in the chapter.

Psychological flexibility and functional coherence

Psychological flexibility is the ability to respond to stimuli in a manner that is functional given a particular context, and that is congruent with personal values (Kashdan & Rottenberg, 2010). It has been solidly linked to both positive health outcomes and, in its negative form (i.e., psychological *in*flexibility), to psychopathology. [For reviews see Kashdan and Rottenberg (2010) and Whiting, Deane, Simpson, McLeod, and Ciarrochi(2017)]. Low psychological flexibility has been associated with greater posttraumatic stress symptom severity in multiple studies (e.g., Boykin, Anyanwu, Calvin, & Orcutt, 2019; Bryan, Ray-Sannerud, & Heron, 2015; Meyer et al., 2019). Psychological flexibility has also been negatively linked to distress and positively linked to quality of life in cancer patients, as well as to moderate the effect of their physical symptoms (McAteer & Gillanders, 2019).

While there is some overlap between psychological flexibility and processes that have been described to promote it, and different aspects of positive psychology, there are some considerable and important differences. Where positive psychology has traditionally focused on the presence of "positive" emotions and experiences, psychological flexibility research is based in the functional contextualist paradigm that emphasized that there are more or less *functional* behaviors and responses to situations and sensations. Functional, here, refers to how well it serves to increase behavior in line with long-term, valued goals. For example, behaviors such as avoidance can be highly effective in terms of reducing immediate distress, but if they end up creating further unwanted consequences they would not be considered functional. Similarly, the efforts to restore cohesion following stressful events can be successful without being very functional. For example, a survivor of childhood sexual abuse can conclude that she was entirely to blame for the abuse which may decrease discrepancy between global and situational meaning and thus decrease distress short-term, but this conclusion is likely to be detrimental to her sense of self and emotional health long-term.

When applied to processes of making sense of the world, the term *functional coherence* has been used to describe a flexible approach to meaning-making. Functional coherence focuses on what works in a particular context; by increasing attention to and tracking of actual experience, coherence is formed predominantly on the basis of *conditional* relational frames and responses can be chosen and engaged in more effectively with individual goals in mind (Villatte et al., 2015). Statements that indicate functional coherence often include conjunctions such as "if," or "when" and seemingly contradictory aspects can be held in mind. A statement exemplifying functional coherence might be "although I really value independence, I can accept help from others when tasks are too physically demanding." In this case, the act of accepting help serves the function of increasing independence long-term by refraining from activities in the short-term that negatively impact health.

In contrast, *essential coherence* refers to seeking a kind of absolute truth with symbolic equivalency and consistency to reduce discomforts of cognitive dissonance and incoherence. To achieve essential coherence, it is suggested that we must often ignore important aspects of our experiences in favor of defending simplified conceptualizations and descriptions. For example, people who see themselves as "healthy" might ignore early signs of heart disease, as they believe that this could not apply to them. Similarly, *social coherence* refers to an abandonment of personal experience in favor of rigid rules and conceptualizations that are socially reinforced (Villatte et al., 2015). An example of social coherence for a person who prefers not to work out might be "I should exercise because the doctor told me to." Although this might seem like a good enough reason to exercise, this is unlikely to be motivating in the moment as the potential reinforcer (doctor) is not in close proximity of the actual activity. Furthermore, any failure to do so might lead to avoidance of going to the doctor.

Using acceptance and commitment therapy to increase adaptive meaning-making

Psychological flexibility has been well studied in the context of ACT which centers around the premise that psychological health and well-being is largely a function of psychological flexibility, and that psychological distress is maintained and increased by experiential avoidance and overreliance on rigid rules and limited behavioral repertoires. ACT is a transdiagnostic psychological treatment and behavioral change method that deploys a set of evidence-based processes to increase psychological flexibility in the service of increased vitality and pursuit of valued goals. The idea that engagement in meaningful activities and emotional range is a cornerstone of psychological well-being has been long argued in existential and humanistic therapies (e.g., Frankl, 1985; Hoffman, 2009).

ACT has a solid research foundation of core processes and over 300 RCTs have been conducted to test its effectiveness. ACT has been found effective in the treatment of a wide range of health conditions such as chronic pain (for review see Hann & McCracken, 2014), epilepsy (Lundgren, Dahl, & Hayes, 2008), cancer (e.g., Feros, Lane, Ciarrochi, & Blackledge, 2013), and fibromyalgia (Wicksell et al., 2013). Although large-scale, controlled trials of ACT for PTSD are still limited, there are good preliminary findings (see Bean, Ong, Lee, & Twohig, 2017) and ACT has been shown to be as good or better than standard treatments for mental health conditions such as anxiety (including health anxiety) and depression (see Twohig & Levin, 2017), as well as for behavioral change interventions such as smoking cessation, weight loss, and increased physical activity (e.g., Brown, Lejuez, Kahler, Strong, & Zvolensky, 2005; Butryn, Forman, Hoffman, Shaw, & Juarascio, 2011; Lee, An, Levin, & Twohig, 2015; McClure, Bricker, Mull, & Heffner, 2018). Acceptance and mindfulness-based therapies also have been successful in reducing long-term disability in high-risk medical populations (Dahl, Wilson, & Nilsson, 2004),treating relationship distress in the context of medical concerns (Fischer, Baucom, & Cohen, 2016) and reducing distress for cancer survivors as they transition back to work (Arch & Mitchell, 2016).

This broad evidence base including both promotion of health behaviors and improvements in psychological well-being lends support for ACT as a promising intervention for survivors of acute cardiac events.

Through the use of interventions targeted at acceptance, values exploration, flexible perspective taking and committed action, adaptive meaning-making can be targeted and supported through a multidimensional approach that harnesses the healing power of meaning and purpose while reducing the rumination and adherence to rigid conceptualizations of meaning associated with increased distress and poor adjustment.

Core processes

Six core processes associated with psychological flexibility have been identified through systematic research. These six core processes are interrelated, and typically presented in the ACT "hexaflex." The six core processes and how they relate to the process of meaning-making are described below.

Acceptance

In ACT, acceptance is generally defined as a willingness to experience difficult private experiences (thoughts, emotions, memories) in the service of valued action (Hayes, Strosahl, & Wilson, 2012). The opposite of acceptance is experiential avoidance. Acceptance is not a goal in ACT, but rather a process and method to increase engagement in committed action toward valued goals. Acceptance has been identified with positive outcomes for women with heart disease who were seeking meaning (Fleury et al., 2001; Rosenfeld & Gilkeson, 2000). Suppression of emotion has been linked to decreased emotional coherence (Dan-Glauser & Gross, 2013) while acceptance has been linked to increased MIL over time for patients with congestive heart failure (Park, Malone, Suresh, Bliss, & Rosen, 2008). Furthermore, acceptance has been found predictive of emotional well-being and physical functioning among cardiac patients (Karademas & Hondronikola, 2010). When formulated as distress tolerance, acceptance has also been mentioned as an important aspect of adhering to heart-healthy behaviors such as smoking cessation (Brown et al., 2005), diet, and physical activity (e.g., Butryn et al., 2011; Falk, Bisogni, & Sobal, 2000).

Present moment awareness/mindfulness

In ACT, being present means being aware and actively experiencing what is happening without trying to predict, change, or make judgments about the experience. Mindfulness practice and nonjudgmental acceptance has been found to decrease posttraumatic hyperarousal symptoms (Chopko & Schwartz, 2013), and different mindfulness-based therapies have been found effective with cardiac populations in terms of reducing perceived stress and psychopathology. Although mixed findings have been reported, there are some empirical evidence of mindfulness reducing blood pressure, symptoms of chronic heart failure, and mental fatigue (e.g., Abbott et al., 2014; Momeni, Omidi, Raygan, & Akbari, 2016; Sullivan et al., 2009).

Defusion

Cognitive defusion refers to the ability to separate oneself from one's thoughts, to see "thoughts as thoughts" rather than as truth. Unlike cognitive interventions used in traditional CBT therapies, defusion interventions are intended to change how an individual reacts to or interacts with their thoughts and feelings rather than the content of the thoughts and feelings. Defusion techniques aim to change the function of thoughts and help clients hold contradictions in experience more easily. It has been suggested defusion can aid adaptive meaning-making by reducing the impact of discrepancies of meaning (Steger & Park, 2012).

Self-as-context

The self-as-context process, sometimes known as the transcendent self or the "observing self," refers to the concept that an individual is more than her experiences, thoughts, or emotions—that we are not what happens to us, but rather the ones experiencing what happens to us (e.g., Hayes et al., 2012). Self-as-content, on the other hand, refers to the conceptualized self that is made up of the elaborate, descriptive and evaluative relational frames we have constructed based on our history (I'm shy, I'm a good/bad mother, I'm a tough guy). While these descriptions are based on past behavior and experiences, they can become rigid when future behavior is guided by them in order to maintain coherence. Self-as-context work is targeted at developing flexible perspective taking and a stable sense of self from which meaning can be experienced.

Values

Perhaps the most obviously overlapping process between ACT and the MIL literature lies in what ACT calls values—the qualities and ideals that each person believes in and that we find fulfillment in when we choose to work toward them and uphold them in our lives. In ACT, therapists assist clients in applying techniques that help them live their lives according to the values they have identified as central. The values work in ACT is closely linked to the literature on purpose and the experience of being guided and motivated by valued life goals; a sense of striving toward which has been linked to increased well-being (e.g., Sheldon & Elliot, 1999). Values and goals are, however, not synonymous. ACT and RFT suggest that values be positively stated such that specific goals can be tied to them and committed action taken.

Committed action

In ACT, committed action refers very specifically to "a values-based action that occurs at a particular moment in time and that is deliberately linked to creating a pattern of action that serves the value" (Hayes et al., 2012, p. 328). At the core, ACT is a behavioral therapy—the goal of which is behavioral change. Behavioral changes associated with improved physical health have been found to be more likely and more sustainable when they are personally meaningful and freely chosen (e.g., Anderson, Funnel, & Arnold, 2002). Purpose and meaning function both as motivators for behavior, as well as arise as a result of behavior. For example, purposiveness has been linked to increased physical activity in cardiac patients, which in turn has predicted increased subjective health and meaning (e.g., Holahan, Holahan, & Suzuki, 2008). Perceived interference with attainment of personal goals has been associated with reduced quality of life in patients following coronary angioplasty procedures (Echteld, van Elderen, & van der Kamp, 2003).

Vignette

Jenny is a 36-year-old married woman with two children aged 5 and 8. Eight months ago Jenny suffered a sudden cardiac arrest (SCA) as she was cleaning up after dinner. Jenny's husband found her unresponsive in the kitchen, called 911, and delivered CPR until paramedics arrived. Jenny's heart was in ventricular fibrillation, a condition where the heart is quivering rather than pumping blood. Her heart function resumed after three defibrillator shocks and she was transported to the nearest hospital where she was placed in an induced coma for 3 days with her body temperature reduced in an effort to preserve brain and cardiac functioning. Upon awakening, Jenny had no memory of the week prior to her cardiac arrest and she struggled greatly with short-term memory, needing to be told repeatedly what had happened during the first days. Jenny had no identified health problems before her SCA; she was of normal weight and exercised regularly. After a series of tests, including invasive procedures such as a catheterization for an angiogram, she was diagnosed with Long QT Syndrome (LQTS)—a genetic disorder that often goes undetected but can lead to sudden cardiac death. While there is no cure for LQTS, Jenny was fitted with an internal defibrillator (ICD) before she left the hospital. Although she began to feel better after a few days in the hospital, she remained concerned about her husband and children who were very distressed about her SCA. Jenny reported enormous gratitude that she survived, as she had learned how rare this was, and she initially felt reassured by the insertion of the ICD. After returning home, however, Jenny grew increasingly concerned that it would happen again. She stated that her husband coped by talking a lot about the event, describing what had happened in great detail. As Jenny had no memories of the event, it seemed unreal and she did not want to talk about it. Despite feeling very tired, she tried to "return to normal for the children's sake." As time went on, however, Jenny started avoiding time with her family as it would provoke painful thoughts about how her death would hurt them and feelings of guilt. She reported thinking about the event "constantly." Jenny also became hypervigilant to any physical symptoms of cardiovascular activity such as changes in heart rate or feeling light headed and she avoided all forms of exercise. After canceling multiple follow-up appointments with her cardiologist, Jenny was referred for counseling.

Jenny's search for meaning

When Jenny started therapy she displayed many of the typical reactions to trauma. The SCA had shattered her assumptions of safety built on an assumption of control, the echoes of which could be found in statements such as "I was healthy, I was taking care of myself, this wasn't supposed to happen," as well as in her continued fear. She was desperately trying to hold on to previously made meaning, which resulted in rigidity in her self-concept. She displayed self-as-content views, including frequent insistence that she wasn't herself anymore, that this person who was "always tired," struggled with concentration, and was "such a coward" was not actually her. Jenny had made sense of her world largely in accord with the dominant cultural perspective that "good things happen to good people" and that she had made her way in the world by being a hard worker and a "doer." She had found meaning through her role as a "good" mother, wife, friend, and employee, but she was fused with rigid rules about what that meant. Jenny reported that she felt broken and "completely stuck" trying to figure out why this had happened to her. She reported that she often couldn't sleep at night, trying to figure out how to "just be grateful and get over it."

Receiving a diagnosis of a life-threatening illness has been found to commonly challenge assumptions of mastery, meaning, and self-worth (Janoff-Bulman, 1992), which was evident in Jenny's case. She was clearly struggling with the massive trauma she had experienced, as well as with adjusting to her diagnosis. The meaning aspect was particularly salient for Jenny, and an area where she expressed a desire for help to get "unstuck." Her therapist, however, also worked from the assumption that these domains are related and that adaptive meaning-making would both influence and be influenced by self-concepts and agency, and she worked together with Jenny to increase flexibility and move from a search for an "essential truth" toward a more functional coherence.

Values clarification

When first asked about what she valued in life, Jenny would state "being a good mother," "being healthy," and "having a good life." While these were somewhat informative as to areas that mattered, they were rather vague. To aid in clarifying Jenny's values, her therapist used a variety of techniques anchored in RFT. One approach when exploring values in ACT is to extract meaning from pain. By exploring what hurts we can use opposition framing to find what matters. Rather than just ask "what is important to you," Jenny's therapist used reports of pain and tearful moments to help identify an overarching value of "being available to offer love, support, and guidance to my children" as one of Jenny's most important values. For Jenny, this was the value that made the thought of dying the most painful, that made "being healthy" truly matter. The problem with "being healthy" was of course that it was largely out of Jenny's control. Together with her therapist, Jenny reframed this value to make "staying as healthy as possible" and "living longer" as goals to strive toward in the service of the larger value of being present for her daughters in a loving, supporting, and guiding manner. Jenny and her therapist began to identify actions that she could take toward realizing these values. While doing this, Jenny also began to expand her appraisal of the cardiac arrest as an opportunity to model resilience to her daughters.

Committed action

As Jenny had identified the qualities of action that she wished to embody, her therapist helped her explore concrete steps that she could take. When doing this, Jenny's therapist made sure to identify a broad set of actions requiring a varying amount of time and effort so that Jenny had a choice of many actions serving a few functions. For example, Jenny's goal of staying as healthy as possible included actions such as exercise—which could take the form of going to the gym, but also taking a walk or going for a bike ride with her family. As engagement in physical activity was something that triggered unpleasant sensations and difficult feelings such as fear, Jenny had felt very unmotivated to take these actions. By strengthening the relational frame between the actions and the function they served, she came into closer contact with their meaning and engagement became more rewarding.

Acceptance

Jenny had grown up with a mother who struggled with addiction, and Jenny had coped with the unpredictable caregiving and overwhelming feelings she experienced as a child by never asking for help.

She had developed different strategies to avoid feeling such as "day-dreaming" and "not thinking about it." As a child, this had been functional as it had helped her survive when no other options were available. However, by continuing to avoid her distressing feelings, Jenny did not realize that they were safe to experience as an adult. Her attempts to avoid activities and situations that would bring up thoughts about her cardiac arrest or the realities of living with LQTS were moving her further away from things that mattered to her. In fact, the dissociative strategies that helped her before now increased her distress by decreasing contact with her experiences and added to a sense of confusion and lack of cohesion. In the short-term, "pretending I don't even have this thing, like it never really happened," was very effective in reducing her distress. However, she also described experiencing moments of "just feeling panicky, like out of the blue."

When exploring what it would mean to accept the SCA and her diagnosis, Jenny's therapist made sure to explain that acceptance was not the same as liking it, and Jenny described fear that the feelings that might arise would overwhelm her such that she would "not be able to function." With the painful consequences of her previous strategies more clearly defined the therapist asked if Jenny thought she would be willing to open up to her feelings in session and see what happened. When talking about the SCA and the lack of control she had felt, Jenny became very tearful, but also learned that she could be emotional without "falling apart" and that she was able to "function" afterward. Jenny learned that accepting rather than avoiding her feelings made it possible for her to engage in meaningful activities since she was less dictated by automatic responses. As she accepted unpleasant emotions and events as part of her reality, she also learned that as an adult she now had the power to respond to these in effective ways, such as asking for help from her husband. As she began to engage with her husband in new ways that allowed for more vulnerability, Jenny experienced greater intimacy with him.

Present moment awareness

When Jenny first came to therapy, she was dominated by past experiences and fear of future events, and she had little contact with the present. Jenny's therapist utilized various mindfulness exercises to practice nonjudgmental noticing and worked toward Jenny tolerating regular symptoms of arousal and discriminating these from cardiac symptoms. As Jenny's willingness to experience her full range of emotions increased, she also worked to identify these as they arose and make sense of them. Jenny, like many trauma survivors, developed a strong symbolic relationship between "feeling afraid" and "danger," which created some challenges for her. It is highly functional to remove oneself from life-threatening situations; however, when Jenny became fearful, she would escape from situations and activities intended to keep her safe such as doctor's appointments or exercise. Through the use of mindfulness interventions, as well as tracking during exposures, Jenny learned to attend to somatic cues of fear and comprehend them in the context in which they appeared. She could experience her emotions as "making sense," and thus reduce the influence of the symbolic relationship between fear and danger.

Self-as-context

The therapist worked with Jenny to develop more flexible perspective taking and a stable sense of self. Jenny initially had a very difficult time holding opposing ideas and experiences at once. For example, she held the belief that she had to feel only gratitude at all times, and that momentary experiences of not feeling grateful defined her as a not-grateful person. Through therapy, she learned that it was possible to grieve the loss of the life she had before while also feeling grateful for surviving and that there was a stable, "transcendent" self to experience these thoughts and emotions without being defined by them. Through a long history of practice, Jenny had become "a master of silver linings," something that on the surface looked like a successful strategy for coping with adversity, but was based in a symbolic equivalence between vulnerability and rejection developed in childhood when expressions of sadness or discontent were met with abandonment. Rigid adherence to rules such as "never bother other people with your feelings," meant Jenny rarely shared negative feelings. New experiences in therapy, but especially through exposure in her everyday life, taught Jenny that expressing sadness could also lead to increased support and understanding from others, and that showing vulnerability could be experienced as meaningful even when she could not be certain of the outcome.

Conclusion

Despite what is now a significant body of research highlighting both the impact of psychological distress and well-being on cardiovascular health and the centrality of existential questions concerning meaning and purpose for survivors of acute cardiac events, little has been translated into general practice. Inspiration for this chapter has come in part from the experience of one of the authors following such an event, and the lack of professional support to address the emotional sequelae. Suggested here is an idiographic approach that can meet a range of needs among survivors by targeting core processes to increase psychological flexibility. Jenny's narrative of her cardiac arrest changed over the course of treatment in ways that indicated increased flexibility. She had an increased ability to hold opposing experiences at once, such as seeing positive aspects that had come out of her experience without denying pain that it had inflicted on her and her family. Toward the end of such a treatment we might expect conclusions such as "I don't know why this happened, and in some ways it still feels very unfair, but that's how life is... I guess I don't feel that same need anymore, to figure that out. Now I feel like the best I can do is to live my life the way I want to while I can. Some days that's still really hard."

A more traditional CBT approach might be to challenge painful thoughts, such as perhaps whether her children would be "scarred for life" by the early loss of their mother through examples of children recovering well from parental loss. The ACT therapist would rather respond with validation of that thought and the pain as making sense, and then move toward exploring how the client would like to respond to it. While there might be some comfort in reappraising a situation to a more palatable one, and there is room in ACT to expand relational frames in this verbal way, one risk is that we instead strengthen them through engagement in an internal debate with them. It is possible that a more effective approach is to work to accept painful feelings—even lean into them—to find the purpose and meaning that makes living worth the pain that inevitably comes along with life and love.

References

Abbott, R. A., Whear, R., Rodgers, L. R., Bethel, A., Coon, J. T., Kuyken, W., ... Dickens, C. (2014). Effectiveness of mindfulness-based stress reduction and mindfulness based cognitive therapy in vascular disease: A systematic review and meta-analysis of randomised controlled trials. *Journal of Psychosomatic Research, 76*(5), 341–351.

Agarwal, S., Presciutti, A., Verma, J., Pavol, M. A., Anbarasan, D., Brodie, D., ... Stern, Y. (2018). Women have worse cognitive, functional, and psychiatric outcomes at hospital discharge after cardiac arrest. *Resuscitation, 125*, 12–15.

American Psychiatric Association. (2000). *Diagnostic and statistical manual of mental disorders* (4th ed., text revision). Washington, DC: American Psychiatric Association.

American Psychiatric Association. (2013). *Diagnostic and statistical manual of mental disorders* (5th ed.). Washington, DC: American Psychiatric Association.

Anderson, R., Funnel, M., & Arnold, M. (2002). Using the empowerment approach to help patients change behavior. *Practical Psychology for Diabetes Clinicians, 2*, 3–12.

Antonovsky, A. (1987). *Unraveling the mystery of health: How people manage stress and stay well*. San Francisco, CA: Jossey-Bass.

Appel, J. E., Park, C. L., Wortmann, J. H., & van Schie, H. T. (2019). Meaning violations, religious/spiritual struggles, and meaning in life in the face of stressful life events. *The International Journal for the Psychology of Religion*, 1–17.

Arch, J. J., & Mitchell, J. L. (2016). An Acceptance and Commitment Therapy (ACT) group intervention for cancer survivors experiencing anxiety at re-entry. *Psycho-Oncology, 25* (5), 610–615.

Baumeister, R. F. (1991). *Meanings of life*. New York, NY: Guilford Press.

Bean, R. C., Ong, C. W., Lee, J., & Twohig, M. P. (2017). Acceptance and commitment therapy for PTSD and trauma: An empirical review. *The Behavior Therapist, 40*(4), 145–150.

Benjamin, E. J., Virani, S. S., Callaway, C. W., Chamberlain, A. M., Chang, A. R., Cheng, S., ... de Ferranti, S. D. (2018). Heart disease and stroke statistics-2018 update: A report from the American Heart Association. *Circulation, 137*(12), e67.

Boehm, J. K., & Kubzansky, L. D. (2012). The heart's content: The association between positive psychological well-being and cardiovascular health. *Psychological Bulletin, 138*(4), 655.

Boykin, D. M., Anyanwu, J., Calvin, K., & Orcutt, H. K. (2019). The moderating effect of psychological flexibility on event centrality in determining trauma outcomes. *Psychological Trauma: Theory, Research, Practice and Policy, 12*(2), 193–199.

Brown, R. A., Lejuez, C. W., Kahler, C. W., Strong, D. R., & Zvolensky, M. J. (2005). Distress tolerance and early smoking lapse. *Clinical Psychology Review, 25*(6), 713–733.

Bryan, C. J., Ray-Sannerud, B., & Heron, E. A. (2015). Psychological flexibility as a dimension of resilience for posttraumatic stress, depression, and risk for suicidal ideation among Air Force personnel. *Journal of Contextual Behavioral Science, 4*(4), 263–268.

Butryn, M. L., Forman, E., Hoffman, K., Shaw, J., & Juarascio, A. (2011). A pilot study of acceptance and commitment therapy for promotion of physical activity. *Journal of Physical Activity and Health, 8*(4), 516–522.

Chopko, B. A., & Schwartz, R. C. (2013). The relation between mindfulness and posttraumatic stress symptoms among police officers. *Journal of Loss and Trauma, 18*(1), 1–9.

Cohen, S. R., Mount, B. M., Tomas, J. J., & Mount, L. F. (1996). Existential well-being is an important determinant of quality of life: Evidence from the McGill quality of life questionnaire. *Cancer: Interdisciplinary International Journal of the American Cancer Society, 77* (3), 576–586.

Dahl, J., Wilson, K. G., & Nilsson, A. (2004). Acceptance and commitment therapy and the treatment of persons at risk for long-term disability resulting from stress and pain symptoms: A preliminary randomized trial. *Behavior Therapy, 35*(4), 785–801.

Dan-Glauser, E. S., & Gross, J. J. (2013). Emotion regulation and emotion coherence: Evidence for strategy-specific effects. *Emotion, 13*(5), 832.

Echteld, M. A., van Elderen, T., & van der Kamp, L. J. T. (2003). Modeling predictors of quality of life after coronary angioplasty. *Annals of Behavioral Medicine, 26*(1), 49–60.

Edmondson, D. (2014). An enduring somatic threat model of posttraumatic stress disorder due to acute life-threatening medical events. *Social and Personality Psychology Compass, 8* (3), 118–134.

Edmondson, D., Richardson, S., Falzon, L., Davidson, K. W., Mills, M. A., & Neria, Y. (2012). Posttraumatic stress disorder prevalence and risk of recurrence in acute coronary syndrome patients: A meta-analytic review. *PloS One, 7*(6), e38915.

Edmondson, D., Rieckmann, N., Shaffer, J. A., Schwartz, J. E., Burg, M. M., Davidson, K. W., ... Kronish, I. M. (2011). Posttraumatic stress due to an acute coronary syndrome increases risk of 42-month major adverse cardiac events and all-cause mortality. *Journal of Psychiatric Research, 45*(12), 1621–1626.

Falk, L. W., Bisogni, C. A., & Sobal, J. (2000). Personal, social, and situational influences associated with dietary experiences of participants in an intensive heart program. *Journal of Nutrition Education, 32*(5), 251–260.

Fischer, M. S., Baucom, D. H., & Cohen, M. J. (2016). Cognitive-behavioral couple therapies: Review of the evidence for the treatment of relationship distress, psychopathology, and chronic health conditions. *Family Process, 55*(3), 423–442.

Feros, D. L., Lane, L., Ciarrochi, J., & Blackledge, J. T. (2013). Acceptance and Commitment Therapy (ACT) for improving the lives of cancer patients: A preliminary study. *Psycho-oncology, 22*(2), 459–464.

Fleury, J., Sedikides, C., & Lunsford, V. (2001). Women's experience following a cardiac event: The role of the self in healing. *Journal of Cardiovascular Nursing, 15*(3), 71–82.

Foa, E. B., & Rothbaum, B. O. (2001). *Treating the trauma of rape: Cognitive-behavioral therapy for PTSD*. New York: Guilford.

Fors, A., Dudas, K., & Ekman, I. (2014). Life is lived forwards and understood backwards—Experiences of being affected by acute coronary syndrome: A narrative analysis. *International Journal of Nursing Studies, 51*(3), 430–437.

Frankl, V. E. (1985). *Man's search for meaning*. New York: Simon & Schuster.

George, L. S., & Park, C. L. (2016). Meaning in life as comprehension, purpose, and mattering: Toward integration and new research questions. *Review of General Psychology, 20*(3), 205–220.

Gulliksson, M., Burell, G., Vessby, B., Lundin, L., Toss, H., & Svärdsudd, K. (2011). Randomized controlled trial of cognitive behavioral therapy vs standard treatment to prevent recurrent cardiovascular events in patients with coronary heart disease: Secondary Prevention in Uppsala Primary Health Care project (SUPRIM). *Archives of Internal Medicine, 171*(2), 134–140.

Hann, K., & McCracken, L. (2014). A systematic review of randomized controlled trials of Acceptance and Commitment Therapy for adults with chronic pain: Outcome domains, design quality and efficacy. *Journal of Contextual Behavioral Science, 3*(4), 217–227.

Hayes, S. C., Barnes-Holmes, D., & Roche, B. (Eds.), (2001). *Relational frame theory: A post-Skinnerian account of human language and cognition*. New York: Plenum.

Hayes, S. C., Strosahl, K. D., & Wilson, K. G. (2012). *Acceptance and commitment therapy: The process and practice of mindful change* (2nd ed.). New York: The Guilford Press.

Hoffman, L. (2009). Introduction to existential psychology in a cross-cultural context: An east-west dialogue. In L. Hoffman, M. Yang, F. J. Kaklauskas, & A. Chan (Eds.), *Existential psychology east-west* (pp. 1–67). Colorado Springs, CO: University of the Rockies Press.

Holahan, C. K., Holahan, C. J., & Suzuki, R. (2008). Purposiveness, physical activity, and perceived health in cardiac patients. *Disability and Rehabilitation, 30*(23), 1772–1778.

Janoff-Bulman, R. (1992). *Shattered assumptions*. New York: Free Press.

Janoff-Bulman, R., & Yopyk, D. J. (2004). Random outcomes and valued commitments: Existential dilemmas and the paradox of meaning. In J. Greenberg, S. L. Koole, & T. Pyszczynski (Eds.), *Handbook of experimental existential psychology* (pp. 122–140). New York: Guilford.

Junehag, L., Asplund, K., & Svedlund, M. (2014). A qualitative study: Perceptions of the psychosocial consequences and access to support after an acute myocardial infarction. *Intensive and Critical Care Nursing, 30*(1), 22–30.

Karademas, E. C., & Hondronikola, I. (2010). The impact of illness acceptance and helplessness to subjective health, and their stability over time: A prospective study in a sample of cardiac patients. *Psychology, Health & Medicine, 15*(3), 336–346.

Kashdan, T. B., & Rottenberg, J. (2010). Psychological flexibility as a fundamental aspect of health. *Clinical Psychology Review, 30*(7), 865–878.

Keyes, C. L. (2005). Mental illness and/or mental health? Investigating axioms of the complete state model of health. *Journal of Consulting and Clinical Psychology, 73*(3), 539.

Kim, E. S., Sun, J. K., Park, N., Kubzansky, L. D., & Peterson, C. (2013). Purpose in life and reduced risk of myocardial infarction among older US adults with coronary heart disease: a two-year follow-up. *Journal of Behavioral Medicine, 36*(2), 124–133.

Kronish, I. M., Edmondson, D., Goldfinger, J. Z., Fei, K., & Horowitz, C. R. (2012). Posttraumatic stress disorder and adherence to medications in survivors of strokes and transient ischemic attacks. *Stroke, 43*(8), 2192–2197.

Kubzansky, L. D., Huffman, J. C., Boehm, J. K., Hernandez, R., Kim, E. S., Koga, H. K., ... Labarthe, D. R. (2018). Positive psychological well-being and cardiovascular disease: JACC health promotion series. *Journal of the American College of Cardiology, 72*(12), 1382–1396.

Lee, E. B., An, W., Levin, M. E., & Twohig, M. P. (2015). An initial meta-analysis of Acceptance and Commitment Therapy for treating substance use disorders. *Drug and Alcohol Dependence, 155*, 1–7.

Lundgren, T., Dahl, J., & Hayes, S. C. (2008). Evaluation of mediators of change in the treatment of epilepsy with acceptance and commitment therapy. *Journal of Behavioral Medicine, 31*(3), 225–235.

McAteer, G., & Gillanders, D. (2019). Investigating the role of psychological flexibility, masculine self-esteem and stoicism as predictors of psychological distress and quality of life in men living with prostate cancer. *European journal of cancer care, 28*(4), e13097.

McClure, J. B., Bricker, J., Mull, K., & Heffner, J. L. (2018). Comparative effectiveness of group-delivered acceptance and commitment therapy versus cognitive behavioral therapy for smoking cessation: A randomized controlled trial. *Nicotine & Tobacco Research, 22*(3), 354–362.

Meyer, E. C., La Bash, H., DeBeer, B. B., Kimbrel, N. A., Gulliver, S. B., & Morissette, S. B. (2019). Psychological inflexibility predicts PTSD symptom severity in war veterans after accounting for established PTSD risk factors and personality. *Psychological Trauma: Theory, Research, Practice, and Policy, 11*(4), 383.

Momeni, J., Omidi, A., Raygan, F., & Akbari, H. (2016). The effects of mindfulness-based stress reduction on cardiac patients' blood pressure, perceived stress, and anger: A single-blind randomized controlled trial. *Journal of the American Society of Hypertension, 10*(10), 763–771.

Motzer, S. U., & Stewart, B. J. (1996). Sense of coherence as a predictor of quality of life in persons with coronary heart disease surviving cardiac arrest. *Research in Nursing & Health, 19*(4), 287–298.

Park, C. L. (2010). Making sense of the meaning literature: An integrative review of meaning making and its effects on adjustment to stressful life events. *Psychological Bulletin, 136*(2), 257.

Park, C. L. (2012). Meaning, spirituality, and growth: Protective and resilience factors in health and illness. In A. Baum, T. A. Revenson, & J. Singer (Eds.), *Handbook of health psychology* (pp. 405–429). New York: Psychology Press.

Park, C. L., & Folkman, S. (1997). Meaning in the context of stress and coping. *Review of General Psychology, 1*(2), 115–144.

Park, C. L., Malone, M. R., Suresh, D. P., Bliss, D., & Rosen, R. I. (2008). Coping, meaning in life, and quality of life in congestive heart failure patients. *Quality of Life Research, 17* (1), 21–26.

Rosenfeld, A. G., & Gilkeson, J. (2000). Meaning of illness for women with coronary heart disease. *Heart & Lung, 29*(2), 105–112.

Ryff, C. D. (1989). Happiness is everything, or is it? Explorations on the meaning of psychological well-being. *Journal of Personality and Social Psychology, 57*(6), 1069–1081.

Schneider, S. M., & Morris, E. K. (1987). A history of the term *Radical Behaviorism*: From Watson to Skinner. *The Behavior Analyst, 10*(1), 27–39.

Sheldon, K., & Elliot, A. (1999). Goal striving, need-satisfaction, and longitudinal well-being: The self-concordance model. *Journal of Personality and Social Psychology, 76*, 482–497.

Steger, M. F., Frazier, P., Oishi, S., & Kaler, M. (2006). The meaning in life questionnaire: Assessing the presence of and search for meaning in life. *Journal of Counseling Psychology, 53*(1), 80–93.

Steger, M. F., Kashdan, T. B., Sullivan, B. A., & Lorentz, D. (2008). Understanding the search for meaning in life: Personality, cognitive style, and the dynamic between seeking and experiencing meaning. *Journal of Personality, 76*(2), 199–228.

Steger, M. F., Oishi, S., & Kashdan, T. B. (2009). Meaning in life across the life span: Levels and correlates of meaning in life from emerging adulthood to older adulthood. *The Journal of Positive Psychology, 4*(1), 43–52.

Steger, M. F., & Park, C. L. (2012). The creation of meaning following trauma: Meaning making and trajectories of distress and recovery. In R. A. McMackin, E. Newman, J. M. Fogler, & T. M. Keane (Eds.), *Trauma therapy in context: The science and craft of evidence-based practice* (pp. 171–191). Washington, DC: American Psychological Association.

Sullivan, M. J., Wood, L., Terry, J., Brantley, J., Charles, A., McGee, V., ... Adams, K. (2009). The Support, Education, and Research in Chronic Heart Failure Study (SEARCH): A mindfulness-based psychoeducational intervention improves depression and clinical symptoms in patients with chronic heart failure. *American Heart Journal, 157*(1), 84–90.

Sumner, J. A., Kubzansky, L. D., Elkind, M. S., Roberts, A. L., Agnew-Blais, J., Chen, Q., ... Suglia, S. F. (2015). Trauma exposure and posttraumatic stress disorder symptoms predict onset of cardiovascular events in women. *Circulation, 132*(4), 251–259.

Tagney, J., James, J. E., & Albarran, J. W. (2003). Exploring the patient's experiences of learning to live with an implantable cardioverter defibrillator (ICD) from one UK centre: A qualitative study. *European Journal of Cardiovascular Nursing, 2*(3), 195–203.

Twohig, M. P., & Levin, M. E. (2017). Acceptance and commitment therapy as a treatment for anxiety and depression: A review. *Psychiatric Clinics, 40*(4), 751–770.

Vilchinsky, N., Ginzburg, K., Fait, K., & Foa, E. B. (2017). Cardiac-disease-induced PTSD (CDI-PTSD): A systematic review. *Clinical Psychology Review, 55*, 92–106.

Villatte, M., Villatte, J. L., & Hayes, S. C. (2015). *Mastering the clinical conversation: Language as intervention*. New York: Guilford.

Wicksell, R. K., Kemani, M., Jensen, K., Kosek, E., Kadetoff, D., Sorjonen, K., ... Olsson, G. L. (2013). Acceptance and commitment therapy for fibromyalgia: A randomized controlled trial. *European Journal of Pain, 17*(4), 599–611.

Whiting, D. L., Deane, F. P., Simpson, G. K., McLeod, H. J., & Ciarrochi, J. (2017). Cognitive and psychological flexibility after a traumatic brain injury and the implications for treatment in acceptance-based therapies: A conceptual review. *Neuropsychological Rehabilitation, 27*(2), 263–299.

PART 5

Conclusions

CHAPTER

10

Finding and creating meaning in life during reversals and revisions

Elizabeth M. Altmaier

Department of Psychological and Quantitative Foundations, College of Education, University of Iowa, Iowa City, IA, United States

Our lives contain many transitions. The authors in this text analyzed a sample of transitions from among discernable types. The text considered transitions of *development*, including life stage; within developmental transitions are identity transitions, which intersect with life stage transitions. Transitions of *role*, including work role and social role, were examined. Finally, transitions within *health*, including chronic illness and cancer survivorship, were evaluated. Each of these transitions have the potential to challenge individuals' meaning in life since the transitions affected or altered aspects of life that significantly influence both global and situational meaning. This chapter will consider six challenges to meaning in life posed by transitions: physiological changes, disruption of norms, overreliance on social network for validation, stressful autonomy, psychosocial vulnerability, and biographical disruption.

Before considering transitions in more detail, it is important to return to the definition of meaning in life. As was noted in Altmaier (in press), *meaning in life* poses definitional difficulties. An individual's response to an item stem of "My life is meaningful" is a subjective appraisal that fails to provide specificity regarding the bases on which people make these judgments. Recent models (see George & Park, 2017; Martela & Steger, 2016) have advanced the study of meaning in life by recommending its multidimensionality, usually composed as appraisals of

Navigating Life Transitions for Meaning
DOI: https://doi.org/10.1016/B978-0-12-818849-1.00010-2

coherence, purpose, and mattering. *Coherence* is making sense of one's own experiences, *purpose* is an organizing structure that confers motivation for the future, and *mattering* is having significance in one's larger world.

A recent investigation (Costin & Vignoles, 2020) of these three aspects of meaning—coherence, purpose, and mattering—evaluated whether these aspects are conceptually and empirically distinct and then tested their influence on judgments of meaning in life. The authors first analyzed measurement items testing purpose, mattering, control, belonging, self-esteem, and mood and established that coherence, purpose, and mattering were empirically distinct from each other and unrelated to potentially similar concepts of self-liking, self-competence, control, and belongingness. The authors then developed a new measure of meaning in life to investigate reciprocal influences on meaning. In a final study with a longitudinal design, they established that mattering was the primary influence on meaning in life measured at a later time and meaning in life itself predicted coherence and purpose. The authors argued for the importance of mattering, which has been less fully investigated in research on meaning in life.

As an example of understanding the importance of mattering, Pernice, Biegel, Kim, and Conrad-Garrisi (2017) examined mattering to others as a mediator of the relationship between social support and internalized stigma among recovering adults. Their data revealed that mattering, perceptions of one's value to others, explained the relationship between support and internalized stigma, underling the significance of mattering. Mattering, essentially, is a relational construct. We view ourselves from the point of view of others, whether that other is an individual or a social group. Although that external viewpoint is what we perceive to be present rather than how we are actually perceived by others, mattering to others is critical to judgments of meaning in life.

We turn now to a consideration of aspects of life transitions that may, or are likely to, influence meaning in life. One basic element of transitions present in some, but not all, transitions are the *physiological changes* within the transition. For example, Eivers and Kelly (in press) discussed the many significant physical changes experienced during the transitions of adolescence. The onset of puberty exists in the body, and changes in the body are frequent and can be unsettling. There are also significant cognitive changes, including increased complexity in mental scripts. Physiological changes are evident in health transitions as well. Park, Dibble, Sinnott, Sanft, and Bellizzi (in press) consider the transition from active treatment to survivorship. And Bigony and Keitel (in press) outlined the many physical disruptions posed by inflammatory bowel disease, where symptoms that are intrusive and isolating are unpredictable and uncontrollable.

Physical components of transitions are related to each of the elements of meaning in life. Coherence, making sense of life, is challenged by bodily changes and by intrusive symptoms that contrast abruptly with earlier bodily selves. Purpose can be altered when the future feels predetermined by one's own body. And mattering can be called into question when physical changes result in actual or perceived loss of social networks. Some transitions discussed in this text are experienced in a less physiological way. But transitions that exist partially in physiological changes or that alter the body itself can pose a threat to all components of meaning in life.

A second element of transitions is *disruption of norms*. Norms, unwritten rules of behavior expected of a group or unit, organize our experience across contexts and time. We look to norms for guidance on how to enter a new setting or role, we feel validated when we adhere to norms, and we may judge ourselves or others when norms are not followed. Neibergall and Sanchez (in press) described the many ways in which male norms conflict with realities of late life transitions. For example, the norm of "Big Wheel" emphasizes success and status and the norm of "Sturdy Oak" emphasizes physical strength and appearance. When aging results in lower production of any type, and when physical changes conflict with norms, depression, isolation, and loneliness result. Similarly, acute cardiac events described in Bergman and Keitel (in press) affect norms as well where enduring somatic threats interfere with social and occupational functioning.

When norms that have guided the perception of experience are out of reach, a series of results follow. A negative value is placed on the transition that has resulted in a new inability to reach valued goals. Failure to achieve norms equates wrongly to challenges to mattering, a key component of meaning in life. Finally, as Chen, Sugarman, and Brenman (in press) discussed, self-stigma begins to warp perceptions of reality and of personal value. Tension grows between concealing changes versus openness about changes. If norms have been the basis of coherence and purpose in meaning judgments, failure to meet them threatens those components of meaning in life.

The third aspect of transitions that influence meaning in life is *overreliance on social networks for personal validation*. When those networks are the prime or only source for personal validation, a transition that affects access to those networks poses major challenges. First, the transition may affect the social network itself. For example, transitions that relate to job change cancel out the occupationally based network that was previously available. Second, the transition may be stigmatizing, or appear stigmatizing to the person in the transition, and thus results in isolation from social support.

5. Conclusions

Milman and Neimeyer (in press) analyze the transition of bereavement which is a social role transition experienced by virtually all persons. Certain types of bereavement, such as deaths that are tragic or violent, may be damaging to the bereaved sense of self. If meaning-making is dependent on social network for validation, then judgmental or antagonistic contexts in that network disenfranchise meaning. There is also the potential for destruction of a life narrative that contained elements of coherence, purpose, and mattering, as might occur in situations where the bereaved was dependent on the deceased. Thus, not only is there a loss of another important person, but there is the grief that comes about from lost possible interactions.

A fourth aspect of transitions that influence meaning in life is the increase of *stressful autonomy*. Allan and Liu (in press) discuss in detail the ways in which current labor market trends threaten meaningful work. Meaningful work is understood by the worker to be valuable, significant, important, and worthwhile and thus contains all the components of meaning in life—coherence, purpose, and mattering. Labor market trends of industrialization, precariousness of jobs, and uncertainty in conditions of work lead to situations where an individual is completely responsible for occupational success. An example is the "gig economy" where individuals become contract workers and have no long-term identification with a company or job. This new work environment requires individuals to identify, prepare for, and pursue their own career success across a lifetime of jobs. Another way in which transitions force increased responsibility for autonomy was described by Bergman and Keitel (in press) where individuals must reshape their lives after acute cardiac events. Meaning is threatened by enduring somatic threats and overly rigid belief systems. Flexibility is key to the development of new meaning.

An important aspect of a transition that challenges meaning in life is its impact on an individual's sense of *psychosocial vulnerability*. For example, Park et al. (in press) describe the loss of a treatment team and its supportive care as one aspect of the trajectory into cancer survivorship. Another vulnerability is caused by fear of recurrence of cancer. There may also be a vulnerability in social roles, in unrealistic expectations from others for the resumption of normal life. Chen et al. (in press) analyze another type of vulnerability, that of an individual in transitions of identity. If stigma is experienced or becomes internalized, which can occur as a negative response is enacted, felt, anticipated, or internalized, a deep sense of personal vulnerability can result. A new identity must be negotiated which entails possibility of concealment or disclosure, a threat to social networks.

The last aspect of a transition that poses challenges to meaning in life is the degree of *biographical disruption* caused by the transition. If the arc

5. Conclusions

of a personal narrative is irretrievably interrupted by the transition, then meaning in life is also interrupted. Many of the chapters in this text considered this type of challenge. Chen et al. (in press) outlined the importance of personal identity to meaning. Bigony and Keitel (in press) identified biographical disruption as a key influence on meaning-making: the unpredictability of the disease, and its lack of a discernable cause. There is a loss of "self" and a parallel loss of others. Biographical disruption threatens all the components of meaning in life. Purpose, motivation for the future, is disrupted by uncertainty. Coherence of a life story is dismantled because the future will look nothing like the past. And mattering, if predicated on social, occupational, or personal roles, is reduced.

It is worth noting that the challenges of a transition can lead to decline but can also lead to growth. Meaning reconstruction (see Altmaier, 2017) has been documented to occur in conditions of extreme trauma as well as transition. Recovery does not mean unchanged. The opportunity is existent in all transitions for elements of meaning reconstruction. An example is the construct of *finding benefit*. There is a growing literature on the ways in which people, after a negative or traumatic stressor, identify a new, durable change in their lives, a benefit. A meta-analysis of studies of benefit finding (Helgeson, Reynolds, & Tomich, 2006) revealed that benefit finding was associated with improved mental health outcomes of lower depression and higher positive well-being. A study (Cheng et al., 2017) of benefit finding within the transition to the role of caregiving for persons with Alzheimer's disease revealed that participants who received a benefit finding intervention reported lower depression and less role overload compared to caregivers who received psychoeducation.

The authors of this text have begun the important work of considering how life transitions, most of which are frequent and unavoidable, may threaten meaning in life. That threat may come about within physical, social, or personal domains of life and against meaning in life judgments of coherence, purpose, and mattering. Park, Currier, Harris, and Slattery (2017) noted that we know very little about how global meaning systems develop. While increased research attention on trauma's effect on meaning in life, and now transition's effect on meaning in life, has considered a deconstruction process, we cannot assume that construction is only the opposite. Similarly, reconstruction of meaning may not resemble initial construction. A challenge ahead is to integrate understanding of the intersection of life event with meaning in life with the development of meaning.

So, too, there is a need to more fully understand mattering. Flett (2018) analyzed mattering from a variety of perspectives. He set out seven components of mattering. Attention is feeling that I am noticed by others. Importance is feeling that I am significant to others and that they care for me. Dependence is knowing that others rely on me. Ego extension is recognizing the someone is invested in me, and that my experience impacts them as well. Noted absence is feeling that when I am not present, I am missed. Appreciation is feeling that I am valued by someone else. And individuation is that I am unique and special and that my true self is known and valued.

These components have not been empirically validated but serve as an outline of ways in which mattering exists between me and others. How they may contribute to my own meaning in life is less clear. It is exciting that the study of meaning in life can be enriched by many viewpoints within psychology and also supplied by other disciplines. Given the importance of meaning in life to well-being and flourishing, continued research and application can be eagerly anticipated.

References

Allan, B. A., & Liu, T. (in press). Transitions in an uncertain labor market: Implications for meaningful work. In E. M. Altmaier (Ed.), *Navigating life transitions for meaning*. New York: Elsevier.

Altmaier, E. M. (Ed.), (2017). *Reconstructing meaning after trauma: Theory, research, and practice*. New York: Elsevier.

Altmaier, E. M. (in press). Meaning in life amidst life transitions. In E. M. Altmaier (Ed.), *Navigating life transitions for meaning*. New York: Elsevier.

Bergman, M., & Keitel, M. (in press). At the heart of meaning making: An acceptance and commitment approach to developing adaptive meaning following acute cardiac events. In E. M. Altmaier (Ed.), *Navigating life transitions for meaning*. New York: Elsevier.

Bigony, C. E., & Keitel, M. (in press). Meaning making and chronic illness: Understanding through narratives. In E. M. Altmaier (Ed.), *Navigating life transitions for meaning*. New York: Elsevier.

Chen, E. C., Sugarman, H., & Brenman, M. (in press). Transitions and transcendence: Transgender individuals' identity negotiations and meaning construction in context. In E. M. Altmaier (Ed.), *Navigating life transitions for meaning*. New York: Elsevier.

Cheng, S. T., Maik, E. P. M., Fung, H. H., Kowk, T., Lee, D. T. F., & Lam, L. C. W. (2017). Benefit-finding and effect on caregiver depression: A double-blind, randomized controlled trial. *Journal of Consulting and Clinical Psychology*, *85*, 521–529.

Costin, V., & Vignoles, V. L. (2020). Meaning is about mattering: Evaluating coherence, purpose and existential mattering as precursors of meaning in life judgments. *Journal of Personality and Social Psychology*, *118*, 864–884.

Eivers, A., & Kelly, A. B. (in press). Navigating the teenage years: What do we know about how adolescents find meaning and purpose? In E. M. Altmaier (Ed.), *Navigating life transitions for meaning*. New York: Elsevier.

Flett, G. L. (2018). *The psychology of mattering: Understanding the human need to be significant*. San Diego, CA: Elsevier Press.

George, L. S., & Park, C. L. (2017). The Multidimensional Existential Meaning Scale: A tripartite approach to measuring meaning in life. *The Journal of Positive Psychology*, *12*, 613–627.

Helgeson, V. S., Reynolds, K. A., & Tomich, P. L. (2006). A meta-analytic review of benefit finding and growth. *Journal of Consulting and Clinical Psychology*, *74*, 797–816.

Martela, F., & Steger, M. F. (2016). The three meanings of meaning in life: Distinguishing coherence, purpose, and significance. *The Journal of Positive Psychology*, *11*, 531–545.

Milman, E., & Neimeyer, R. A. (in press). Meaning making in bereavement transitions: Review and clinical relevance. In E. M. Altmaier (Ed.), *Navigating life transitions for meaning*. New York: Elsevier.

Neibergall, N. C., & Sanchez, F. J. (in press). Men's transitions in late life: Exploring the influence of male norms. In E. M. Altmaier (Ed.), *Navigating life transitions for meaning*. New York: Elsevier.

Park, C. L., Currier, J. M., Harris, J. I., & Slattery, J. M. (2017). *Trauma, meaning, and spirituality: Translating research into clinical practice*. Washington, DC: American Psychological Association.

Park, C. L., Dibble, K. E., Sinnott, S., Sanft, T., & Bellizzi, K. (in press). Resilience trajectories of cancer survivors: A meaning-making perspective. In E. M. Altmaier (Ed.), *Navigating life transitions for meaning*. New York: Elsevier.

Pernice, F. M., Biegel, D. E., Kim, J. Y., & Conrad-Garrisi, D. (2017). The mediating role of mattering to others in recovery and stigma. *Psychiatric Rehabilitation Journal*, *40*, 395–404.

Index

Note: Page numbers followed by "*f*" refer to figures.